This *"Journey of a Healer"*

Volume III

is presented to

_____

*By*_____

this _____ *Day*

of _____ *20*____

City _____, *State*_____

Whispers from within…

Unconditional Love – Unselfishness – Forgiveness

Prayer – Persistence

Is the Only Paths that Lead to …

True Success – True Happiness

Understanding of Man and God's True Nature

And Ultimately to Eternal life:

To God and His Kingdom!

Paolo Ficara

To harvest, first you need to sow!
But, don't ever forget ...
Whatever you sow is what you harvest!

To get, first you need to give!
But, always remember ...
Whatever you give is what you get back!

To be loved, first you need to love!
The truth and the greatest news is ...
The more you love,
the more you will be loved!

Paolo Ficara

LOVE...

Is the flowing and the expression
of our emotions, conveying feelings of goodwill and kindness toward the people who are dear to us...
Is the path that leads to the realization of what we define as Divine
Love.

Divine Love is synonymous with God.
Is the essence of what we call
Light, Life, and Creation.
Is the source, the cause and the ruler
of everything that exists.
Is harmony, peace, and joy combined.
Is all there is.

To search for it should be our most important priority.
To find it, remains our greatest challenge.
To consciously experience it,
should be our ultimate goal.

Paolo Ficara

A Note for the Reader

I hope the reading of *Journey of a Healer Volume III* will bring you a better awareness and understanding of this complex and mysterious life that we are all living, that will awaken in you new hope for the future, and most important, will help you to fulfill all your goals and dreams, and fills your life with new joy and everlasting peace.

Sincerely
Paolo Ficara

Reviews and Testimonials

Dr. Robert Harmon M.D.
Palm Desert, California.
Approximately twenty-nine years ago, Paolo and I became friends. On occasion, he would recount his experience in healing through prayer, which he referred to as "concentration." These healings defied conventional medical belief.

As amazing as some of them were, I, however, believed them without any doubt or hesitation.

Reading his books have been a joy and profound learning experience for me. Paolo's journey has a message for every reader.

Gessie Palazzi
Businesswoman
Montreal, Canada.
What can I say about your manuscript? I thoroughly enjoyed it! I couldn't put it down. I am fascinated with your story (your life)!

It has led me to understand many things which I didn't before. Thank you for this. And thank you for sharing your story with me.

"Volere significa Potere!" "To want, means to be able to!"

This is so true in life. It is a rule that everyone should apply in their lives.

Brian & Michelle Faulkner
Banning, California.
The life story of Paolo Ficara is an uplifting memoir of a life well-served and the amazing story about the power of prayer and the ability to heal the ill. This book will make you laugh, cry and look at life in a whole new light. A must-read for anyone interested in alternative therapy!

Ken and Elaine Osborne
Retired
Joshua Tree, California.
The quest for knowledge and unimaginable love of family gives author Paolo Ficara strength to persevere through life's conflicts and confusion.

Questions that we ask deep within ourselves are a constant conflict in his life.

Is there a God?

Where is He?

Why doesn't He handle things the way we think He should?

Is there a bigger picture?

You will tread through each day with the author, feeling his fear, disappointments, excitement, financial security, and most importantly, true love.

An inspiring and life-changing read!

Giuseppe Sutera Sardo
V.P. Production Cheese Industry
Montreal, Canada.
Journey of a Healer is the marvelous biography of Paolo Ficara. From the very first pages, you enter into a different world. Adventures, mysticism, religions, meditation, healings, belief in a supernatural world and understanding are what make his life-story unique. Anybody belonging to any type of religion can read this book, because no particular religion is preferred.

I consider myself very lucky because I had the chance to read the complete story when I needed it most. It helped me to change and improve my life and the lives of my family.

I hope that after publishing the first volume the author will publish the other two immediately, because I believe they can do a lot of good for a lot of people.

Debbie Williams
Yucca Valley, California
June 23, 1981

Because of a childhood injury, I had to have a knee operation in which they had to completely remove my right kneecap. The bone was deteriorating and it had to be scraped. It was extremely painful and I was limping. I could not bend my knee at all or put any pressure on it whatsoever. Paul Ficara discussed my leg operation and disability with me. He asked if he could help me. He said that through his healing ability and God's help he thought he could help me to heal and walk.

I went over to Paul's. He told me to completely relax in a chair and to pray and concentrate that my leg would get better. (This would happen only if I believed in God.)

I relaxed, and as Paul helped me, I could feel my leg completely relax. I became so relaxed that I fell into a semi-sleep. I would hear some background noises, but it was like I was in a deep sleep.

As we prayed and concentrated on my leg, it became warmer and warmer.

When I woke up, I felt refreshed. I got up to walk and I could walk with no limp.

It also didn't hurt as it had. The leg felt warm on the inside but still cold on the outside.

The next morning my leg felt great.

It has been two weeks and it still does not hurt as it did and it isn't stiff.

I went to my physician today, and he said since I had seen him last I had made remarkable improvement and I was completely released from his care. The doctor helped my leg, but I truly feel that it was Paul who healed it

Lori Nelson
(Testimony)

I met Paolo (Paul) Ficara and his wife in 2003. I had just graduated from business college. I was applying for jobs that I wasn't even sure if I was qualified for. I was feeling good about myself because I was thirty-five years old when I had gone back to school and never thought in a million years I would be successful. I proved myself wrong and actually loved being in school. Now, once again I was back to feeling vulnerable about where I fit in the working world.

When I met Paolo (Paul), he was like nobody I had ever had the pleasure to encounter in my whole life. I felt so welcome in his home and we hit it off immediately. I was very interested in what he had to say. He told me that he was a spiritual person and helped people to achieve their goals. He was also a healing man. People went to him for many personal reasons.

He asked me what my goals were in life, where I wanted to be as a person. I told him about the job that I applied for at a local hospital in my community. He said that I needed to focus on wanting the job and to pray and ask for what I wanted. I always thought that it was selfish to ask for something for yourself. But I did what he told me, and darn if I didn't get that job! For the first time in my life I took a different approach at going after what I wanted. This was new to me. I felt on top of the world.

I now stay focused on my life and concentrate on where my life is going. Do I feel it is going in the direction that I want it? Yes, I am in control now and it feels great. I pray for what I want and am grateful everyday for the gifts that I receive. Thanks to Paolo (Paul), he has shown me the good side of life and even myself. I like the person that I've become. I do believe "If you ask you shall receive." I don't feel selfish as long as I'm asking for help to become a better me.

I may have only met Paolo (Paul) once for a brief moment in my life, but I will never forget him; his words stay with me always. I think of him and his wife often. He was definitely a positive impact in my life and the best way I can thank him is to be the best that I can be. I wish him and his family all the happiness life has to offer and I hope that one day I can talk with him again.

Mrs. May Paquette
Professor Emerita
Banning, Ca.

Although I had read Paolo Ficara's *Journey of a Healer, Volume I and II,* the insight he has shared with his readers, in *Volume III* is both deeply provocative yet also very meaningful and rewarding. As I shared with Paolo during in January 2012, when we visited him and Pina at their lovely home, I, too, have been overwhelmed with mystical, profound, and unanswered questions over the years, which I had often asked God about. Paolo's spiritual revelations and perceptions in this book were indeed intriguing and reached the very depths of my heart, body, soul, and mind in trying to understand the "consubstantial" existence of God with Energy, Creative Power, Omnipotence, and Omniscience as described by Paolo.

Paolo's reflection of our deeper, inner union with God being achieved only trough love and deep prayer, and hence the true essence of His Divinity, which brings about a transformation in our lives, was indeed revealing and challenging to me.

However, a transformation is necessary in order for each of us to find peace, joy, and happiness. I understand that I most avoid *ignorance,* and instead, seek understanding and truth to experience less suffering and more tranquility in life. I also believe that forgiveness is part of this equation, only then will my heart rejoice and feel secure with an indescribable peace that manifests a fulfillment of my prayers through God's divine love.

Paolo's book has awakened a new awareness in me: only with a daily, spiritual life with God in my soul and innermost region of my heart will be fulfilled.

March 1, 2010
James Di Cesare
University Student
Montreal, Canada

Journey of a Healer is an absolutely extraordinary book! It showed me that you can achieve anything you put your mind to, as long as you have the will and desire to do so.

After reading the book, the phrases "I wish," "I can't," and "It's too difficult," have been eliminated from my vocabulary and now have become "I want," "I will," and "I can do anything."

This book has also given me new insight into my own personal beliefs. As a Catholic, I have always asked myself some of the same questions asked by Paolo in his book, never expecting to get answers. But through Paolo's experiences, most of those questions are now answered.

It is one thing to tell someone that the mind is very powerful, capable do doing extraordinary things. But it is another thing demonstrating it through your own personal experiences. This is what makes *Journey of a Healer* such a credible book.

Thank you, Paolo, for sharing your life experiences with us. It has inspired me, and I am sure it will inspire many others.

Roberta Edgar
Editor
Beverly Hills, California

Journey of a Healer was an extraordinary experience for me, since, not only did I read the book many times over, I also edited the compelling manuscript for the author, Paolo Ficara. Because it is the story of Mr. Ficara's life and the miraculous healings he was able to manifest through the power of his mind and the purity of his heart, its ultimate completion was never in doubt. This work is no less than the culmination of Paolo's life goal, to provide inspiration and insight into the human potential for personal healing. There is no question that *Journey of a Healer* accomplished its mission with me. It changed my life forever.

Chau Le
Retired
Palm Springs, California
March 1, 2010
Dear Paolo,

I have read *Journey of a Healer* Volume I with great interest. It took me one night and one day to finish the book. You write very well.

The story of your life, i.e. the early part of it in Volume I, is so absorbing I could not put the book down until I finished it. You have a very close-knit family, and the love and support you received from all members of your family and friends is truly edifying.

On the other hand, I found the way you used boldface type to emphasize the important questions you raised about life and faith a little bit unusual. This is a very small matter, however.

All in all, your readers must be thankful to you for bringing your life story to the public. There are many lessons to be learned from your book.

I am very anxious to read the next volumes of your memoir, particularly about your healing experiences.

Thank you very much for sharing your book with me.

Dee Richhart
President & C.E.O.
William Insurance Service. Inc.
Twentynine Palms, California
March 4, 2010
Mr. Ficara's book is not only a chronicle of his fascinating life, but also of his gradual awakening to the power that lies within each of us. This encouraging and thought-provoking book is a peasant read that leaves one curious about the next installment and anxious to know what happens next. I recommend this book to anyone who has goals or dreams, or wishes they did.

Fannie Gomez
Housewife
Chula Vista, California
March 11, 2010
Dear Paolo,

I just finished reading Volume I of *Journey of a Healer*, I was so inspired that I decided to give a set of all tree volumes to each of my children, hoping they are inspired by it and never give up their goals. I am very anxious to read the second and third volumes.

Keep up the good work and congratulations.

Jerry Mattos
Insurance Broker
5592 Oasis Avenue
Twentynine Palms, California
March 5, 2010
Paolo,

For me, reading your book was a grand experience on several levels: the immigrant's experiences, the importance of family, and the discovery of God and church.

My grandparents, both' sides, mother and father, came from the old country, Azores Islands of Portugal. By reading your book I was provided and understanding of their experiences and a window into their lives. I did appreciate your sharing the importance of family and telling us what you did to maintain family. The asking of yourself those tough questions about the church and what they were saying was another appreciated witness.

Your choice in sharing your story had a wonderfully uncomplicated integrity.

Looking forward to Volume II & III

Jerry Mattos
Insurance Broker
5592 Oasis Avenue
Twentynine Palms, California
June 30, 2012
Paolo,

I enjoyed reading *Journey of a Healer,* Volume I & II, an honest witness to the living of life. Everyone should read and think about their life's journey as you have.

Now Volume III is here with definite answers revealed to Paolo through the voice of his heart.

Reading Volume III is an awakening and a worthwhile experience. Paolo, I believe your practice is a truth: pray and listen to the voice in your heart, test the results, remember your past living experiences and weigh them with your current life experiences, and then listen.

Like a biblical prophetic voice in the desert, we hear Paolo's witness. Who would ever have thought that the desert would be in the USA, and even in Southern California? But then again, it is The Desert of Joshua Tree.

Paolo is a prophet whose practice should be thought about and considered by those who seek truth.

Paolo, thank you for bravely sharing your prophetic understandings.

Bob Miller
Construction General Superintendent
Yucca Valley, California
6/20/2011
My Friend Paolo,

There are few people you encounter during your life who you feel you owe a debt you cannot repay. For me, one of those is Paolo Ficara.

My name is Bob Miller and I am employed as a general superintendent by a large construction firm that specializes in military housing. In 2005, my assignment was the renovation of various housing areas at Marine Corps Air Ground Combat Center, Twentynine Palms, California.

The scope of work included removing and replacing several miles of asphalt roadways throughout several housing areas. This would require a qualified subcontractor to mill the existing asphalt, remove excess spoils, grade and compact the base material, and pave and stripe the new surface. This was to be a huge undertaking—and more, the work was to be performed while the roads remained open.

It was 2007, and time to build some road. We would need a highly skilled paving contractor willing to work under these complicated conditions while meeting the stringent requirements of the contract specifications, a firm that was customer oriented. Lucky for me, my boss decided to go with a small, family-owned and operated company—Ficara Paving.

I was very concerned; could this small company do such a large job? I soon met the owner, president, CEO, estimator, truck driver, paver operator, grader operator and all around nice guy Paolo Ficara, A.K.A. Paul (since us native-born Americans cannot properly pronounce his name). Paul's company soon proved to be a perfect fit.

While things at work were in order, at home my wife Paula had been having trouble breathing. We had no family doctor, and like most of us, she figured things would get better soon. She didn't feel sick, just short of breath.

I took her at her word that she was okay. But the complaints became more frequent and my concern for her health grew. I wanted to take her to a doctor or an emergency room, but she continued to refuse. Finally, one day she drove herself to the local ER in Joshua Tree. There she was seen and misdiagnosed with having allergies. She was given medication, but wasn't getting better. I wanted to take her to the ER in Palm Springs, but once again she wanted to wait and see if the medications would begin to work.

It was in the fall, August/September, I'm not sure, I do know it was a Tuesday, and she called me at work to say she was ready to go to Palm Springs. I was at Twentynine Palms, 30 minutes from the house, and the ER in Palm Springs was an additional 40 minutes from there.

I rushed to the house and found her pale and trembling, with her breathing extremely labored. She was in big trouble. We loaded up and headed for Palm Springs. When we passed an urgent care facility, she said to pull in, as she didn't think she could make it to the hospital.

We went in and she was seen by a doctor who after examined her, administered a breathing treatment in an attempt to ease her breathing. Upon completion, he asked how she felt and she responded that she felt no different. The doctor pulled me to the side and told me to take her home because she was exaggerating her symptoms and she would be fine when she calmed down.

We were walking out when her legs gave out on her. I knew we needed to get to the ER now! We still had a 35-minute drive to get to Palm Springs. During the ride she seemed to be stable but still not good. After a series of delays and missed turns, we arrived at Dessert Regional 45-50 minutes after leaving Yucca Valley. I pulled up to the ER entrance, let her out and went to park the car. By the time I got inside, they were getting information from her, and it was not long before the ER staff was seeing her.

They did all the routine stuff; checked her temperature, checked her blood pressure, etc. She sat on a gurney with her legs hanging over the edge, once again doing a breathing treatment, puffing away on this contraption. An attendant stood on each side of her, but they had their backs turned, working on other things. She suddenly turned purple and fell backwards off the gurney. The attendants instantly turned around; one took me by the elbow, while the other began to cut off her blouse. I was ushered to a small waiting area to meet with a counselor.

I was fed minimal information for the next several hours and was finally taken to an area of the hospital where they housed patients who were kept alive by a respirator. I met with her assigned doctor, who told me she had severe emphysema and COPD. I could not bring myself to ask if she was going to die, and he did not say. All I knew for sure was that the machine was keeping her alive.

During the first day, I learned to watch certain things. Her oxygen level was monitored. I was told the ideal oxygen level is 93 and higher. And if the oxygen level falls below 80, brain cells can be destroyed. Paula's level fluctuated between 78 and 82. In my mind, I was losing my wife.

Things were complicated by the fact I had taken Paula to the hospital while my daughter was at school. Kris was sixteen at the time and more than capable of caring for her. But it was a difficult phone call to tell her I would be home to get her and we would be returning to the hospital that evening. Kris had lost her biological mother when she was six and now faced losing the mother she had known and loved for the last ten years.

I believe it was day two or day three that somehow Paul showed up at the hospital. To this day, I don't know how he knew Paula was in trouble. I do know he went from hospital to hospital until he found us.

You can imagine my surprise when I looked up and saw my asphalt subcontractor in the waiting room.

Paul explained that he could help, that he was a faith healer, and he would like to see Paula. I told him I didn't think they would allow it, that it was family only, no more than two at a time and for a limited amount of time.

He told me he needed to be with her so he could help; he instantly became Cousin Paul from Sicily.

When Paul entered her room, Paula's oxygen level was at 78. He pulled a chair up next to her and took her hand. He seemed to go into a relaxed state of meditation. This surprised me, as the constant mechanical sound of the respirator clicking and exhausting with each breath kept me on edge, but it didn't seem to faze Paul.

With him in the room, I took time to go for a walk and just get away for a while. I needed to make phone calls and update everyone on the events—or should I say lack of progress—of the day. I returned to the room probably 40-45 minutes later to find Paul still sitting in his meditative state holding Paula's hand. There was one major difference, though. Paula's oxygen level was at 100% and stayed there until Paul released her hand some 15-20 minutes later. Almost instantly, her levels dropped, but stopped at 84 and never went below that level again. I realized I had witnessed a miracle.

As of today, Paula is alive and well. She still takes daily medications, but no longer needs oxygen or special treatments. The doctors told us when she left the hospital not to expect further improvement. That is not so; Paula is 100 times better than when she first came home.

Everyone has an opinion on how and why my wife is still here today. I know the answer. I was there; I saw it with my own eyes. That night the debt I cannot repay was created.

Paul, I forever will be in your debt. Two people were saved that night— Paula and me.

Gregory Graham Ed. D.
Emeritus Professor
California State University, Los Angeles
"Journey of a Healer" Volume I, is an amazing family story of an Italian immigrant boy and his commitment to his God, family and future. His unwavering desire to establish a successful business to support his family is driven by his core beliefs, ethics and talent.

August 30/2017
Cerresa Jacobs
Cathedral City, California
My name is Cerresa Jacobs. I went to Paolo Ficara on Thursday 8/24/2017. A good friend had recommended that I see him for a healing session.

I had broken my back when I was thirteen years old. I fell from an open trap door that opened over the main staircase of our Victorian home. As I dropped through the opening I hit my head on the wood frame knocking myself out. I fell with my legs in the air and landed on the stairs below with my tailbone making the first and bounced down the stairs to the first landing, where I collapsed in a pile. My sister found me and brought me downstairs to the bed in my father's study on the ground floor. I remained in that bed for two weeks recovering. When I stood up after this healing period I was crooked, my shoulders were no longer level and my spine was tipped at an odd angle. When I was then x-rayed it was I was found that I had shattered my L4 and L5 vertebrae. This happened 1959, it is now 2017 so for 58 years I suffered with progressively worse back pain with every I aged. I had recently had an x-ray and the report was that a great deal of arthritis had settled in the joints of my lower back. The doctor candidly reported that it was certainly that I had back pain and they were surprised that I was able to manage my life without high dosages of painkillers.

Over the years I had been on many medications for pain including Oxycontin, Methadone and Gabapentin. I found that the pain pills added side effects, such as extreme fatigue, sleepiness, sluggishness, brain fog and addition that deteriorated the quality of my life. As a result I was better equipped to live my life with the pain, rather than living with muffled, masked pain while ingesting these chemical poisons. However, as you can clearly imagine, this meant I lived an abbreviated life. I eliminated many activities that others considered essential to life because I always needed to return home, recharge and get off my feet. I kept my socializing to a minimum and stayed away from intimacy with family members to keep the fires of emotional drama dampened down to the smallest of sparks; since all activities drained my energy banks quickly and human drama was lethal to my supply of good energy. I would start out strong and run out of energy in three hours or less which necessitated the need to return home. Of course as soon as the energy supply dwindled, my enthusiasm for activities vanished while my irritability, negativity and depression increased.

The misalignments in my spinal column pulled the muscles in my thighs until my knees were also pulled out of alignment. My left knee had been surgically replaced while my right knee lost more and more cartilage. My doctors had reported that my right knee was completely worn down and each time I bent I was rubbing bone on bone, they declared that the only solution was a second knee replacement surgery, now on my right knee.

I took a few minutes with Paolo to sketch my skeletal and muscular disabilities and then we sat down together to pray and meditate on the healing power of God, seeking His face and His love for this healing. When the hour was up, I got out of the chair to check out my body. After thousands of church services and many efforts at healing by my friends and lovers, I got out of that chair healed. For the first time since I smashed my vertebrae at thirteen years of age, I was out of pain. My knee was completely restored as well. I moved quickly around the room, feeling a freedom of movement like that of my childhood years. When I was led to squat, I sat down on my knees and swung my hips using my newly restored right knee to bounce up and down. You might see a body-builder do this movement, not a 72 year old woman and certainly not me who just a few minutes earlier was old, crippled and infirm. I was crying, laughing and breathing deeply. I was in shock and amazement and joy! *HEALED!* <u>made whole, after 58 years of suffering.</u>

Thank you, Paolo Ficara, and the healing spirit that flows through him to heal our bent and broken bodies, restoring them to vibrant health and necessary function.

Journey of a Healer Volume III

Journey of a Healer Volume III

Jesus' Teachings & Questions Answered

Paolo Ficara

For information contact:

Paolo Ficara

2645 Rice Rd.

Joshua Tree, CA 92252

Or write to: ficarapaolo@hotmail.com

ISBN: 0984436901
ISBN 13: 9780984436903

Dedication

*I dedicate this work of mine to the memory of my beloved
parents, Pellegrino (Pino) and Rosa Ficara ...*

*... for having instilled in my mind and my heart the basic
principles of honesty, love and respect for mankind.*

*Grazie di Cuore Papa Grazie di Cuore Mamma
Your loving son,*

Paolo

The Author

Since my childhood in Sicily, I have searched for the key to understand this life on earth. I have questioned God's existence and what seems to be His mysterious and at time senseless and contradictory behavior.

At the age of fourteen, I witnessed the miraculous healing of my terminally ill mother. This experience profoundly affected my life, instilling in me the desire to learn how healing occurs and who God is in His true essence and nature.

Born to a poor family of farmers, my older brother hoped to help the family financially by immigrating to Germany at the young age of eighteen.

This caused my brother, my entire family and myself a lot of pain. It was during this period that I promised myself to reunite my family in a place where we could live, work and prosper together.

In the hopes of fulfilling this promise, I emigrated to Montreal, Canada in September of 1967 at the age of twenty-one. There I met my wife Pina with whom I had three children.

In August 1979, I moved my family to Joshua Tree, a small town in the southern California desert. Here, in the peace and harmony of this new and different environment, I learned how to pray, how to forgive and most importantly, how to love. As a result, I was able to fulfill all my dreams-including my quest to find the answers to the questions I'd been asking myself and others for most of my life.

I discovered that the limitations man puts on himself and the problems man encounters – including those of health, finances, love and discontent – are solely the fruits of ignorance. I strongly believe that anyone can attain success, good health and happiness.

Now that I retired as owner of a small asphalt paving company, I am working on my next book, named *"A Ray of Hope for Mankind"* and look forward to spending more time nurturing the *"Universal Center for Self-Enlightenment and Self-Healing,"* a foundation I have established to help others find fulfillment and success.

I humbly pray that my life story can inspire and help each reader to find his own journey through this life and that he would experience a brighter and more successful future.

I thank all those who, after reading my words, will take the time to share their learning's with as many people as they can. I believe that in so doing, not only they will be more fulfilled, but they also will contribute to improve other people's lives, making this world a better place to live.

Finally, I hope that everyone's desires will be fulfilled and that the peace, the harmony and the joy of God will abide with them today, tomorrow and forever.

God Bless,
Paolo Ficara
May – 14 - 2014

Acknowledgements

I would like to thank the people who have influenced the course of my life. I will start with my family.

I thank my wife Pina, my three children, Pellegrino (Pino), Antonino (Nino) and Paolo Jr., my parents Pellegrino (Pino) and Rosa Ficara, and my brothers Gioacchino and Ignazio for their deep, unconditional and unselfish love that always showed. I also thank them for always believing in me; for being there when I needed them the most; for giving me support and hope in my darkest and most difficulty moments; and for the joy they continuously give me. It is impossible to express in words the immensity of my love and the infinity gratitude I always felt for all of them. For that I ask their forgiveness.

I thank Zia (aunt) Carmela, my mother's only sister, and her husband Zio (uncle) Salvatore Piazza, for having sponsored my parents and my brother Ignazio, helping them to settle in their new land, and for their love for all of us. They have been instrumental in making our dreams become reality. Without their help, the course of our lives would have been completely different.

I thank Zio Joe Piazza, Zio Agostino Piazza and Zio Luca Piazza, Zio Salvatore's brother, and their family for accepting us as part of their family and making us fell welcome and at home.

I thank Zio Lillo; my father's younger brother, and Zia Lina, his wife, for being like second parents to me; and their two sons Gioacchino and Antonio for always treating me like a brother.

I thank Zio Pasquale Salvo and his wife, Zia Antonina, their children Pietro and his wife Nena, Joe and his wife Angie, Giovanni and his wife Angela, Mattia and her husband Zio Nino Gentile, and Antonietta and her husband Nino Caci, for accepting me as one of their family and for always being there for us.

I thank my cousin Francesca and her husband Giovanni Sciangula, my cousin Maria and her husband Pasquale Terrasi, and my cousin Teresa and her husband Carmelo Tortorici, and my friends Liborio Zambito, Vincenzo D'Anna and Emanuele Territo for helping me overcome the difficult times I went through during my first few months in Montreal.

Other people who have influenced the course of my life are some of my closest friends. I would like to give thanks to Enzo Tortorici, Giuseppe Zabbara, Nino Zabbara, Pippo Sutera, Franco Sferra, Giuseppe Cortese and Pippo Ferrera for their brotherly friendship.

A special thanks go to:

- My friend Joe Catalano, for having treated me as a brother from the very first moment we met in Palm Springs, and for helping me to establish my paving company when first I arrived in Southern California.
- My friend Edoardo Federico, for helping me to settle in Joshua Tree when we moved to California.
- My friend, Professor Eliseo Franco Amico, PhD, for putting all his heart, passion, love and talent in translating my manuscript from its original Italian format into English, and for having over the course of the years challenged my experiences and my thoughts. He has been more a brother than a friend.
- My friend Robert Harmon, M.D., for believing in my healing stories and for tirelessly encouraging me to pursue my life's natural vocation.

- My friend Dr. Beverly Marie Rumsey. Thanks to her highly developed sense of clairvoyance, she helped our family avoid what could have been a very unpleasant experience.
- Thanks to my editors, Roberta Edgar and Sandy Tritt, for helping me to edit the manuscript.

I would like to thank all my relatives, friends, and acquaintances that directly or indirectly, in a positive or negative way, influenced and shaped the course of my life. I forgive and thank all the people who directly or indirectly have caused me grief and pain, because I know, without those experiences, I could not have become the person I am today. To everyone I give my eternal appreciation, gratitude and love.

- I acknowledge and thank Thomas Nelson Bibles, a Division of Thomas Nelson Inc., for allowing me to include verses from the: *The Holy Bible, New King James Version,* Copyright 1992, by Thomas Nelson, Inc.
- I acknowledge and thank Wikipedia, the Free Encyclopedia from the Internet, for allowing me to include reports and notations about characters.

I would also like to thank the following people who through their works and their writings have immensely influenced the outcome of my life:

- Joseph Murphy, author of *The Power of Your Subconscious Mind,* for teaching me the importance of our thoughts.
- Baird T. Spalding, author of *Masters of the Far East,* for explaining the endless capability of Man.
- Paramahansa Yogananda, author of *Autobiography of a Yogi,* and founder of Self Realization Fellowship, for teaching me how to pray and meditate.

A special acknowledgement and thanks go to:

- Lord Jesus
- Lord Buddha
- Lord Krishna
- Prophet Mohammed
- Prophet Moses

I thank Them for teaching me that the path that deliver us from the bondage of ignorance, limitation, poverty, misery, and sufferance, and that will lead us to experience successes, riches, freedom, and Divine Joy, is one and the same and can only be achieved through prayer, love and forgiveness.

I was astonished to learn that the essence of their teachings, messages, ideal and ideas, although expressed in different words and different ways, are expressing the same truth; which when interpreted and accepted correctly and lived faithfully, will lead and take us to the same destination, to the source where we all come from, to God, so we can learn to understand Him, so we can learn to know Him, and so finally, we can be reunited to His essence for eternity.

Finally, I give my thanks to the Omniscience of the Christ Consciousness, - the Creative Power of the Holy Spirit of God, - that abides within me, that abides within every living man and women, that abides in every living creature, and that abides in every atom existing in the universe, for having:

- Inspired me every moment of my life;
- Guided me in every step of my life;
- Paved the right path for me to follow;
- Assisted me in all my pursuits;
- Fulfilled all my dreams, desires, aspirations, goals and prayers;

- And most importantly, for having unfolded to me the apparent mystery of life, allowing me to perceive what is the true essence and nature of man, what is the true essence and nature of God, and what is the relationship existing between them.

Once more, to all of them go my love, my devotion and my gratitude.

Paolo Ficara
Joshua Tree, CA.
May 14, 2014

Paolo Ficara
North America Journey

Paolo Ficara
European Journey

Contents and Chapters

Introduction

Journey of a Healer Volume III encompasses the journey of my life from my mid-thirties to the present—some of my most formidable years, and without doubt, the most challenging and gratifying time of my life thus far.

During this period, I began to consciously develop a close relationship with what at the time I called the *"voice of my heart."*

As a result, I was able to:

- **Fulfill my goals and dreams;**
- **Develop a deeper understanding of Jesus' teachings and work, as well the teachings and work of other prominent enlightened people;**
- **And find the answers to all the questions that I have been searching during the course of my life.**

It is with great joy that I share what I have learned.

But, due to the depth and complexity of the contents, I recommend that prior to reading *Volume III* please read *Volume I The Struggle,* and *Volume II Healings Experience.*

I take this opportunity to emphasize that *Journey of a Healer* does not have a specific religious orientation or affiliation.

The message is scientific, spiritual, and universal and can be lived by anyone, regardless of his/ her professed faith, or religious belief.

Reading of *Journey of a Healer Volume I…, II…, and III…* can bring awareness and understanding of the teachings and works of Jesus, as well of the teachings and works of all the enlightened Masters of the past and present.

Moreover, if the reader will follow, accept, and live the teachings of the Masters, will be lead to:

- **A brighter future;**
- **Will experience what man considers and calls miracles;**
- **And most important, his life will be blessed and filled with true peace and pure joy.**

God Bless
Paolo Ficara

CHAPTER 1

CONSTRUCTION OF THE R. V. PARK

The work I have done throughout my adult life has been strenuous and certainly not conducive to the practice of my lifelong calling— prayer and healing. Spurred by the desire and need to pursue healing as a way of life, I considered the possibilities of looking into a new type of work that would be less labor intensive and would allow me time to practice the vocation for which I had yearned all these years. I wondered what sort of work I could do that would provide for my family's financial needs and at the same time satisfy my personal goals.

In September 1983, my brother Gioacchino and I were doing the grading and paving for a new R.V. Park located in the city of Desert Hot Springs. As we worked, we discussed the idea of building our own R.V. Park in the City of Twentynine Palms, where we owned approximately twenty acres of land adjacent to a golf course. Once we established a campground, we could earn enough money to lead a decent lifestyle without breaking our backs every day doing manual labor. Furthermore, since most tourists came to the desert during the fall, winter, and spring when the climate was superb, I could dedicate the hot summer months to prayer and healing.

The idea was certainly worth thinking about, and gradually my brother and I became charged with enthusiasm. We researched how to activate our plan. To start things moving, we hired an architect, who drew up all the necessary plans to put before the Twentynine Palms City planning commission.

For over a year, we attended meetings at city hall. Finally, in late 1984, our project was approved and the city gave us the permit to start building.

At this point, we shopped for a bank loan to finance our project. I went to just about every bank I could find in Southern California, but all of them, for one reason or another, refused to grant us the needed loan.

Throughout this process, I felt nervous and uncertain, but I never sought the source of my feelings. I logically reasoned that since our property was located next to a golf course and since the temperature in that specific area was ideal during the winter months, our project would be successful enough to bring an end to our asphalt-paving career.

Unfortunately, our hopes for the project were fueled by my reason and logic, and I overlooked why, deep in my heart, I continued to have negative feelings. Instead of investigating my feelings, I concentrated all my strength and determination on working extremely hard and unceasingly with Gioacchino to make our dream a reality.

After several years of struggling, in the spring of 1988, Mercury Savings and Loan, a bank whose main office was located in the City of Long Beach, finally granted us a $550,000.00 loan. We began the construction work and finished about a year-and-a-half later.

After the inauguration, September 1990, it occurred to me that I had forgotten one important thing—how we were going to get people to stay at our resort. In our area, there were no other campgrounds, and the City of Twentynine Palms was not recognized as a winter destination for tourists. We realized the only way to promote our resort was through heavy advertising in Canada and in the northern United States, where, because of the harsh winters, a large segment of the population traditionally goes south in search of warmer temperatures. But that kind of advertising would require considerable time and money.

I asked myself if we were financially prepared to face this new challenge, and the answer was "no."

The nervousness, the uncertainty, and the doubts I had perceived deep in my heart all along now turned out to be well - founded. I grew angry with myself for having been instrumental in programming what was turning out to be a resounding fiasco. However, what could I do at this point?

Turning our backs on the project would mean losing all our savings and putting our reputation in jeopardy. We realized we had no choice but to try to overcome the difficulty that lay before us. After considerable reflection, we decided that Pina and Rosa could run the camp during the daytime while my brother and I continued to lay asphalt to earn extra money. Then, Gioacchino and I would swap places with our wives and take over at night, so they could take care of our respective families.

After about three years of this business, it became apparent that what we had imagined to be an easy ticket to financial success and a better life turned out to be a nightmare, as every passing moment brought nothing but uncertainty and fear of the future.

This state of affairs particularly distressed Gioacchino and his family. They were disheartened and disappointed as they became increasingly convinced that nothing could change the negative course of events that had taken place, and concluded that eventually we would be forced to give up the business. This, of course, would mean losing everything we had striven to accumulate, maybe even outright bankruptcy. Daunting as this situation was, it generated enormous tension in our relationship.

It is easy to criticize in retrospect and to point a finger at those we deem responsible for what turned out to be costly mistakes. Since I had always been the one to make decisions of major importance in the family, that finger was constantly pointed at me, holding me responsible for the negative turn of events.

We asked three real estate agents specializing in R.V. resorts if they were interested in selling our property, and how much we could get for it.

After they reviewed our financial books, all three came to the same conclusion. Since we operated on a negative balance and were keeping the property afloat with money out of our pockets, it had no market value, and it would therefore be very hard to find a buyer. They suggested our only options were either to find someone willing to take over the property for whatever we owed the bank, or to abandon the project entirely, and let the bank take it over.

One way or the other, we would end up losing our entire investment and, worse yet, our reputations - something that could have dire repercussions in the future if we were to seek another bank loan or some such thing. What could we do?

Gioacchino and Rosa were no longer interested in the business and wanted a way out at any cost, even if that meant giving it away.

In principle, I could not agree with them, since accepting their alternative meant losing not only all our savings and all the hard work we had put into the operation, but also all our hopes and whatever psychological stability I retained. I felt certain that if I followed the course suggested by my brother and his wife, I would never be at peace with myself and would end up feeling like a flop for the rest of my life.

In 1993, after a long period of negotiations, Pina and I agreed to buy out Gioacchino and Rosa's interest. Since we did not have the money on hand, it was agreed that we would pay them off as we could. This set of circumstances gave rise to a period of bewilderment and insecurity for both our families, leaving our futures hanging by a very thin string.

In October 1994, we bought a manufactured home on credit, which we placed at the camp entrance. Then we temporarily left our beautiful house on the hill in Joshua Tree, to set up residence at our campgrounds in Twentynine Palms. Thus, we began one of the most difficult periods of our lives, working seven days a week, from morning until late in the evening, which caused me to lose touch with all those things that had occupied a prominent place in my life—particularly time to be with my family and my spiritual research and prayer. Without knowing how, I plunged myself into a deep pit in which I became inescapably trapped.

Memories
from the
R.V. Park

I take this occasion, to recognize, and thank the many people, that in the course of the years helped us at the R.V. Park. Making it a fun, enjoyable and beautiful place to spend the winter vacation.

Some of them are:

Don and Lois Peterson (Nebraska)
Rex and RaNa Hopper, (Oregon)
Remo and Marnie Quarin (British Columbia, Ca.)
Bill and Claire Stock (Washington)
Jim and Marci Kerr (Nevada)
Ted and Donna Maddux (Washington)
Dick and Maryland Rood (Washington)
Lois and Less Alexander (Illinois)
Shirley and Larry Miller (Washington)
Ron Erwin (Oregon)
Shirley and Steve Nash (Washington)
Norm and Norma Cox (Oklahoma)
Chuck and Pat Ruth (Oregon)

Don and Judy Bush (Washington)
Irene and Harold Erwin (Alberta, Canada)

These are, very few, when compared to the one who actually helped; my apology, my appreciation and my love to those whose name is not mentioned in the above list.

Entrance of the Club House
29 Palms, Ca. 1995

The Making of the Spaghetti Sauce
From the left: Barry, Paolo, Jim, Jim P. and Remo
29 Palms, Ca. 2000

Friends and Guests of the R.V. Park.
From the left: Paolo, Barry, Pina, Lorry, Jim, Jan, Jim
P., Remo In front: RaNae and Rex Hopper,
29 Palms, Ca. 2000

Pina Serving Spaghetti
29 Palms, Ca. 2002

Pina displaying her beautiful apron from Sicily
29 Palms, Ca. 2001

Marnie, RaNae, Pina and Paolo
29 Palms, Ca. 2000

From the left, our sons:
Nino and Pino, Pina, Paolo and Paolo Jr.
29 Palms, Ca. 2004

Don and Lois Peterson, Pina and Paolo Ficara
Puerto Vallarta, Mexico, 1995

Vicki Kane, Marietta Rio, Al Rio, Pina and Paolo
29 Palms, Ca. 2003

Donna and Ted Maddoux
29 Palms, Ca. 2002

Bill and Clair Stock
29 Palms, Ca. 1998

CHAPTER 2
PURCHASE OF THE GOLF COURSE

Meanwhile, the condition of the golf course, which was owned by the City of Twentynine Palms and was adjacent to our campgrounds, steadily deteriorated. Dissatisfied, our customers, who were mostly golfers, shortened their stays at our resort, significantly curtailing our profits.

I complained about the problem to the city manager one day, and he informed me that each year the city sustained approximately $80,000.00 in losses from the course. "There is no way," he said, "that I could ask city council to pour more money into improvements. In fact, some members of the council have already suggested we close the course permanently."

I couldn't help but feel discouraged by his words, as I was sure that without the golf course, our resort simply could not survive.

"I'm really sorry about the situation, but there isn't much I can do to help you," he said. Then, he lowered his head as if in thought, and when he raised it, he asked, "Would you be interested in leasing the course?"

Shrugging my shoulders, I replied that I didn't know. "Why should I take over the responsibility for the golf course when I already know it's a losing proposition?"

He replied that the city, being a public agency, had to pay workers far more than would be expected of a private outfit. "My thinking is that you could run the golf course at a far lower cost and with greater efficiency than the city has been able to do. If you're interested, I could speak with the mayor and the city council and see what they think."

I said that if the council helped me by making a favorable offer, I might consider it. He asked for some time to assess the situation, after which he promised to give me an answer.

A few days later, he called to set up a meeting with me at city hall. When I arrived, he told me the council members had responded favorably to his proposal of leasing out the golf course, subject to some provisions. I would be required to sign a twenty-five year lease in exchange for which the city would agree to contribute monies for the first five years, starting with $25,000.00 the first year and reducing incrementally by $5,000.00 each year. Also, I'd be required to improve the general condition of the golf course.

Knowing that it would take lot money to improve the golf course, I told him I was not in the position to accept the proposal.

"In that case," he said, "the city will entertain other offers."

About two months after this meeting, the city leased out the golf course to a local. Unfortunately, the new lessee lacked both the necessary experience to run such an operation and the money to implement any improvements. Consequently, by the end of the first year, conditions at the course had worsened.

Concerned because the situation was affecting my own operation, I went to see the city manager.

He replied that he was well aware of the circumstances and was just as worried as I was. He informed me that the lessee had not complied fully with the agreement, thus giving the city the right to rescind its contract. "Would you reconsider taking it over if we nullify the contract with the present lessee?"

Truly, I did not know what to do. After a few seconds of reflection, I told him to give me a few days so I could think about the matter and discuss it with my family.

Pina, the children, and I spent a lot of time discussing the pros and cons of the situation, and were convinced there was no easy solution.

If we decided not to take over the golf course and it remained in its present disastrous condition, our camping resort would eventually close down.

After considerable reflection, we decided that leasing the golf course was not in our best interest. However, if the city decided to sell us the course at a good price and under favorable conditions, then, perhaps, we would choose to buy it. That would give us the possibility of borrowing the money to make the improvements, and, in time, conditions permitting, we could recover our initial investment.

Soon after reaching that decision, I went to speak with the city manager, who patiently listened to my proposal and replied that he would speak to the mayor and members of the council about it, letting me know their decision as soon as possible.

A few days later, he called me to come to his office, where he told me that the mayor and city council had discussed my proposal and the city wanted to sell. The only hitch was that, according to their lawyer, we were dealing with public property, which meant they could not sell the property directly to me, but would be required to put it up for public auction. Whoever submitted the highest bid would get it. At this point, the problem was that the city needed a year to prepare the papers for the auction, which meant they had to manage the golf course during that time. That also meant the city would lose more than $80,000.00.

To avoid that, they proposed they lease the property to me for one year; in return, they would be willing to give me the right of first refusal. In other words, if I were able to match the highest bid at the time of the sale, they would be legally bound to sell me the golf course.

I said that under those terms, I would be interested in leasing it and eventually buying the property, even if I hadn't the slightest idea where I would find the money to do so.

With this understanding, the city administration granted me a year's lease and began the process of selling the property. At the end of the one-year lease, we matched the bid the city officials accepted and we bought the golf course.

In order to acquire the money necessary for us to buy the golf course, and improve it, we had to sell our interest in a few lots from our campgrounds. We obtained a bank loan for the remainder.

At this point, I had the problem of finding someone to run the day-to-day operation at the golf course. I couldn't do it, because that would mean I'd have to stop working with the paving company, thereby cutting off my income that allowed us to pay our bills and survive.

One night while I was trying to find a solution to this problem, my son Pino, who had already graduated from the University of San Diego with a degree in Business Administration and was then working in the city of Rancho Santa Fe for an investment company, phoned me to say he had quit his job and would come home and help us. Later on, when Paolo Jr. graduated from the same university with the same degree in Business Administration, he followed Pino's example and came to work with us, as well. Nino quit school and joined us. Experiencing so much love and loyalty from our children overwhelmed Pina and me with joy.

Thus, we began the reconstruction of the course, which was completed in 2003.

As all of this was taking place, time was inexorably flying by.

One evening over supper, about three years after we purchased the golf course, Nino expressed his desire to go back to school and study agriculture, with special emphasis on the construction and maintenance of golf courses, so that he could pursue a degree in the field. When I heard what he had to say, I told him that all of us would be happy to make whatever sacrifices were necessary to send him back to school so that someday, with a degree in hand, he could have a better chance of finding security in the workplace. Thus, he re-enrolled in school.

Memories
from the
Golf Course

Ribbon cutting at Road Runner Dunes Golf Course
From the left: Jim Bagley (City counsel, City of 29 Palms), Liz Meyer
(City counsel, City of 29 Palms), Pina, Paolo, M. C. Dube (Mayor of the City
of 29 Palms) Paolo Jr., Pino, Judy Bush, Jim Hart (City manager of 29 Palms),
29 Palms, Ca.
October, 1997

Pino, Kelly Overton, Paolo
29 Palms, Ca.
October, 1997

Pino, Paolo Jr., Pina and Paolo
29 Palms, Ca.
October,1997

CHAPTER 3

FAITH - HOPE - PRAYER KEEPS MY DREAM ALIVE

During those three years, I spent all my time working extremely hard. The meditation, prayer, and healing that had once occupied a very important place in my life remained on hold.

Although I was no longer praying for the sick or for spiritual advancement, my thoughts were often directed to God - that God I still could not understand. I incessantly prayed to Him to help me confront and resolve the problems I faced each day. Without any doubt, those difficult years put to trial all my patience, perseverance, determination, and willpower - and, above all, my hope and faith. Today, more than ever, I am convinced that without my constant prayers to God, and without His help, I never could have overcome all the hardships that confronted me during those difficult years.

At this time, due mainly to the extremely high interest rates, the construction industry was practically non-existent.

The only thing that kept our asphalt company going was the small repair jobs property owners consigned to us for maintenance of their real estate. Although we never really knew where the money would be coming from to meet our financial responsibilities, somehow, by the end of each month, we always managed to pay our bills.

I cannot emphasize enough that if it had not been for my continuous prayer and unfailing faith in God, we never could have overcome the difficulties we faced during those arduous years. In retrospect, I have to admit that in some ways, they were a mixed blessing.

For example, had we not been in such dire financial straits, our boys, after finishing the university, never would have decided to head back home and help us when we needed them the most—thereby demonstrating their great love and attachment to us. Watching them grow each day from young adults into mature independent men became a great source of joy and satisfaction to Pina and me. Another positive note arising from our difficult situation was that the continuous pressure of hard work and the problems we faced on a daily basis tempered our personalities and character, making us emotionally stronger than ever. We were thus able to meet challenges with greater ease and serenity.

CHAPTER 4

REKINDLING THE HOPE TO FULFILL MY DREAM - I
LEARN TO TYPE AND TO USE THE COMPUTER

On September 25, 2000, something unexpected happened. As I worked on the golf course getting the soil ready to seed for the winter grass, gas accumulated in my stomach. Unable to pass the gas, the pressure in my stomach grew stronger and stronger, with the consequence that it put a lot of pressure on my diaphragm. Pain developed and grew in my chest. I thought I was having a heart attack. As my indisposition continued to grow, I became weaker and paler to the point that my symptoms were visible to my sons, who promptly asked if I were feeling okay.

Trying not to frighten them, I just told them I was feeling some discomfort in my stomach. They told me to go home and rest. I followed their advice.

When Pina came inside the house from the office next door and saw me lying down, she became alarmed and wanted to know what was wrong. I said I was tired and wanted to rest a bit. But I must not have sounded too convincing, as she kept on barraging me with questions. When I finally told her the truth, she became very frightened and insisted that I go immediately to the hospital. I told her not to be so dramatic and assured her it was just a slight case of fatigue. She kept insisting I go to the hospital, but I kept refusing.

My symptoms persisted throughout the day, and I became increasingly more frightened. It occurred to me that if I really had heart problems,

I wouldn't be able to keep up the kind of demanding physical work I was doing and could die at any moment. That would mean leaving my family to face the misery and problems we were going through on their own. I wondered if all the work and sacrifices of the past years were for naught.

The more I thought about it, the more frightened and depressed I became. In the midst of this panic, I managed to get to the window and look out at the open skies above. I implored God to help me during that extremely precarious hour of my life. After praying for about half an hour, I felt the need to use the bathroom. After that, I released most of the gas accumulated in my stomach. The pains in my chest slowly subsided until they were completely gone.

The next morning, at Pina and my sons' insistence, I went to see my friend, Dr. Harmon. After a thorough examination, he assured me that in his opinion, my symptoms did not reflect the symptoms of a heart attack, but for precaution, he referred me to a cardiologist, who I saw that same day. The cardiologist, after hearing my symptoms, performed an E.K.G., a stress test and an echocardiogram. At the end, he informed me that all the tests were negative, that my heart was fine, and that my chest pain was caused by an excess of gas in my stomach pushing up the diaphragm and putting a lot of pressure on my chest.

He told me the accumulations of gas in my stomach had its origin in a combination of stress, spicy food and overeating, and if I would control those things, I had nothing to worry about. I felt relieved and optimistic about my future once again.

That evening, after supper, while I was watching T.V., suddenly, from the depths of my heart, I felt a desire to read one of the spiritual books I had not read for years.

When we had moved to our new home in Twentynine Palms, due to lack of space, I placed some of my books under the bed. Now I had to lower myself to the floor and reach underneath to search for the books.

Instead, I put my hand on two old folders containing my manuscript and my briefcase with all the notes I had jotted down several years before.

After cleaning off the thick layer of dust, I glanced through the pages and noticed that the last entry I'd made was back in April 1987 - more than thirteen years before. As I read through those dusty pages, I felt in my heart a joy I hadn't experienced in years—a joy that rekindled in me a strong desire to complete that work.

That, of course, was more easily said than done.

Where would I find the necessary time to dedicate to writing? Moreover, how would I finish this monumental project when I could neither type nor use a computer?

Writing the material out by hand would be too time consuming, and having someone else type it would inhibit me from externalizing and describing my emotions the way I felt them deep in my heart. What was I to do?

The next day, I talked about my dilemma to a man from Oregon named Gerald Pike, who, at the time, was staying at the R.V. Park. He told me the best solution was for me to learn to type and to use a computer.

"I've tried," I said, "But I failed."

"Why?" he asked.

I shrugged. "It's not easy to learn to type. I tried, but I found it very hard, so I quit. It's difficult for me to learn things like that."

Gerald refused to give up. "If more than half the population can learn, you can. It is really not that difficult. You just need a bit of motivation, patience, perseverance and a little time to practice."

He told me that typing cannot be learned overnight, and if I would stop thinking that I was not able to learn and instead began to practice, he would prove that he was right. At the end, he convinced me that I could do it. Therefore, I tried it.

Thanks to Gerald's help, I was eventually able to learn how to type and operate the computer, and thus finally resumed the writing of my autobiography.

I dare say that my writing was so slow I wondered if I would live long enough to finish the project. Whenever I told Gerald about my difficulties and problems, he would simply laugh as if I were telling him a joke and caution me against being nervous and impatient. "Practice is all it takes, Paolo. I promise you that you'll be able to learn in spite of yourself."

It has been approximately four years since that conversation with Gerald, and I have to admit he was right. I have since entrusted my entire manuscript to my computer and feel confident it will accelerate the writing process to completion.

I thank you, Gerald, and I shall always be grateful for your precious help, your inspiration, and your encouragement, and above all, for having been a dear friend.

CHAPTER 5

More Doubts

W hile typing my manuscript into the computer, I experienced a renewal of the enthusiasm that initially led me to undertake the work. Now, with fresh determination, I became so impatient to finish the project that I even considered taking a few weeks of vacation at a location where I wouldn't be disturbed.

After going to bed one night, unable to fall asleep, I thought about setting a date for my *escape*. Just as I was going over my destination plans, from the voice of my heart, I perceived that I was wasting my time. Surprised, I asked why.

The response was that I was not yet prepared to finish my book.

I asked why, and perceived that:

- **I had not yet succeeded in understanding the mechanism of my healing experiences.**
- **More importantly, I still didn't know who, in His true essence and form, is that being we commonly call God.**

Reflecting on the above, my perceptions seemed well founded. What was I supposed to do?

I prayed to God constantly, asking Him to somehow let me perceive the truth about His true identity. As my appeals failed to bring results,

I grew impatient and nervous, a state that had negative repercussions on every facet of my daily existence.

One Saturday evening while watching TV with Pina, and still befuddled about the fate of my writing, I became conscious of my nervousness. The television irritated me, so I retreated to the bedroom. I lay in bed and thought intensely about God, trying to conjure up an image of who He was and what He looked like.

As I concentrated on these thoughts, from the depths of my heart I felt a great need to pray. I sat on the bed with my legs crossed and repeated the following prayer:

> *"My God, I know at this moment that You are perfectly aware of the desire that is wrenching my heart. I entreat You, therefore, with all the sincerity my heart can muster, to manifest Yourself, so that I can finally know who You are and thus appease this flame that is constantly burning inside me. This fire in my heart will never be extinguished until such a time as You satisfy my wish and allow me to finish writing my book."*

I repeated this simple prayer slowly, trying to let it sink deep into my heart. After praying for about twenty minutes, I noticed the nervousness I had experienced earlier gradually dissipated.

After I prayed for about an hour, I felt overwhelmed by a great sense of peace and joy. I continued praying for a long time, maybe an hour or two. The only thing I remember is that at a certain point, the joy and tranquility I felt elevated to pure bliss. Even in this ecstatic state, from deep in my heart I perceived that God still couldn't appear to me.

I then fervently asked why.

After numerous appeals to the voice of my heart, I perceived that God couldn't appear to me for the simple reason that He didn't have a clearly defined form through which to reveal Himself.

After this perception, I inquired:

- **How is it possible that God has no form?**
- **Could it mean there is no God, and that man, confronted by nature's baffling riddles, found it expedient to create the illusion of a superior, mysterious being he called and is still calling God?**

In other words:

- **Was the term *God* concocted for the simple reason of holding someone responsible for all the things man himself could not understand or explain through reason?**
- **If this were true, then why have people throughout the world and down through the ages worshipped—in every conceivable form and in every imaginable way—this being we refer to as God?**
- **Could everyone, always, have been wrong?**

Unable to find adequate answers to my perplexing questions, my peace of mind vanished and I fell into a deep state of psychological turmoil that overwhelmed me with fears and doubts, making me endure one of the darkest periods of my life.

From time to time, as if to exorcise the bleak thoughts filling my mind, I tried to analyze my healing experiences. I had always thought and believed, without ever really knowing it, that my healing experiences were accomplished through God's divine intervention. But, if God had no shape or form, how was He able to help me?

Where was I to find scientifically verifiable evidence of His existence and intervention in my life?

As I explored this riddle, the voice of my heart somehow made me perceive there was an explanation to the puzzle, but my insufficient spiritual development hindered my comprehension.

I perceived, that instead of hastily seeking a resolution, I should patiently continue praying and wait for the time when I would be capable of understanding the truth—and at that point, the truth would be revealed to me.

Instead of reassuring me and giving me peace of mind, this new revelation increased my anxiety and confusion, leading me to ask:

- **How would I recognize the truth when it was revealed to me?**
- **How would I know, with a reasonable degree of assurance, that I would not mistake something else for the truth?**
- **Would I be able to perceive God when He came to me?**
- **How would I recognize God's identity?**

Unable to find satisfactory answers, my existence was plunged into a state of acute agitation from which I could find no respite.

From left: Prof Mike Murillo, Pina, Pino,
Bob Delacy, and Paolo
Joshua Tree, Ca. June 1993
Pino's graduation from junior College

Pino, Greg and Paolo
Joshua Tree, Ca. June 1993
Pino's Graduation from Junior College

Pino Ficara
Washington DC, 1993

Nino Ficara
San Diego, Ca. 2000

Pina, Paolo Jr. and Paolo
Vancouver, B.C., Canada
August 1999

Paolo Jr. Ficara
Graduate from University of San Diego
San Diego, Ca.
May 2000

Paolo and Pina
Morongo Valley, Ca.
25th Wedding Anniversary
December 12, 1995

Paolo and Pina
Puerto Vallarta, Mexico
March 1996

From left: Mercurio Falco, Nino Ficara, Pino Ficara, Luca Falco, Francesca
Falco, Andrea Falco, Fiorella Falco, Paolo Jr. Ficara, Pinuccia Falco,
Santangelo Muxaro, Sicily, Italy
August 1999

From left: Paolo, Mercurio Falco (Pina's Brother), Fiorella,
(Mercurio's wife), Pina, and Sheila Kennedy
Milano, Italy, 2001

Rosa Ficara (Paolo's Mother) and Pina
29 Palms, CA. 2005

Robert and Sheila Kennedy & Paolo and Pina Ficara
Milano, Italy, 2001

Paolo and Pina Ficara
Seattle, Washington
August 2005

Paolo and Pina Ficara
29 Palms, CA. 2005

CHAPTER 6

I Am Inspired to Read the Bible

Over coffee one Sunday morning, Pina announced, "I haven't been to church for a long time, and I'd really like to attend Mass today. Would you like to come along?"

I said I would, and off we went.

During the service, I noticed that although I was in church physically, my mind roamed elsewhere, thinking about matters that had nothing to do with the rite of Holy Mass. The priest's words abruptly called me back to reality when he spoke of the mystery of the Holy Trinity and explained that God the Father, Jesus the Son, and the Holy Ghost were three persons in one. Those words brought to memory the question I had been asking myself since I was a child:

How was it possible that three persons could be fused into one?

I analyzed the priest's words. If I accepted his hypothesis according to the mystery of the Holy Trinity, God had to have an individuality of His own, as well as a form and shape. Since He was one with Jesus, and since Jesus had a human form, it followed that God also had to have a human form.

It also followed that God had a place in which to dwell, located probably somewhere in space - a location we call heaven or paradise - where, like a great monarch, he reigned over the universe.

Was such a thing possible?

I thought about the earlier revelation I had from the voice of my heart, informing me that God had no shape or form.

- **Who was right?**
- **What was the truth behind this mystery?**
- **How could all this confusion ever be reconciled?**

As I wrestled with these thoughts, the priest announced the end of Mass, giving me the impression the ritual was over in the blink of an eye. Pina and I went home, where she started cooking dinner and I sat on the sofa watching TV. After a few minutes, I felt so nervous that I shivered all over. Unable to stay put, I began to walk in the house as if searching for something, but without the slightest idea of what I was looking for.

Seeing the restless state I was in, Pina advised me to go meditate, hoping I could relax.

I followed her advice and went into the bedroom, where I sat on the floor and began to pray as follows:

"My God, if You really do exist, I'm sure You already know what is ailing my heart. I ask You, therefore, to help me understand the truth about Your nature."

After continuously repeating the above prayer for about an hour, my nervousness had not abated in the least, and I felt I was wasting my time. I stopped praying and went into the kitchen, where Pina had dinner ready. As I sat down to join her and the kids, she asked if I felt any better, and I shook my head.

After we finished eating, while we were talking, all of a sudden and for no apparent reason, I got up and went straight to the bedroom, where I stretched out on the floor and pulled out all my books from under the bed. I glanced at the titles and flipped through pages, looking for something that would awaken memories.

Finally, I set my eyes on a book my mother had given me many years before.

The name of that book was:

THE HOLY BIBLE
New King James Version
Thomas Nelson Bibles
A Division of Thomas Nelson, Inc.
Copyright 1992 by Thomas Nelson, Inc.

As soon as I took the volume in my hands, my anxiety rescinded. In its place, I felt the familiar sensation of joy, peace and harmony that would fill me whenever I immersed in prayer and became perfectly attuned to the voice of my heart.

Getting up from the floor, Bible in hand, I related to Pina the reaction I had the moment I touched the book. She thought it seemed strange, but added, "I think the voice of your heart is trying to tell you to read the Bible."

I walked over to the sofa, where I shut my eyes and asked the voice of my heart if I should follow Pina's advice. After a moment, I perceived as true without a doubt what Pina had intuited.

I began to read the Gospel attributed to Matthew, and then I continued with the ones attributed to Mark, Luke, and John, and then the Epistles of Paul.

At the beginning of my research, if I may call it such, I saw Jesus' doctrine strange and His message ambiguous, leaving me in a protracted state of uncertainty.

During this perplexing period, I would often ask myself why Jesus, who appeared so great, powerful and wise, had not expressed Himself in a simpler and more direct manner.

Had He done so, He would have helped, in my opinion, people understand and accept His teachings with ease, conviction, and certainty?

Following my initial skepticism, I had the blessing and good fortune to realize that what had initially seemed strange, mysterious, complex and ambiguous was surprisingly and amazingly simple and direct.

Before sharing my results, I want to point out that in the following commentary of the Gospels, I shall only cite the biblical passages that have contributed the most to my understanding of the message Jesus passed down to us through His life, works, and teachings.

After reading the Gospels repeatedly, I concluded that the message could be divided into three different parts:

- **Jesus' doctrine**
- **Jesus' prodigious power**
- **Jesus' purpose on earth**

PART ONE
Jesus' Doctrine

CHAPTER 7

The Old and the New Law

Matthew, Chapter 5

17: "Do not think that I came to destroy the law or the prophets. I did not come to destroy but to fulfill . . . .

21: "You have heard that it was said to those of old, *'You shall not murder*, and whoever murders will be in danger of the judgment.'

22: "But I say to you that whoever is angry with his brother without a cause shall be in danger of the judgment. And whoever says to his brother, 'Raca!' shall be in danger of the council. But whoever says, 'You fool!' shall be in danger of hell fire.

23: "Therefore, if you bring your gift to the altar, and there remember that your brother has something against you,

24: "Leave your gift there before the altar and go your way. First be reconciled to your brother, and then come and offer your gift.

25: "Agree with your adversary quickly, while you are on the way with him, lest your adversary deliver you to the judge, the judge hand you over to the officer, and you be thrown into prison.

26: "Assuredly, I say to you, you will by no means get out of there till you have paid the last penny.

27: "You have heard that it was said to those of old, 'You shall not commit adultery.'

28: "But I say to you that whoever looks at a woman to lust for her has already committed adultery with her in his heart...

39: "But I tell you not to resist an evil person. But whoever slaps you on your right cheek, turn the other to him also.

40: "If anyone wants to sue you and take away your tunic, let him have your cloak, also . . .

43: "You have heard that it was said, 'You shall love your neighbor and hate your enemy.'

44: "But I say to you, love your enemies, bless those who curse you, do good to those who hate you, and pray for those who spitefully use you and persecute you,

45: "that you may be sons of your Father in heaven; for He makes His sun rise on the evil and on the good, and sends rain on the just and on the unjust.

46: "For if you love those who love you, what reward have you? Do not even the tax collectors do the same?

47: "And if you greet your brethren only, what do you do more than others? Do not even the tax collectors do so?

48: "Therefore you shall be perfect, just as your Father in heaven is perfect."

In verse seventeen, Jesus states that He didn't come to abolish the law and the prophets, but to fulfill the law. This affirmation gave me a lot to think about, but despite all my efforts, I couldn't understand how Jesus could have fulfilled the law.

Then, in verse twenty-one, Jesus says that He who kills will be called to judgment. I had no doubt about that.

But I couldn't understand the message contained in verses twenty-two, twenty-three, twenty-four, twenty-five, and twenty-six where Jesus states that anyone who gets angry at another person or who offends another by uttering angry words would be condemned and must immediately try to reconcile with that person—or he would remain stuck in his predicament until he has *paid up to the last penny.*

I knew that He was not referring to money, but if not money, what was it that Jesus meant?

With whom were we to square up?

Now, if the message of the above verses was difficult for me to fathom, verses twenty-seven and twenty-eight were even more incomprehensible. In those, Jesus accuses of adultery anyone who even dares to look lustfully at a woman. Why did Jesus equate the thought of having sex with the actual physical act?

In verses thirty-nine and forty, Jesus instructs that anyone who is wronged should turn the other cheek. I certainly didn't agree with this form of passive resistance. I believed at that time that failure to react to an offense by another was a sign of weakness that encouraged persecutors to perpetuate their actions. I felt it was more expedient to exchange the slap on the face with two or three blows to the offender's head, possibly accompanied by a few kicks.

At that moment, I asked myself:

If Jesus' teachings appeared to be impractical from a logical standpoint, why then did He insist on reinforcing such ideas in the minds of His followers?

What seemed to me stranger and more absurd was the statement in verse forty-four:

"Love your enemies, and pray for those who curse you." Matthew 5:44

- **Why should we love our enemies and pray for them?**
- **If that were truly the right thing to do, why did He not discuss and explain in detail the benefits to be gained by following and applying these teachings to our daily life?**
- **Why didn't Jesus clearly explain the mechanism—if there were one—of the laws governing His doctrine, so that everyone could easily understand and believe?**

Going on to verse forty-eight, where Jesus prompts us to be perfect like our Heavenly Father, I presumed that by *Heavenly Father*, Jesus was referring to God. Therefore, I asked myself:

- **Is God also our Father?**
- **How could that be possible?**

God is referred again to as our *Heavenly Father* in *The Lord's Prayer.*

CHAPTER 8
The Lord's Prayer

Matthew Chapter 6

1 "Take heed that you do not do your charitable deeds before men, to be seen by them. Otherwise you have no reward from your Father in heaven.

2 "Therefore, when you do a charitable deed, do not sound a trumpet before you as the hypocrites do in the synagogues and in the streets, that they may have glory from men. Assuredly, I say to you, they have their reward.

3 "But when you do a charitable deed, do not let your left hand know what your right hand is doing,

4 "that your charitable deed may be in secret; and your Father who sees in secret will Himself reward you openly.

5 "And when you pray, you shall not be like the hypocrites. For they love to pray standing in the synagogues and on the corners of the streets, that they may be seen by men. Assuredly, I say to you, they have their rewards.

6 "But you, when you pray, go into your room, and when you have shut your door, pray to your Father who is in the secret *place*; and your Father who sees in secret will reward you openly.

7 "And when you pray, do not use vain repetitions as the heathen do. For they think that they will be heard for their many words.

8 "Therefore do not be like them. For your Father knows the things you have need of before you ask Him."

In the above verses, Jesus explained that whenever performing a charitable deed, one should avoid making a public display of it, and that we should not publicize our supposed kindness. He also appears to be teaching the apostles where to pray and how to pray.

He states that there is no need to attend synagogue or church services in order to pray, which contradicts the religious leaders of those times as well those of our time who consider it a sin not to do so. In fact, Jesus says that all we need in order for our prayers to be heard is to pray in a secluded, quiet place.

He states further that our prayers should be expressed in silence and need not be long and repetitious, but simple and short, and should express the essence of our desires and needs.

I had prayed in this kind of atmosphere on many occasions and benefited accordingly - even though I still didn't fully understand the mechanism through which God was hearing my prayers and granting my wishes.

Matthew Chapter 6
9: "In this manner, therefore, pray: Our Father in heaven, Hallowed be Your name.
10: Your kingdom come. Your will be done On earth as it is in heaven.
11: Give us this day our daily bread.
12: And forgive us our debts, As we forgive our debtors.
13: And do not lead us into temptation. But deliver us from the evil one. For Yours is the kingdom and the power and the glory forever. Amen.

Then Jesus said:

14: "For if you forgive men their trespasses, your heavenly Father will also forgive you.
15: "But if you do not forgive men their trespasses, neither will your Father forgive your trespasses."

For the very first time in my life, I approached *The Lord's Prayer* from a different perspective. In the past, I had spoken the words automatically, but now I was analyzing them very carefully, hoping that I could grasp their true meaning and message.

I could discern that:

- **Heavenly Father and God were the same entity;**
- **That God was not only Jesus' Father, but also the Father of all humanity;**
- **That in addition to asking God to provide for our bodily sustenance and to forgive us our sins, we were to ask for His help and protection to avoid temptation.**

Upon further analysis, I noted that Jesus addresses His Father - that is to say God - as an individual with a precisely defined form who dwells in the kingdom of Heaven.

Taking this into consideration, I couldn't help wondering how - if what Jesus taught about God was true - I could have previously perceived from the depths of my heart that God couldn't appear to me because He had no definite form.

Moreover, if we were to accept Jesus' hypothesis that God is the common Father to us all, wouldn't it mean that we humans were on a par with Jesus, and that we should have been endowed with the same powers?

Is this the reality of human existence?

No!

The reality is that a significant number of human beings, for one reason or another, find themselves powerless and incapable of reacting to the vast sea of problems with which they are confronted over the course of their lives, with the consequence being that their lives more often than not are transformed into a living hell.

So, if this is the reality of life, where then is the truth of Jesus' teachings?

As I continued to analyze the verse of *The Lord's Prayer* that says:

"And forgive us our debts, as we have also forgiven our debtors,"

I found it easy to follow Jesus' supplication to His Father God to forgive us our wrongs, as we are to forgive those who commit wrongs against us.

But as I read Jesus' comment, the meaning became murkier, giving me pause. In fact, in verses fourteen and fifteen, Jesus states:

"For if you forgive men their trespasses, your heavenly Father will also forgive you." Matthew 6:14
"But if you do not forgive men their trespasses, neither will your Father forgive your trespasses." Matthew 6:15

What I couldn't understand was:

- **Why would the heavenly Father (God) forgive us only on condition that we forgive those who wrong us?**
- **Why, if we chose not to forgive, would God not forgive us?**
- **Should we infer from this verse that God is a vengeful being?**

This question gave rise to more questions:

- **If God didn't forgive us our sins, wouldn't He be acting and reacting in the same vengeful manner as most humans do?**
- **Wouldn't His actions show inconsistency with what we consider the goodness of His divine nature and the nature of His direct teachings?**
- **Don't most human beings love and respect only those who love and respect them, despising instead those who hate and mistreat them?**
- **Why was God, in the form of Jesus, preaching and teaching two completely different ideas with contradicting messages?**

God, in the form of Jesus, teaches us to love our enemies and to pray for those who persecute us.

"But I say to you, love your enemies, bless those who curse you, do good to those who hate you, and pray for those who spitefully use you and persecute you." Matthew 5:44

Was it possible that God, the creator of this complex and marvelous universe, and appearing in the perfect form of Jesus, contradicted Himself in such a puerile way?

After debating the point considerably and attempting to understand Jesus' message, I sensed there were no contradictions in Jesus' teachings and the reason I found them contradictory was due to the simple fact that I did not yet understand.

However, if there were no contradictions in Jesus' teachings, I asked myself:

- **Who is God in His true essence and nature?**
- **What kind relationship exists between God, Jesus and man?**

While pondering those questions, I sensed that I should not give in to despair, but should continue my quest, for eventually - when I was ready - the truth would be made known to me.

With this hope in heart and mind, I continued my search.

CHAPTER 9
CHRIST'S SERMON ON THE MOUNT TO THE MULTITUDE

Matthew, Chapter 6

19: "Do not lay up for yourselves treasures on earth, where moth and rust destroy and where thieves break in and steal;
20: "But lay up for yourselves treasures in heaven, where neither moth nor rust destroy and where thieves do not break in and steal.
21: "For where your treasure is, there your heart will be also."

I thought that what was stated in verse nineteen, seemed perfectly understandable, because every human being could relate to it. I could not say the same for verse twenty, which was totally in conflict with my sense of reason. I could not understand the nature of those treasures that Jesus talked about that we have to *lay up for ourselves* in Heaven, nor what *Heaven* is.

I asked myself:

- **How does one could accumulate treasure in Heaven, if we do not even know of what it might consist?**
- **Is there a place called Heaven?**
- **Where is it located?**

Further along in verse twenty-one, Jesus states:

"For where your treasure is, there your heart will be also." Matthew 6:21

I asked myself:

- **What do** *treasure* **and** *heart* **truly represent for Jesus?**
- **What does He mean by** *"Where your treasure is, there your heart will be also?" Matthew 6:21*
- **What is the true nature of this** *treasure* **that is located in the same place as our heart?**
- **Why did Jesus not explain in simple detail the nature of those treasures and the means by which they could be obtained?**

Matthew, Chapter 6
22: "The lamp of the body is the eye. If therefore your eye is good, your whole body will be full of light.
23: "But if your eye is bad, your whole body will be full of darkness. If therefore the light that is in you is darkness, how great is that darkness!"

The message in verses twenty-two and twenty-three was just as mysterious to me as the one in the preceding verse. I could comprehend that the term *eye* was not used in literal reference to one of our physical organs; but if not that, then what is it?

- **What did Jesus mean by the words,** *The lamp of the body is the eye…? Matthew 6:22*
- **Why, when this eye was** *sound,* **would our whole body be** *full of light,* **whereas when it was** *not sound,* **our whole body would be full of darkness?**

- In what part of our body was this enigmatic *eye* located?
- How could we check on it, to see if it were sound?

Despite my best efforts, I couldn't decipher the mystery of Jesus' words.

Matthew, Chapter 6.
24: "No one can serve two masters; for either he will hate the one and love the other, or else he will be loyal to the one and despise the other. You cannot serve God and mammon."

Why did Jesus state that men are not able to serve God and riches at the same time?

Matthew, Chapter 6
25: "Therefore I say to you, do not worry about your life, what you will eat or what you will drink; nor about your body, what you will put on. Is not life more than food and the body more than clothing?
26: "Look at the birds of the air, for they neither sow nor reap nor gather into barns; yet your heavenly Father feeds them. Are you not of more value than they?
27: "Which of you by worrying can add one cubit to his stature?
28: "So why do you worry about clothing? Consider the lilies of the field, how they grow: they neither toil nor spin;
29: "and yet I say to you that even Solomon in all his glory was not arrayed like one of these.
30: "Now if God so clothes the grass of the field, which today is, and tomorrow is thrown into the oven, will He not much more clothe you, O you of little faith?
31: "Therefore do not worry, saying, 'What shall we eat?' or 'What shall we drink?' or 'What shall we wear?'
32: "For after all these things the Gentiles seek. For your heavenly Father knows that you need all these things.

33: "But seek first the kingdom of God and His righteousness, and all these things shall be added to you.

34: "Therefore do not worry about tomorrow, for tomorrow will worry about its own things. Sufficient for the day is its own trouble."

In verses twenty-five through thirty-three, Jesus explains that over the course of our lives we should not be constantly worried about what we eat or drink, or how we dress. In other words, we should not worry about material things, but we should concentrate instead on seeking God's kingdom and His justice. When we do that, He (God) - who knows about all our needs - will provide for us, just as He provides for the birds that fly in the air and the grass and flowers that grow in the fields.

This message, though apparently easy to understand, gave me a rough time, since I still couldn't understand what follows:

- How could I look for God's kingdom and His justice if I didn't yet know who God truly is, or where His kingdom is located?
- How and where could I look for something I was still incapable of understanding?

In verse thirty-four, Jesus teaches us that our biggest concern should be today, and that we should not worry about *tomorrow,* because *tomorrow,* the future will take care of itself.

How could that be possible?

Matthew, Chapter 7
1: "Judge not, that you be not judged.
2: "For with what judgment you judge, you will be judged; and with the measure you use, it will be the measured back to you . . ."
7: "Ask, and it will be given you; seek, and you will find; knock, and it will be opened to you.

8: "For everyone who asks receives, and he who seeks finds, and to him who knocks it will be opened . . ."
12: "Therefore, whatever you want men to do to you, do also to them, for this is the Law and the Prophets..."
24: "Therefore, whoever hears these sayings of Mine and does them, I will liken him to a wise man who built his house on the rock . . ."
26: "But everyone who hears these sayings of Mine, and does not do them, will be like a foolish man who built his house on the sand."

In reading and analyzing the above verses, I had the sensation that Jesus was explaining the way God's law works.

In verse one, Jesus explains that if we do not judge, we will not be judged. Verse two, explains and illustrates that if we judge, we will be judged according our own criteria, and we will be treated in the same way we treat others.

In verse seven and eight, Jesus motivates us with the promise that whoever asks receives, whoever looks finds, and whoever knocks will have the door opened.

I had already experienced two of the above principles many times over, but as for seeking and finding, I still entertained serious doubts. Had I not fervently looked most of my life to find an answer to the mystery of God' existence? Yet, after many years of seeking and striving, I was still unable to fathom His true essence and identity.

Verse twelve states:

"Therefore, whatever you want men to do to you, do also to them, for this is the Law and the Prophets." Matthew 7:12

How can that be?

Close to the end of the chapter, Jesus goes on to say that whoever listens to, accepts, and practices His teachings can be likened to a wise man;

whereas whoever hears His words without putting them into practice - that is, without integrating them into their daily lives - can be compared to a fool.

What did Jesus mean by *wise* and *foolish* in this case?

CHAPTER 10

The Main Commandment

Matthew, Chapter 22

34: But when the Pharisees heard that He had silenced the Sadducees, they gathered together.

35: Then one of them, a lawyer, asked Him a question, testing Him, and saying,

36: "Teacher, which is the great commandment in the law?"

37: Jesus said to him, "'You shall love the Lord your God with all your heart, with all your soul, and with all your mind.'"

38: "This is the first and great commandment.

39: "And the second is like it: 'You shall love your neighbor as yourself.'

40: "On these two commandments hang all the law and the prophets."

From the above verses, I could clearly understand that the essence of the two most important commandments of God's law and of the prophets was embodied in the expression of our love for God and our neighbors.

After spending considerable time pondering the message in verses thirty-six, thirty-eight and thirty-nine, I asked myself:

- **Why is *loving God* and our *neighbors* so important as to exemplify nothing less than the essence of the two most important commandments of God's law?**

- Why do we have *to love* with all our *heart*?
- What does Jesus mean by *heart*? Is He referring to the organ that pumps blood through our body, or is the term used to indicate something less tangible?
- Why not connect *love* with a different part of our anatomy - like our feet, stomach, arms, mouth, and say, *"I love you with all my feet,"* instead of, *"I love you with all my heart?"*
- And why should we *love* with all our *soul*?
- What, in its true form and essence, is the *soul*?
- And why should we *love* with all our *mind*?
- What, in its true essence, is our *mind*?
- Why should we *love our neighbor as ourselves*?
- Who is our *neighbor*, and why does he/she deserve to be loved by us as much as we love ourselves?

And most important:

Why do all of God's laws and the prophets' teachings depend on those two commandments?

During this period, whenever I meditated on what I thought to be Jesus' message as set forth in the above verses, I would think intently about the Ten Commandments that Moses passed on to us, and which I quote below:

1   I am the Lord your God; you shall have no other gods before Me.
2   You shall not take the name of the Lord your God in vain.
3   You shall not worship false idols.
4   Remember the Sabbath day, and keep it holy.
5   Honor your father and your mother.
6   You shall not kill.
7   You shall not commit adultery.
8   You shall not steal.

9 You shall not bear false witness.
10 You shall not covet your neighbor's house.

While carefully reading the Ten Commandments, I sensed little difference between the message embodied in them and the basic concepts Jesus teaches in the Gospels. In essence, what Jesus preaches is practically identical to the principles His Jewish predecessors had already made known.

If Jesus says nothing that wasn't already known, why were His teachings considered so innovative and important?

After pondering that for a while, I concluded that the answer lay in Jesus' own words:

"Do not think that I came to destroy the Law or the Prophets. I did not come to destroy but to fulfill." Matthew 5:17

In different words, Jesus states that He came in this world not to bring a new law or doctrine, but to fulfill the one that already existed.
Following this train of thought, I asked myself:

How, in what way, was Jesus fulfilling the law?

After unsuccessfully pondering that issue for some time, I had to set it aside.
Thus far into my studies, Jesus' teachings, even if not entirely original - linked intrinsically as they were to the canons of the Old Testament - infused a new awareness into my spiritual outlook. Moreover, even if I couldn't yet entirely understand all of His doctrine, I could grasp that:

• **The Son** *Jesus* **and the Father** *God* **are the same;**
• **God is not only Jesus' Father but also the Father of mankind;**

- **The most important purpose in our lives is to love the Lord our God with all our heart, soul, and mind, and to love and respect our fellow man as we do ourselves;**
- **We are commanded to forgive and love our enemies and pray for their well - being.**

Setting these principles as a foundation for my research, with the resolution in my mind and my heart that I would pursue my search with more intensity until I found what I was looking for, I felt that I was now ready to continue my analysis of what I consider the second part of the Gospels.

PART TWO
JESUS' PRODIGIOUS POWER

CHAPTER 11

Jesus Heals a Leper - The Centurion's Servant - Peter's Mother in Law is Healed - The Stilling of the Tempest on the Sea - The Paralytic

Matthew, Chapter 8

1: When he had come down from the mountain, great multitudes followed Him.

2: And behold, a leper came and worshiped Him, saying, "Lord, if You are willing, You can make me clean."

3: Then Jesus put out His hand and touched him, saying, "I am willing; be cleansed." And immediately his leprosy was cleansed.

After reading these verses, I concluded that the basic elements that helped the leper to heal were two simple things:

Jesus' uncommon healing powers and the leper's wish to be healed.

Matthew, Chapter 8

5: Now when Jesus had entered Capernaum, a centurion came to Him, pleading with Him,

6: saying, "Lord, my servant is lying at home paralyzed, dreadfully tormented."

7: And Jesus said to him, "I will come and heal him."

8: The centurion answered and said, "Lord, I am not worthy that You should come under my roof. But only speak a word, and my servant will be healed.

9: "For I also am a man under authority, having soldiers under me. And I say to this one, 'Go,' and he goes; and to another, 'Come,' and he comes; and to my servant, 'Do this,' and he does it."

10: When Jesus heard him, He marveled, and said to those who followed, "Assuredly, I say to you, I have not found such great faith, not even in Israel!"

Again, in this episode, it is evident that the elements that corresponded to the healing of the centurion's servant were the same:

Jesus' healing powers as well the desire, hope and faith of the centurion that prompted him to ask for Jesus' help.

Matthew, Chapter 8

14: Now when Jesus had come into Peter's house, He saw his wife's mother lying sick with a fever.

15: So He touched her hand, and the fever left her. And she arose and served them.

16: When evening had come, they brought to Him many who were demon-possessed. And He cast out the spirits with a word, and healed all who were sick…

23: Now when He got into a boat, His disciples followed him.

24: And suddenly a great tempest arose on the sea, so that the boat was covered with the waves. But He was asleep.

25: Then His disciples came to Him and awoke Him, saying, "Lord, save us! We are perishing!"

26: But He said to them, "Why are you fearful, O you of little faith?" Then He arose and rebuked the winds and the sea, and there was a great calm.

The sequence of events in the above verses shows that the basic element for having one's petitions granted by Jesus is the simple belief that He can help and one's willingness to ask for intercession.

Matthew, Chapter 9
1: So He got into a boat, crossed over, and came to His own city.
2: Then behold, they brought to Him a paralytic lying on a bed. When Jesus saw their faith, He said to the paralytic, "Son, be of good cheer; your sins are forgiven you."
3: And at once, some of the scribes said to themselves, "This Man blasphemes."
4: But Jesus, knowing their thoughts, said, "Why do you think evil in your hearts?
5: "For which is easier, to say, '*Your* sins are forgiven you,' or to say 'Arise and walk?'
6: "But that you may know that the Son of Man has power on earth to forgive sins"—then He said to the paralytic, "Arise, take up your bed, and go to your house."
7: And he arose and departed to his house.

After I meditated for quite some time on the above verse, I sensed one more time that the main ingredients in the healing process were the:

Desire to be healed and the unconditional belief and faith in Jesus' power.

Also in the above verses, Jesus stated that:

- *Sickness* **is the consequence of man's sin;**
- *The Son of Man* **has the power to forgive sin and to heal he who has sinned;**
- *Healing* **can be performed with the use of different sentences or words; as long as the meaning is the same, the results will also be the same.**

After reflecting upon the last assertion, I couldn't help asking myself:

- **Who is the *Son of Man*?**
- **Is Jesus speaking about Himself or is He speaking about every human being in general?**
- **If He is referring to Himself, as the Son of God, then it becomes understandable that He can forgive the sins of others. But, if He is referring to mankind, how can a man forgive the sins of his fellow man?**
- **When Jesus tells the man with the palsy, *Your sins are forgiven*, how does the lame man begin to walk? What is *sin* in its true essence?**
- **How could *sin* actually have caused that man's paralysis?**

CHAPTER 12
THE PHARISEES AND THE TRADITION

Matthew, Chapter 15

1: Then the scribes and Pharisees who were from Jerusalem came to Jesus, saying,

2: "Why do Your disciples transgress the tradition of the elders? For they do not wash their hands when they eat bread."

3: He answered and said to them, "Why do you also transgress the commandment of God because of your tradition?

4: "For God commanded, saying, 'Honor your father and your mother,' and 'He who curses father or mother, let him be put to death.'

5: "But you say, 'Whoever says to his father or mother, "Whatever profit you might have received from me is a gift to God . . ."'

6: "Then he need not honor his father or mother. Thus you have made the commandment of God of no effect by your tradition.

7: "Hypocrites! Well did Isaiah prophesy about you, saying:

8: "'These people draw near to Me with their mouth,
And honor Me with their lips,
But their heart is far from Me.

9: "And in vain they worship Me,
Teaching as doctrines the commandments of men.'"

10: When He had called the multitude to Himself, He said to them, "Hear and understand:

11: "Not what goes into the mouth defiles a man; but what comes out of the mouth, this defiles a man."
15: Then Peter answered and said to Him, "Explain this parable to us."
16: So Jesus said, "Are you also still without understanding?
17: "Do you not yet understand that whatever enters the mouth goes into the stomach and is eliminated?
18: "But those things which proceed out of the mouth come from the heart, and they defile a man.
19: "For out of the heart proceed evil thoughts, murders, adulteries, fornications, thefts, false witness, blasphemies.
20: "These are the *things* which defile a man, but to eat with un-washed hands does not defile a man."

As I was reading verses one to ten, I felt that Jesus was warning us not to interpret the scriptures of the Old Testament literally and blindly, urging us to use logic, common sense, and wisdom in deciphering the message of the prophets.

Then, in reflecting on verses eleven through verse twenty, I sensed that Jesus, although in a different way and using different words, was teaching the role our thoughts play and the effect they have on our lives.

CHAPTER 13

*JAIRUS' DAUGHTER AND THE WOMAN
WITH A BLOOD ISSUE*

Matthew, Chapter 9

18: While He spoke these things to them, behold, a ruler came and worshiped Him, saying, "My daughter has just died, but come and lay Your hand on her and she will live."

19: So Jesus arose and followed him, and so did His disciples.

20: And suddenly, a woman who had a flow of blood for twelve years came from behind and touched the hem of His garment.

21: For she said to herself, "If only I may touch His garment, I shall be made well."

22: But Jesus turned around, and when He saw her He said, "Be of good cheer, daughter; your faith has made you well." And the woman was made well from that hour.

23: When Jesus came into the ruler's house, and saw the flute players and the noisy crowd wailing,

24: He said to them, "Make room, for the girl is not dead, but sleeping." And they ridiculed Him.

25: But when the crowd was put outside, He went in and took her by the hand, and the girl arose.

In reading and analyzing the above verses, four specific points affected me strongly:

- **The demonstration of Jesus' incredible power;**
- **Jairus' deep fatherly love and his determination - despite insurmountable odds—not to surrender to the harsh reality of death, but to seek with steadfast faith Jesus' help;**

(Although the circumstances were vastly different, this episode reminded me of my father's unfaltering hope when he took my mother to the old healer in Marsala and to the clinic in Palermo - thus saving her life, even when the town doctors felt sure she was going to die: "Journey of a Healer Volume I)

- **The immense faith shown by the hemorrhagic, who believed that by merely touching Jesus' cloak she could be cured;**
- **Jesus' affirmation to the hemorrhagic:** *Take heart, daughter; your faith has made you well.*

In light of all the above, I wondered:

- **What does Jesus mean when He tells the hemorrhagic woman that it wasn't He who had cured her, but her own** *faith*?
- **How could the woman's** *faith* **have cured her blood condition that had affected her for the previous twelve years of her life?**
- **What is** *faith* **in its true essence?**
- **Why doesn't Jesus explain in clear and simple words the definition of** *faith*?

CHAPTER 14

The Two Blind Men and the
Mute Possessed of the Devil

Matthew, Chapter 9

27: When Jesus departed from there, two blind men followed Him, crying out and saying, "Son of David, have mercy on us."

28: And when He had come into the house, the blind men came to Him. And Jesus said to them, "Do you believe that I am able to do this?" They said to Him, "Yes, Lord."

29: Then He touched their eyes, saying, "According to your faith let it be to you."

30: And their eyes were opened. And Jesus sternly warned them, saying, "See that no one knows it."

31: But when they had departed, they spread the news about Him in all that country.

32: As they went out, behold, they brought to Him a man, mute and demon-possessed.

33: And when the demon was cast out, the mute spoke. And the multitudes marveled, saying, "It was never seen like this in Israel."

In verse twenty-eight, we can see once again how extremely important it is for people seeking help to believe strongly in the fulfillment of their wishes.

Verse twenty-nine, on the other hand, emphasizes that the success of the healing also requires faith in the healer - in this case, in Jesus.

All of this demonstrates that *faith* is an important prerequisite for affecting a cure.

Verse thirty-two introduces us to *diabolical possession*, and in verse thirty-three, Jesus *expels the demon*.

This last miracle prompted me to meditate on the nature of the evil spirit that had taken possession of the mute and consequently made him suffer.

Jesus never explains in simple, understandable words who or what these *demons* or *devils* are;

Or the mechanism by which they take possession of human beings;

Nor does He explain how He casts them out.

I asked myself:

Why?

CHAPTER 15

The Disciples Called, Instructed and Sent Forth

Matthew, Chapter 10

1: And when He had called His twelve disciples to *Him*, He gave them power over unclean spirits, to cast them out, and to heal all kinds of sickness and all kinds of disease.

7: "And as you go, preach, saying, 'The kingdom of heaven is at hand.'

8: "Heal the sick, cleanse lepers, raise the dead, cast out demons. Freely you have received, freely give."

In the first verse, Jesus states that He transferred His powers to His disciples, giving them the power to do the same things He did.

I wondered:

- **How could He do that?**
- **Why does Jesus not explain in clear and simple words the mechanics of how the disciples were empowered?**
- **Could Jesus, if He wished, empower other people besides His disciples?**

In verse seven, Jesus directs the disciples to go about preaching that *the kingdom of heaven is at hand,* but He does not explain what this kingdom of heaven is, where it is located and what we need to do to get there.

- **Why?**
- **Why is He making things more complicated than they should be?**
- **Why doesn't He explain everything in detail once and for all, so that everyone can understand?**

In verse eight, He admonishes His disciples not to *ask* for or *take compensation* for *their services*. It is important that they *dispense freely* what they have *freely received* from God.

This admonishment made me recall the time I was considering charging for my prayers and the negative consequences of those thoughts. Why doesn't Jesus explain why it is wrong to accept compensation?

CHAPTER 16

THE RICH YOUTH

Luke, Chapter 18

18: Now a certain ruler asked Him, saying, "Good Teacher, what shall I do to inherit eternal life?"

19: So Jesus said to him, "Why do you call Me good? No one is good but One, that is, God.

20: "You know the commandments: *'Do not commit adultery,' 'Do not murder,' 'Do not steal,' 'Do not bear false witness,' 'Honor your father and mother.'*"

21: And he said, "All these things I have kept from my youth."

22: So when Jesus heard these things, He said to him, "You still lack one thing. Sell all that you have and distribute to the poor, and you will have treasure in heaven; and come, follow Me.

23: But when he heard this, he became very sorrowful, for he was very rich.

24: And when Jesus saw that he became very sorrowful, He said, "How hard it is for those who have riches to enter the kingdom of God!

25: "For it is easier for a camel to go through the eye of a needle than for a rich man to enter the kingdom of God."

Here again, Jesus teaches that *riches* are an obstacle on the path to spiritual enlightenment, and yet He never explains the reasons why. If *riches* are such a hindrance, why is it that over the centuries and up to the present, a great number of religious figures and most religious organizations work hard to amass material fortunes?

CHAPTER 17
LAZARUS' RESURRECTION

John, Chapter 11

1: Now a certain man was sick, Lazarus of Bethany, the town of Mary and her sister Martha.

2: It was that Mary who anointed the Lord with fragrant oil and wiped His feet with her hair, whose brother Lazarus was sick.

3: Therefore the sisters sent to Him, saying, "Lord, behold, he whom You love is sick."

4: When Jesus heard that, He said, "This sickness is not unto death, but for the glory of God, that the Son of God may be glorified through it."

5: Now Jesus loved Martha and her sister and Lazarus.

6: So, when He heard that he was sick, He stayed two more days in the place where He was.

7: Then after this He said to the disciples, "Let us go into Judea again."

8: The disciples said to Him, "Rabbi, lately the Jews sought to stone You, and are You going there again?"

9: Jesus answered, "Are there not twelve hours in the day? If anyone walks in the day, he does not stumble, because he sees the light of this world.

10: "But if one walks in the night, he stumbles, because the light is not in him."

11: These things He said, and after that He said to them, "Our friend Lazarus sleeps, but I go that I may wake him up."

12: Then His disciples said, "Lord, if he sleeps he will get well."

13: However, Jesus spoke of his death, but they thought that He was speaking about taking rest in sleep.

14: Then Jesus said to them plainly, "Lazarus is dead.

15: "And I am glad for your sake that I was not there, that you may believe. Nevertheless let us go to him."

16: Then Thomas, who is called the Twin, said to his fellow disciples, "Let us also go, that we may die with Him."

17: So when Jesus came, He found that he had already been in the tomb four days.

18: Now Bethany was near Jerusalem, about two miles away.

19: And many of the Jews had joined the women around Martha and Mary, to comfort them concerning their brother.

20: Then Martha, as soon as she heard that Jesus was coming, went and met Him, but Mary was sitting in the house.

21: Now Martha said to Jesus, "Lord, if you had been here, my brother would not have died.

22: "But even now I know that whatever You ask of God, God will give You."

23: Jesus said to her, "Your brother will rise again."

24: Martha said to him, "I know that he will rise again in the resurrection at the last day."

25: Jesus said to her, "I am the resurrection and the life. He who believes in Me, though he may die, he shall live.

26: "And whoever lives and believes in Me shall never die. Do you believe this?"

27: She said to him, "Yes, Lord, I believe that You are the Christ, the Son of God, who is to come into the world."

28: And when she had said these things, she went her way and secretly called Mary her sister, saying, "The Teacher has come and is calling for you."

29: As soon as she heard that, she arose quickly and came to Him.

30: Now Jesus had not yet come into the town, but was in the place where Martha met Him.

31: Then the Jews who were with her in the house, and comforting her, when they saw that Mary rose up quickly and went out, followed her, saying, "She is going to the tomb to weep there."

32: Then, when Mary came where Jesus was, and saw Him, she fell down at His feet, saying to Him, "Lord, if you had been here, my brother would not have died..."

After analyzing all the above, apart from the demonstration of Jesus' enormous power, I noticed again that the basic ingredients for Lazarus' resurrection was inextricably linked to *the hope, conviction, and above all, the belief and faith* that Martha and Mary had in Jesus. They were firmly convinced that if Jesus had wanted to, He could raise their brother from the dead.

Once more, we see that the key elements to getting one's prayers answered are:

Conviction, believe and faith that anything is possible.

CHAPTER 18

HEALING OF THE EPILEPTIC

Matthew, Chapter 17

14: And when they had come to the multitude, a man came to Him, kneeling down to Him and saying,

15: "Lord, have mercy on my son, for he is an epileptic and suffers severely; for he often falls into the fire and often into the water.

16: "So I brought him to Your disciples, but they could not cure Him."

17: Then Jesus answered and said, "O faithless and perverse generation, how long shall I be with you? How long shall I bear with you? Bring him here to Me."

18: And Jesus rebuked the demon, and it came out of him; and the child was cured from that very hour.

19: Then the disciples came to Jesus privately and said, "Why could we not cast it out?"

20: So Jesus said to them, "Because of your unbelief; for assuredly, I say to you, if you have faith as a mustard seed, you will say to this mountain, 'Move from here to there,' and it will move; and nothing will be impossible for you.

21: "However, this kind does not go out except by prayer and fasting."

Let's observe what, in my opinion, were the most important steps in the above sequence of events:

The man brings his son to the apostles, but they fail to expel the demon.

Instead of accepting the apostles' abortive attempt, as the last resort the man rejects the validity of their intercession and asks help from Jesus.

Jesus immediately heals the boy.

Once again, it is important to note that the key ingredients for the boy's healing were the same as those I previously mentioned: Jesus' supreme healing power and the unflinching determination of the boy's father to pursue what he wanted, even when it seemed there was no hope.

After the healing, the thoroughly astonished disciples ask Jesus why they couldn't heal the boy. Because, Jesus replied, they did not have faith, because they did not truly believe they were able to help the boy, and because demons such as the one He expelled from the boy can only be cast out through prayer and fasting.

That affirmation made me wonder.

If the disciples were already empowered by Jesus to do the things that He was doing, including having the ability *to cast out demons,* - *"Heal the sick, cleanse the lepers, raise the dead, cast out demons..." Matthew 10:8*

- **Why then had they failed?**
- **Why then did Jesus state that His disciples were not able to heal the boy because they did not have faith, because they did not believe, and because this particular type of demon could only be cast out through prayer and fasting?**
- **How could prayer and fasting help to cast out demons from that boy's body?**

While I was considering these concepts, I recalled that whenever I tried to pray for healing right after a big meal, I was rarely successful in establishing contact with the voice of my heart, and rarely were my prayers answered.

Was there a connection between my experiences and Jesus' teachings?

Then I asked myself:

- **What exactly are** *demons*?
- **Where did they originate?**
- **Who created them?**

We hear that God is the creator of all things. If this were true, then *demons* are undoubtedly of His making.

Why would He create these entities called *demons* **whose only function seems to be to inflict pain and suffering on humanity?**

CHAPTER 19

FIRST MULTIPLICATION OF THE BREAD -
SECOND MULTIPLICATION OF BREAD -
THE WEDDING IN CANA

Matthew, Chapter 14

13: When Jesus heard it, He departed from there by boat to a deserted place by Himself. But when the multitudes heard it, they followed Him on foot from the cities.

14: And when Jesus went out He saw a great multitude; and He was moved with compassion for them, and healed their sick.

15: When it was evening, His disciples came to Him saying, "This is a deserted place, and the hour is already late. Send the multitudes away, that they may go into the villages and buy themselves food."

16: But Jesus said to them, "They do not need to go away. You give them something to eat."

17: And they said to Him, "We have here only five loaves and two fish."

18: He said, "Bring them here to me."

19: Then He commanded the multitudes to sit down on the grass. And He took the five loaves and the two fish, and looking up to heaven, He blessed and broke and gave the loaves to the disciples; and the disciples gave to the multitudes.

20: So they all ate and were filled, and they took up twelve baskets full of the fragments that remained.
21: Now those who had eaten were about five thousand men, be-sides women and children.

Matthew, Chapter 15
29: Jesus departed from there, skirted the Sea of Galilee, and went up on the mountain and sat down there.
30: Then great multitudes came to Him, having with them the lame, blind, mute, maimed, and many others; and they laid them down at Jesus' feet, and He healed them.
31: So the multitude marveled when they saw the mute speaking, the maimed made whole, the lame walking, and the blind seeing; and they glorified the God of Israel.
32: Now Jesus called His disciples to Himself and said, "I have com-passion on the multitudes, because they have now continued with Me three days and have nothing to eat. And I do not want to send them away hungry, lest they faint on the way."
33: Then His disciples said to him, "Where could we get enough bread in the wilderness to fill such a great multitude?"
34: Jesus said to them, "How many loaves do you have?" And they said, "Seven, and a few little fish."
35: So He commanded the multitude to sit down on the ground.
36: And He took the seven loaves and the fish and gave thanks, broke them and gave them to His disciples; and the disciples gave to the multitude.
37: So they all ate and were filled, and they took up seven large bas-kets full of the fragments that were left.
38: Now those who ate were four thousand men, besides women and children.
39: And He sent away the multitude, got into the boat, and came to the region of Magdala.

John, Chapter 2

1: . . . there was a wedding in Cana of Galilee, and the mother of Jesus was there.

2: Now both Jesus and His disciples were invited to the wedding.

3: And when they ran out of wine, the mother of Jesus said to Him, "They have no wine."

4: Jesus said to her, "Woman, what does your concern have to do with Me? My hour has not yet come."

5: His mother said to the servants, "Whatever He says to you, do it."

6: Now there were set there six water pots of stone, according to the manner of purification of the Jews, containing twenty or thirty gallons apiece.

7: Jesus said to them, "Fill the water pots with water." And they filled them up to the brim.

8: And He said to them, "Draw some out now, and take it to the master of the feast." And they took it.

9: When the master of the feast had tasted the water that was made wine, and did not know where it came from (but the servants who had drawn the water knew), the master of the feast called the bridegroom.

10: And said to him, "Every man at the beginning sets out the good wine, and when the guests have well drunk, then the inferior. You have kept the good wine until now."

11: This beginning of signs Jesus did in Cana of Galilee, and manifested His glory; and His disciples believed in Him.

12: After this He went down to Capernaum, He, His mother, His brothers and His disciples; and they did not stay there many days.

Once again, we were confronted with a demonstration of Jesus' apparent supernatural powers; but are we to believe it was possible to explain in a scientific manner how He was truly able to have multiplied the bread and fish and to change the water into wine?

CHAPTER 20

JESUS WALKS ON WATER

Matthew, Chapter 14

22: Immediately Jesus made His disciples get into the boat and go before Him to the other side, while He sent the multitudes away.

23: And when He had sent the multitudes away, He went up on the mountain by Himself to pray. Now when evening came, He was alone there.

24: But the boat was now in the middle of the sea, tossed by the waves, for the wind was contrary.

25: Now in the fourth watch of the night Jesus went to them, walking on the sea.

26: And when the disciples saw Him walking on the sea, they were troubled, saying, "It is a ghost!" And they cried out for fear.

27: But immediately Jesus spoke to them, saying, "Be of good cheer! It is I; do not be afraid."

28: And Peter answered Him and said, "Lord, if it is You, command me to come to You on the water."

29: He said, "Come." And when Peter had come down out of the boat, he walked on the water to go to Jesus.

30: But when he saw that the wind was boisterous, he was afraid; and beginning to sink he cried out, saying, "Lord, save me."

31: And immediately Jesus stretched out *His* hand and caught him, and said to him, "O you of little faith, why did you doubt?"

32: And when they got into the boat, the wind ceased.

Here are some considerations:

- How was it possible for Jesus to walk on the water without sinking?
- How could Peter have accomplished the same feat?
- Why did Peter begin to sink the moment he doubted?
- According to Jesus, he was sinking because of his *little faith*. Why does Jesus not explain the meaning of faith in its true essence?

CHAPTER 21

JESUS CURSES THE FIG TREE

Among all of Jesus' miracles, the one that intrigued me the most was the story of the *Cursed Fig Tree.*

Matthew, Chapter 21

18: Now in the morning, as He returned to the city, He was hungry.

19: And seeing a fig tree by the road, He came to it and found nothing on it but leaves, and said to it, "Let no fruit grow on you ever again." Immediately the fig tree withered away.

20: And when the disciples saw it, they marveled, saying, "How did the fig tree wither away so soon?

21: So Jesus answered and said to them. "Assuredly, I say to you, if you have faith and do not doubt, you will not only do what was done to the fig tree, but also if you say to this mountain, 'Be removed and be cast into the sea,' it will be done.

22: "And whatever things you ask in prayer, believing, you will receive."

Mark in Chapter 11

12: Now the next day, when they had come out from Bethany, He was hungry.

13: And seeing from afar a fig tree having leaves, He went to see if perhaps He would find something on it. When He came to it, He found nothing but leaves, for it was not the season for figs.

14: In response Jesus said to it, "Let no one eat fruit from you ever again." And His disciples heard it.

19: When evening had come, He went out of the city.

20: Now in the morning, as they passed by, they saw the fig tree dried up from the roots.

21: And Peter, remembering, said to Him, "Rabbi, look! The fig tree which You cursed has withered away."

22: So Jesus answered and said to them, "Have faith in God.

23: "For assuredly, I say to you, whoever says to this mountain, 'Be removed and be cast into the sea,' and does not doubt in his heart, but believes that those things he says will be done, he will have whatever he says.

24: "Therefore I say to you, whatever thing you ask when you pray, believe that you receive *them,* and you will have *them.*"

In reading the above account by the evangelists Matthew and Mark, what particularly drew my attention was that the versions were not identical. Matthew reports that the fig tree withered immediately, whereas Mark tells us that the day after, as they were returning from Jerusalem, they noticed the tree had withered.

So I asked myself:

- Since the fig tree episode is such a unique occurrence, why are the two versions dissimilar?
- Did the fig tree wither immediately or was it a gradual process?
- Why did Jesus - who knew that it wasn't fig season - go to the tree for a fig and then curse it for not having any fruit?
- Was it the fig tree's fault it had no fruits?
- How could Jesus - the son of God, the manifestation of God in human form, who preached love and forgiveness - get so drastically upset with the fig tree to the point of cursing it and letting it die, even though the tree did not do any wrong to Him?

- Given his ability to change water into wine and multiply bread loaves and fish, why did Jesus not use his creative power to command the fig tree to have fruit, even if it were not the season and the time for the tree to bear fruit?
- Was there a striking contradiction between Jesus' words and deeds?

Now if all this appeared odd to me, Jesus' reply to the disciples appeared even more so.

Mark, Chapter 11
22: So Jesus answered and said to them, "Have faith in God.
23: "For assuredly, I say to you, whoever says to this mountain, 'Be removed and be cast into the sea,' and does not doubt in his heart, but believes that those things he says will be done, he will have whatever he says.
24: "Therefore I say to you, whatever thing you ask when you pray, believe that you receive them, and you will have them."

According to Jesus, whatever is asked in *prayer*, if accompanied by *faith* and *certainty*, would not only allow to perform such *simple feats* as making a fig tree wither, but they could command a mountain to plunge itself into the sea and the mountain would obey.

Now the question is:

- To whom was Jesus referring when He said, *Whoever says…?*
- Was He referring only to His disciples, or was He referring to every man and women who comes in this world?

The reference in my opinion is very clear and eloquent, with *Whoever says…* Jesus was referring to every living human being.

This did bring more questions:

- If Jesus' miracles were being performed through the agency of God the Father, an integral part of Jesus' being, how could He affirm that anyone with sufficient belief, faith, and determination could perform the same feats and obtain the same results that He did?
- Would that mean that any human being is capable to do what Jesus was doing?

CHAPTER 22

FAITH - PERSISTENCE IN PRAYER - THE MEMBERS OF JESUS' FAMILY

Luke, Chapter 17

5: And the apostles said to the Lord, "Increase our faith!"
6: So the Lord said, "If you have faith as a mustard seed, you can say to this mulberry tree, 'Be pulled up by the roots and be planted in the sea,' and it would obey you.

In verse five, the apostles admitted they did not have enough faith, and they pled for help from Jesus.

Jesus, in return, instead of helping them to acquire more faith, reproached them for their lack of faith.

- **Did all this make any sense?**
- **Why Jesus ignored His Apostles' request for help?**

Luke, Chapter 18

1: Then He spoke a parable to them, that men always ought to pray and not lose heart.
2: Saying: "There was in a certain city a judge who did not fear God nor regard man.
3: "Now there was a widow in that city; and she came to him, saying, 'Get justice for me from my adversary.'

4: "And he would not for a while; but afterward he said within himself, 'Though I do not fear God nor regard man,

5: "'yet because this widow troubles me I will avenge her, lest by her continual coming she weary me.'"'

6: Then the Lord said, "Hear what the unjust judge said.

7: "And shall God not avenge His own elect who cry out day and night to Him, though He bears long with them?"

Jesus explains that perseverance is the most important prerequisite to getting our prayers answered, and that only after our prayers are answered should we stop pleading for help.

John, Chapter 2

1: On the third day there was a wedding in Cana of Galilee, and the mother of Jesus was there.

2: Now both Jesus and His disciples were invited to the wedding.

3: And when they ran out of wine, the mother of Jesus said to Him, "They have no wine."

4: Jesus said to her, "Woman, what does your concern have to do with Me? My hour has not yet come."

5: His mother said to the servants, "Whatever He says to you, do it."

6: Now there were set there six waterpots of stone, according to the manner of purification of the Jews, containing twenty or thirty gallons apiece.

7: Jesus said to them, "Fill the waterpots with water." And they filled them up to the brim.

8: And He said to them, "Draw some out now, and take it to the master of the feast." And they took it.

9: When the master of the feast had tasted the water that was made wine, and did not know where it came from (but the servants who had drawn the water knew), the master of the feast called the bridegroom.

10: And said to him, "Every man at the beginning sets out the good wine, and when the *guests* have well drunk, then the inferior. You have kept the good wine until now."
11: This beginning of signs Jesus did in Cana of Galilee, and manifested His glory; and His disciples believed in Him.
12: After this He went down to Capernaum, He, His mother, His brothers and His disciples; and they did not stay there many days.

Matthew, Chapter 12
46: While he was still talking to the multitudes, behold, His mother and brothers stood outside, seeking to speak with him.
47: Then one said to Him, "Look, Your mother and Your brothers are standing outside, seeking to speak with You."
48: But he answered and said to the one who told him, "Who is my mother, and who are my brothers?"
49: And He stretched out his hand toward His disciples and said, "Here are my mother and my brothers!
50: "For whoever does the will of my Father in heaven is My brother, and sister, and mother."

After reading those verses many times over, I found the message extremely intriguing and disturbing, making me wonder as I never had before.

This was because John and Matthew, the only direct disciples and witnesses of Jesus, were testifying that Mary was indeed Jesus' mother, and that Jesus had several brothers.

"After this He went down to Capernaum, He, His mother, His brothers and His disciples; and they did not stay there many days."
John 2:12

"While he was still talking to the multitudes, behold, His mother and brothers stood outside, seeking to speak with him . . ." *Matthew 12:46*

Now the shocking questions:

- **Mary did indeed have several children. Now, if we cannot prove in a tangible and unquestionable way that Jesus was indeed the firstborn child, as stated in the Bible, wouldn't Mary's impregnation by God and the mystery of Her virginity and Christ's divine nature simply vanish into thin air?**
- **Wouldn't this also prove that Jesus was a simple human being like everyone else?**
- **However, if Jesus was indeed a normal human being, how does one explain the supernatural feats He accomplished?**
- **Where was He getting His power?**
- **Who is this God, who we have no evidence that anyone has seen face to face, who could make Mary pregnant and allow Her to keep Her virginity?**

If that was hard for me to understand, what I found even more difficult to comprehend was Jesus' response to the man who made Him acknowledge the presence of His mother and brothers.

"… Who is my mother, and who are my brothers?" Matthew 12:48

"And He stretched out his hand toward His disciples and said, "Here are my mother and my brothers!" Matthew 12:49

"For whoever does the will of my Father in heaven is my brother, and sister, and mother." Matthew 12:50

It seems very clear from the experience in Cana of Galilee (John chapter 2, 1-12), which represents the beginning of Jesus' ministry with His first reported public miracle, that Jesus, His Mother and His brothers got along very well.

In fact, they went together first to the wedding, and then to Capernaum.

Yet Matthew's report in chapter twelve, verses forty-six through fifty, during the height of Jesus' ministry implies that Jesus' relationship with His mother and His brothers was not at its best.

Considering the fact that in those days the meaning of communication and transportation were very limited, and that He had not seen His family for quite some time, being away preaching, I imagined that, if they were in good terms, when He saw them, He was going to be very happy. Instead, Jesus chose to ignore them. In my opinion, that was not the right and natural reaction of a person who had a normal relationship with his family.

When the man did bring to His attention their presence, instead of thanking the man for his kindness, He seemed to be irritated:

"… Who is my mother, and who are my brothers?" Matthew 12:48

"And He stretched out his hand toward His disciples and said, "Here are my mother and my brothers!" Matthew 12:49

"For whoever does the will of my Father in heaven is my brother, and sister, and mother." Matthew 12:50

Using different words, in my opinion, Jesus' reaction could have been expressed with the following words:

- **Who cares about them? Leave me alone; do not bother me!**

Now I asked myself:

- **Why did Jesus act the way He did?**
- **Could it have been that Jesus' family did not understand Him, and consequently did not approve the life He was leading, causing Him to be resentful?**
- **Why else would He ignore, and to some extent, disavow them?**

"…Who is my mother, and who are my brothers?" Matthew 12:48

"…Here are my mother and my brothers!" Matthew 12:49

"For whoever does the will of my Father in heaven is My brother, and sister, and mother." Matthew 12:50

- **If this was indeed the reason behind His actions, why then didn't Jesus practice His own message of forgiveness and love for His own family that He preached and taught to others, and which seemed to be the theme of His doctrine and His teaching?**
- **In what way could someone who practiced the will of His Father - as I imagine He referred to God - become Jesus' brother, sister, or mother?**
- **How could anyone, philosophical and religious issues aside, become bound to another person as brother, sister, or mother?**

In summarizing all the above, on the one hand, Jesus demonstrated His enormous supernatural ability and power by healing the sick, raising the dead, changing water into wine, multiplying bread and fish, walking on water without sinking, and causing a fig tree to wither.

On the other hand, His strange behavior toward His mother and His brothers, as well as the fig tree episode, instilled in me a deep sense of doubt and confusion.

Despite my best intentions, I failed to understand the truth behind the apparently contradictory and enigmatic behavior of Jesus.

CHAPTER 23
FAITH AND BELIEVE

Matthew 17

14: And when they had come to the multitude, a man came to Him, kneeling down to Him and saying,

15: "Lord, have mercy on my son, for he is an epileptic and suffers severely; for he often falls into the fire and often into the water.

16: "So I brought him to Your disciples, but they could not cure him."

17: Then Jesus answered and said, "O faithless and perverse generation, how long shall I be with you? How long shall I bear with you? Bring him here to Me."

18: And Jesus rebuked the demon, and it came out of him; and the child was cured from that very hour.

19: Then the disciples came to Jesus privately and said, "Why could we not cast it out?"

20: So Jesus said to them, "Because of your unbelief: for assuredly, I say to you, if you have faith as a grain of mustard seed, you will say to this mountain, 'Move from here to there,' and it will move; and nothing will be impossible for you."

Matthew 21

22: "And whatever things you ask in prayer, believing, you will receive."

Mark 11

21: And Peter, remembering, said to Him, "Rabbi, look! The fig tree which You cursed has withered away."
22: So Jesus answered and said to them, "Have faith in God."
23: "For assuredly, I say to you, whoever says to this mountain, 'Be removed and be cast into the sea,' and does not doubt in his heart, but believes that those things he says will be done, he will have whatever he says."

I f we accept the above explanations, it could be said and concluded that Jesus' enormous power was linked to *His unconditional faith* in God and to *His unshakable belief* that whatever He said was going to happen.

At this point, I asked myself:

- **What is *faith* in its true essence?**
- **Why is so important to believe?**
- **Who is God to whom Jesus refers—in His true essence—*in whom we should have faith*?**
- **When Jesus uses the pronouns *you* and *whoever*, is He referring to every human being?**
- **If that were the case, that would mean that all of the human family, if sufficiently imbued with faith and belief, would be able to accomplish the same feats as Jesus was doing. Is this the reality of life?**
- **No!**
- **There again, how could it be demonstrated—beyond any reasonable doubt—that what Jesus was teaching and preaching was, indeed, the actual truth?**

Oddly, while my mind was apprehensive and in turmoil, deep in my being I felt calm, sensing there was nothing wrong with Jesus' actions and deeds, and that what He was teaching was indeed the truth.

I also sensed that if I were to persist in my search, in time I would perceive the truth and my thirst for understanding would be quenched forever. This comforting thought gave me new hope and the necessary strength to continue in my search.

PART THREE
Jesus' Purpose on Earth

CHAPTER 24

PROLOGUE AND DIVINITY OF THE WORD

John 1

1: In the beginning was the Word, and the Word was with God, and the Word was God.

2: He was in the beginning with God.

3: All things were made through Him, and without Him nothing was made that was made.

4: In Him was life, and the life was the light of men.

5: And the light shines in the darkness, and the darkness did not comprehend it.

9: That was the true light which gives light to every man coming into the world.

10: He was in the world, and the world was made through Him, and the world did not know him.

11: He came to his own, and his own did not receive him.

12: But as many as received him, to them He gave the right to become children of God, to those who believe in His name:

13: who were born, not of blood, nor of the will of the flesh, nor of the will of man, but of God.

14: And the Word became flesh and dwelt among us, and we beheld his glory, the glory as of the only begotten of the Father, full of grace and truth.

17: For the law was given through Moses, but grace and truth came through Jesus Christ.

18: No one has seen God at any time. The only begotten Son, who is in the bosom of the Father, He has declared *Him*.

Despite my best efforts, I couldn't understand the meaning or the message the above verses conveyed.
Here is the outcome:

"In the beginning was the Word, and the Word was with God, and the Word was God." John 1:1

What is this *Word* that was with God and at the same time was God?

"All things were made through Him, and without Him nothing was made that was made." John 1:3

How could it be that all that exists was created, *made through Him*?

"In Him was life, and the life was the light of men." John 1:4

- **What is meant by *life* and the *light*?**
- **Is *life* and *light* the same thing?**
- **Was it possible that the *light* was indeed the *life* of all mankind?**

"And the light shines in the darkness, and the darkness did not comprehend it." John 1:5

What does this mean?

"That was the true light which gives light to every man coming into the world." John 1:9

- How, in which way, does the *light* give *light* to every man?
- What does that mean?

"He was in the world, and the world was made through Him, and the world did not know Him." John 1:10

Now I asked myself, in a figurative, tangible, and practical way:

- What is God's role in the *world?*
- How was the world *made through Him?*
- If the *world was made through Him* and if *He was in the world*, to whom/what did God refer when He says that *the world didn't know Him?*
- What is the *world* to which He is referring?

"He came to His own, and His own did not receive Him." John 1:11

- Who were those who *did not receive Him?*
- To what does the phrase *His own* refer?

"But as many as received Him, to them He gave the right to become children of God, to those who believe in His name" John 1:12

Although the above verse seemed easy, I had a problem understanding the message. I asked myself:

- Does the word *many* refer to mankind?
- How can we receive Him (God)?
- What is the true meaning of ... *believe in His name?*
- What does *become children of God* mean in a practical way?

"who were born, not of blood, nor of the will of the flesh, nor of the will of man, but of God." John 1:13

- **What exactly is the message of the above verse?**
- **How is it possible to be *born* without the will of man and without the participation of the *flesh* or the *body* of a man and a woman?**
- **What does it mean to be *born of God*?**

"And the Word became flesh and dwelt among us, and we beheld His glory, the glory as of the only begotten of the Father, full of grace and truth." John 1:14

John, in the above verse, states:

The *Word*, which is to say *God*, became *flesh*, which is to say, *human*, and *dwelt* (lived) among *us*, which is to say with *the people* of the time. The reference is clear: *Jesus*. In reading the above verse, I could not understand:

- **Why God, to be able to live with us had to become flesh in the form of Jesus?**
- **Why, didn't He present Himself in the form that truly is, so would have been easier for everybody understand?**

"For the law was given through Moses, but grace and truth came through Jesus Christ." John 1:17

- **In what way did Jesus bring *grace* and *truth*?**
- **What does *grace* and *truth* represent?**

"No one has seen God at any time. The only begotten Son, who is in the bosom of the Father, He has declared Him." John 1:18

In this verse, John affirms that no one has ever seen God at any time and that *His only begotten Son, who is in the bosom of the Father, He has declared Him.* The reference is unquestionably to *Jesus*.

Another thing that is unquestionable in analyzing verses fourteen, seventeen and eighteen is the fact that Jesus indeed, according to John, is the only *begotten Son*, who is in the *bosom* (who is part) of the *Father* (of God), who became *flesh* (man).

How was possible that in the above verses, John states that Jesus was part of God, was God, and was a Divine Being, while in chapter two, verse one through verse twelve, he states that He was the son of Mary and had several brothers?

Matthew, in Chapter twelve, verses forty-six to forty-eight, as the reader may remember, is attesting to the same thing - that Jesus was indeed the son of Mary and had several brothers.

Jesus, Himself, in Matthew, chapter twelve, verses forty-seven to fifty, although indirectly, admits that Mary is His mother and that He had several brothers.

- **How could that be?**
- **Was Jesus the *begotten son* of the Father God - part of God - that is to say God Himself, a Divine Being?**
- **Or, was the son of Mary a common human being like everyone else?**

After long periods of intense concentration, as when I previously asked myself the same question, from the voice of my heart, I perceived that Jesus was both: Divine and human.

- **How could Jesus be both?**
- **How could I demonstrate and prove to myself, behind any reasonable doubt, that what I sensed was the truth?**

After long debating the point, again from the voice of my heart I perceived that if I were to continue to read the Gospels—and if I were to pray with greater constancy and intensity— in time I would find the answers to all my questions and the truth for what it really is.

Comforted by these thoughts, I promised myself that henceforth I had to try harder, and with that in mind, I continued my search.

CHAPTER 25

NICODEMUS

John, Chapter 3

1: There was a man of the Pharisees named Nicodemus, a ruler of the Jews.

2: This man came to Jesus by night and said to him, "Rabbi, we know that You are a teacher come from God; for no one can do these signs that You do, unless God is with him."

3: Jesus answered and said to him, "Most assuredly, I say to you, unless one is born again, he cannot see the kingdom of God."

4: Nicodemus said to him, "How can a man be born when he is old? Can he enter a second time into his mother's womb and be born?"

5: Jesus answered, "Most assuredly, I say to you, unless one is born of water and the Spirit, he cannot enter the kingdom of God.

6: "That which is born of the flesh is flesh, and that which is born of the Spirit is spirit."

7: "Do not marvel that I said to you, 'You must be born again.'

8: "The wind blows where it wishes, and you hear the sound of it, but cannot tell where it comes from and where it goes. So is everyone who is born of the Spirit."

9: Nicodemus answered and said to Him, "How can these things be?"

10: Jesus answered and said to him, "Are you the teacher of Israel, and do not know these things?

11: "Most assuredly, I say to you, We speak what We know, and testify what We have seen, and you do not receive Our witness.

12: "If I have told you earthly things and you do not believe, how will you believe if I tell you heavenly things?

13: "No one has ascended to heaven but He who came down from heaven, that is, the Son of Man who is in heaven.

14: "And as Moses lifted up the serpent in the wilderness, even so must the Son of Man be lifted up,

15: "that whoever believes in him should not perish but have eternal life.

16: "For God so loved the world that He gave his only begotten Son, that whoever believes in Him should not perish but have everlasting life.

17: "For God did not send His Son into the world to condemn the world, but that the world through Him might be saved.

18: "He who believes in Him is not condemned; but he who does not believe is condemned already, because he has not believed in the name of the only begotten Son of God.

19: "And this is the condemnation, that the light has come into the world, and men loved darkness rather than light, because their deeds were evil.

20: "For everyone practicing evil hates the light and does not come to the light, lest his deeds should be exposed.

21: "But he who does the truth comes to the light, that his deeds may be clearly seen, that they have been done in God."

In analyzing the third verse…

"Jesus answered and said to him, "Most assuredly, I say to you, unless one is born again, he cannot see the kingdom of God." John3:3

…like Nicodemus, I too, found it difficult to understand Jesus' message.

- **How could one be** *born again of water and spirit?*
- **What does** *born of water and spirit* **mean?**

Another thing I failed to understand was the message of verse thirteen, in which Jesus affirms:

"No one has ascended to heaven but He who came down from heaven, the Son of man who is in heaven." John3:13

If verse thirteen were to be taken literally, then it means that only that person who comes from heaven may go back to heaven, and that person was the Son of man.

Now I wondered:

- **Whom Jesus meant when He referred to** *the Son of man?*
- **Is He alluding to Himself or to humanity as a whole?**
- **If He refers to Himself exclusively, doesn't that mean that He is the only one who could ascend to heaven?**
- **And if He is referring to all humanity, is He implying that we all came from heaven?**
- **In that case I wondered how—considering the question from a practical, and scientific perspective rather than philosophical or religious perspective - can we come down from heaven, when in fact we are conceived on earth by our parents?**
- **Is Jesus the only begotten Son of God? Or, since on many occasions Jesus mentions that God is the Father of us all, does that mean that we are all God's children?**
- **Now if the response to the second question were positive, wouldn't it contradict the tenet that Jesus is the only begotten Son of God?**
- **Wherein lies the truth?**

Going over verses sixteen, seventeen, eighteen and nineteen, I noticed that once again I could not decipher Jesus' message:

"For God so loved the world that He gave his only begotten Son…" John3:16

The questions that had boggled my mind since childhood came to mind.

- **If God the Father and Jesus the Son are one and the same, wouldn't it have been easier and clearer to say that God came to earth in the form of Jesus to sacrifice Himself for the sake of humanity?**
- **Why did God try to dramatize the situation by saying that He sacrificed His only begotten Son, when according to the *Holy Trinity*, His only begotten Son was Himself?**

Other things that perplexed my mind at that time were:

- **If God, as commonly believed, is the creator of the universe, including man's body;**
- **If God is truly all powerful, and He can do anything and everything, why He needed to come on earth in the form of Jesus, and die, to help man to be delivered from his sufferance?**
- **Why, with an act of His will didn't He erase all human problem?**
- **Why He (God) had to die on the cross?**
- **If God is life, and is eternal, how could He die?**
- **Can God actually die?**
- **Did His sacrifice and death, helped mankind?**
- **Humanity was suffering before His coming, was suffering after His coming and continue to suffer in our days;**
- **So, what did He accomplish?**

In continuing with the second part of verse sixteen:

"...that whoever believes in Him should not perish but have everlasting life." John1:16

I wondered:

- **What the phrase** *believes in Him* **signified?**
- **What, in fact, did one have to believe?**
- **In what way would those who believe in Jesus have** *everlasting life*?
- **What does** *everlasting life* **really mean?**

Verses seventeen, eighteen and nineteen state:

> *"For God did not send His Son into the world to condemn the world, but that the world through Him might be saved." John 1:17*

> *"He who believes in Him is not condemned; but he who does not believe is condemned already, because he has not believed in the name of the only begotten Son of God." John 1:18*

> *"And this is the condemnation, that the light has come into the world, and men loved darkness rather than light, because their deeds were evil." John 1:19*

What I understood from the above verses was that God sent His Son into the world to redeem it, not to punish it; in fact, whoever believes in *His son* (Jesus), will be saved; but he who does not, will be condemned.

And the condemnation meant not seeing the *light* that came into the world, because they chose the *darkness* instead.

At this point, I pondered the following:

- **What represents the** *light*?
- **What represents the** *darkness*?

- Why did God stipulate that in order for man to be saved they had to believe in His Son?
- What happened to all those people who—either before or following Jesus' coming - did not have knowledge of Jesus and Jesus' teachings?
- If God condemned them, wouldn't it amount to condemning innocent people?
- What is going to happen to all those people who made the choice to follow a different spiritual path - perhaps a different religion?
- Would they also be condemned?
- Could or would God really operate in such an inequitable manner?

CHAPTER 26

JESUS PROCLAIMS HIS DIVINE MISSION

John, Chapter 7

14: Now about the middle of the feast Jesus went up into the temple and taught.

15: And the Jews marveled, saying, "How does this Man know letters, having never studied?"

16: Jesus answered them and said, "My doctrine is not Mine, but His who sent Me.

17: "If anyone wills to do His will, he shall know concerning the doctrine, whether it is from God or whether I speak on My own authority."

I couldn't help but wonder, and I explain why.

According to the Holy Trinity, the Father God, the son Jesus and the Holy Spirit were three persons in one, which to me meant that God the father and Jesus the son and the Holy Spirit were one entity.

Now:

- **If they were one entity, why did Jesus say that His doctrine was not His own but was of his father God, and that He was doing His Father's (God's) will?**

- Why instead didn't He say that the doctrine He was teaching was His and that He was doing His own will?
- Were they one entity or two entities?

My inability to understand was causing growing frustration.

John, Chapter 8

12: Then Jesus spoke to them again, saying, "I am the light of the world. He who follows Me shall not walk in darkness, but have the light of life."

13: The Pharisees therefore said to Him, "You bear witness of Yourself; Your witness is not true."

14: Jesus answered and said to them, "Even if I bear witness of Myself, My witness is true, for I know where I came from and where I am going; but you do not know where I come from and where I am going.

15: "You judge according to the flesh; I judge no one.

16: "And yet if I do judge, My judgment is true; for I am not alone, but I am with the Father who sent Me."

17: "It is also written in your law that the testimony of two men is true.

18: "I am One who bears witness of Myself, and the Father who sent Me bears witness of Me."

19: Then they said to Him, "Where is Your Father?" Jesus answered, "You know neither Me nor My Father. If you had known Me, you would have known My Father also."

24: "Therefore I said to you that you will die in your sins; for if you do not believe that I am He, you will die in your sins."

25: Then they said to Him, "Who are You?" And Jesus said to them, "Just what I have been saying to you from the beginning.

28: Then Jesus said to them, "When you lift up the Son of Man, then you will know that I am He, and that I do nothing of Myself; but as My Father taught Me, I speak these things.

29: "And He who sent Me is with Me. The Father has not left Me alone, for I always do those things that please Him."

31: Then Jesus said to those Jews who believed Him, "If you abide in My word, you are My disciples indeed.
32: "And you shall know the truth, and the truth shall make you free."

In verse twelve Jesus affirms that He is the *light of the world* and that *who follows Him* shall no longer walk *in darkness*, but will receive the *light of life* instead.

Now I had new questions:

- **What does Jesus mean when He says that He is** *the light of the world?*
- **What in essence is that** *light* **that gives** *the light of life?*
- **What actually is** *the light of life?*
- **What is the** *darkness?*
- **Why does Jesus not explain in a simpler way and in detail what He was trying to convey so that everyone might understand without wondering and becoming frustrated?**

In verse sixteen, Jesus states that He was not alone and that He was with the Father (God), who had sent Him.

But when the Pharisees ask Him where His Father is in verse nineteen, Jesus does not give them the simple and direct reply that would solve the puzzle once and for all. Instead, He answers that…

> *"If they had recognized Him, they would have known His Father as well; but since they hadn't recognized Him, neither could they know the Father," John 8:19*

…implying once again that He and God are one and the same.

Why doesn't Jesus demonstrate in detail how He and the Father are the same, thereby dispelling not only the Pharisees'

doubts, but those of many people in the generations to follow, myself included?

In verse twenty-four, Jesus lets the Pharisees know that if they did not believe in Him they would die in their sins.

But in verse twenty-five, when the Pharisees openly ask, *Who are You?* Jesus replies that *He is what He has been saying from the beginning,* implying that He is part of God and is God.

Once again I wondered, and I do not tire of repeating it, that if Jesus and God were really one entity, and They really knew everything there was to know - as every believer presumes - They also had to know They were expressing Themselves in a vague and obscure way.

That the Pharisees, as well the most of the people of future generations, would not be able to understand Their teachings.

And that They were wasting Their time and ours as well.

Why, I asked myself once again, didn't They use a more straightforward teaching style that would have made it easier for the Pharisees and for the rest of us to understand Their principles?

In verses twenty-eight and twenty-nine, Jesus states that whatever He was doing and saying, He learned from the Father God - that what He was doing, He was doing to please Him, Who in return, never left Him. There again, the whole thing is very confusing.

In verses thirty and thirty-one, Jesus states that those who believe in Him, follow His teachings and abide in His word would be His disciples and would learn the *truth*, and the *truth would make them free.*

- **What constitutes the *truth* of which Jesus speaks?**
- **In what way would the *truth* free us - and from what?**

CHAPTER 27

JESUS AT THE FEAST OF THE DEDICATION -
THE GENTILES' HOMAGE - THE JEWS' DISBELIEF

John, Chapter 10
**24: Then the Jews surrounded Him and said to Him, "How long do
You keep us in doubt? If You are the Christ, tell us plainly."
25: Jesus answered them, "I told you, and you do not believe. The
works that I do in My Father's name, they bear witness of Me."
28: "And I give them eternal life, and they shall never perish…"
30: "I and My Father are one."
38: "…believe the works, that you may know and believe that the
Father is in Me, and I in Him."**

I n verse twenty-four, Jesus gives a straight answer to the Jews and states
that He is the Christ. In verse twenty-five, He admits that He is the
Son of God.

"…The works that I do in My Father's name…" John 10:25

In verse thirty, Jesus states that He and God are one *"I and My Father are
one". John 10:30*, proclaiming, although indirectly, that He is God, while
in verse thirty-eight, once again, He states that He is in the Father God,
and the Father God is in Him, urging the people to believe.

Does Jesus' affirmation make any sense?

On one hand, He affirms that He and the Father God is one single person and that basically He is God.

On the other, He says that He is the Son of God.

How could Jesus and God be the same person while being Father and Son at the same time?

Despite my efforts to seek the answers in my mind, I could not reconcile the single/dual entity that Jesus was claiming and proclaiming. My thinking was that if Jesus and God were Father and Son, then by definition they were two distinct entities, not one.

Rather than bringing enlightenment, these reflections succeeded only in deepening my already profound sense of frustration and confusion. I had no choice but to patiently continue my quest for answers.

John, Chapter 12
23: …Jesus answered them, saying, "The hour has come that the Son of Man should be glorified."
32: "And I, if I am lifted up from the earth, will draw all peoples to Myself."
34: The people answered Him, "We have heard from the law that the Christ remains forever; and how can you say 'The Son of Man must be lifted up?' Who is this Son of man?"
35: Then Jesus said to them, "A little while longer the light is with you. Walk while you have the light, lest darkness overtake you; he who walks in darkness does not know where he is going."
36: "While you have the light, believe in the light, that you may become sons of light…"

In verse twenty-three, Jesus states, *"The hour has come that the Son of Man should be glorified." John 12:23*

- Was Jesus referring to Himself as a human being, the Son of Mary, or as a Divine Being, the Son of God?
- Was He speaking only about Himself, or was He speaking about mankind in general?

To me, His statement is confusing.

In verse thirty-two, Jesus announces that if He is put to death, He will be *lifted up from the earth,* and *will draw all peoples to Myself.*

Now, to say the least, I argued Jesus' statement just as the Jews did 2,000 years ago, asking myself:

- If Jesus were really the Christ, that is to say, the actual incarnation and manifestation of God, how could He die?
- Could God, the creator of the universe, actually die?
- If that were the case, would it not be a thorough contradiction of what people had always accepted and believed?
- Why would God - in the form of Jesus - have to die to *draw* people to Him?
- Had God - in the form of Jesus - remained on earth performing miracles and preaching, and had been more specific and detailed about His true nature and the nature of His teachings, wouldn't that have helped people understand better, and He would have had greater luck in drawing them to Him?

I became increasingly confused.

John, Chapter 12
35: Then Jesus said to them, "A little while longer the light is with you. Walk while you have the light, lest darkness overtake you; he who walks in darkness does not know where he is going.
36: "While you have the light, believe in the light, that you may become sons of light..."

In verses thirty-five and thirty-six, Jesus goes on to say, without giving a detailed explanation, that He is the *light* and that He will remain with the people only for a short time. For that reason, He calls upon them to believe in Him - that is to say, in *the light* - so that they can become the *sons of the light.*

As confusing and contradictory as all this seemed, I moved forward in my search for the answers.

John, Chapter 12
44: Then Jesus cried out and said, "He who believes in Me, believes not in Me but in Him who sent Me.
45: "And he who sees Me sees Him who sent Me.
46: "I have come as light into the world, that whoever believes in Me should not abide in darkness.
47: "And if anyone hears My words and does not believe, I do not judge him; for I did not come to judge the world but to save the world.
48: "He who rejects Me, and does not receive My words, has that which judges him—the word that I have spoken will judge him in the last day.
49: "For I have not spoken on My own authority; but the Father who sent Me gave Me a command, what I should say and what I should speak.
50: "And I know that His command is everlasting life. Therefore, whatever I speak, just as the Father has told Me, so I speak."

Jesus continues to affirm what I stated earlier - that whoever believes in Him will also believe in the Father who sent Him, and whoever sees Him, sees also He who sent Him - God.

He asserts that His doctrine originated not from Him, but from God, and that He would not condemn whoever listens to His teachings without following them, since He had not come into this world to condemn, but to save.

Moreover, those who would not observe His teachings would in the end be condemned by those very teachings they refused to accept.

- **In what way would Jesus' teachings condemn those who did not follow them?**
- **How could believing in Jesus' doctrine make us children of the Light, and, therefore, sons of God?**
- **If all this were true, how can we explain that the majority of people who claim to believe in Jesus' teachings, and who commit themselves to teach the teachings of Jesus, do not appear to acquire the same powers as Jesus and God - including members of the Christian clergy, who preach the Gospel every day of their lives?**
- **Wherein, then, does the truth of Jesus' words lie?**

CHAPTER 28

THE COMING OF THE KINGDOM OF GOD

Luke, Chapter 17

20: Now when He was asked by the Pharisees when the kingdom of God would come, He answered them and said, "The kingdom of God does not come with observation;

21: "nor will they say, 'See here!' or 'See there!' For indeed, the kingdom of God is within you."

After meditating on the above verses for a long time, I was not able to understand Jesus' message.

What does Jesus mean by the statement:

"The kingdom of God does not come with observation"? Luke 17:20

- **What does He mean by the word** *observation*?
- **Could He mean the kingdom of God does not exist in the way we humans perceive it—a physical place where God and His entourage live?**
- **But if the kingdom of God is not a physical place, of what does it consist?**

This hypothesis seems to be confirmed by Jesus in verse twenty-one, where He states:

"Nor will they say, "See here"! or "See there"! Luke 17:21

In different words, it cannot be said, *It is here*, or *It is there*.

However, what did not make any sense to me was what Jesus states at the end of verse twenty-one, *"…For indeed, the kingdom of God is within you." Luke 17:21*

- **Does Jesus mean that the** *Kingdom of God* **is inside the body of every human being that exists on the face of the earth?**
- **How could that be?**
- **I always thought the** *Kingdom of God* **is a place where God resides, so how can it be located inside of the human body, as part of the human body?**
- **Does that mean the** *Kingdom of God* **- and therefore God - abides inside every human body?**

This notion seems to be corroborated by the Apostle Paul, who states:

1 Corinthians Chapter 3
16: "Do you not know that you are the temple of God and that the Spirit of God dwells in you?"

1 Corinthians Chapter 6
15: Do you not know that your bodies are members of Christ …?
19: Or do you not know that your body is the temple of the Holy Spirit who is in you, whom you have from God, and you are not your own?
20: …therefore glorify God in your body and in your spirit which are God's.

The statements of the Apostle Paul seem to be very simple, clear, and without ambiguity. According to Paul, The Holy Spirit of God inhabits the human body and, with it, constitutes a single unit.

Now, looking at it from a practical standpoint, I asked myself:

- **In what way could the cells that compose the organs of our bodies ever be a part of Christ, which is to say, a part of God?**
- **What shape or form does the essence of God, the Holy Spirit, take in the human body?**
- **Exactly in what part of the body could He be found?**

After giving the above matter a lot of thought, I began to think, once again, that Jesus' teachings seemed inconsistent and contradictory. While in the above verses He states and teaches that God dwells in the human body - His temple - and is an integral part of mankind, in the following verse He gives the impression that Heaven is a specific place located somewhere in the cosmos, and that it is, indeed, where God resides.

Matthew, Chapter 5
45: "that you may be sons of your Father in heaven…"
48: "Therefore you shall be perfect, just as your Father in Heaven is perfect."

Matthew, Chapter 6
9: "In this manner, therefore, pray: Our Father in Heaven, Hallowed be Your name.
10: "Your kingdom come. Your will be done On earth as it is in Heaven…"
20: "but lay up for yourselves treasures in heaven…"
33: "But seek first the kingdom of God . . ."

Now the question is:

- **Does God reside in Heaven or in the human body?**
- **What is the truth?**

CHAPTER 29

THE GOOD SEED - THE MUSTARD SEED - THE LEAVEN - THE HIDDEN TREASURE - THE PEARL - THE FISHING NET

Matthew, Chapter 13

24: ". . . The kingdom of heaven is like a man who sowed good seed in his field..."

31: ".....The kingdom of heaven is like a mustard seed, which a man took and sowed in his field..."

33: ". . . The kingdom of heaven is like leaven, which a woman took and hid in three measures of meal till it was all leavened."

44: "Again, the kingdom of heaven is like treasure hidden in a field, which a man found and hid; and for joy over it he goes and sells all that he has and buys that field."

45: "Again, the kingdom of heaven is like a merchant seeking beautiful pearls..."

47: "Again, the kingdom of heaven is like a dragnet that was cast into the sea and gathered some of every kind. ..."

Matthew, Chapter 25

1: "Then the kingdom of heaven shall be likened to ten virgins who took their lamps and went out to meet the bridegroom..."

Reading the above verses perpetuated the sense of mystery for me, and I could neither understand nor perceive Jesus' message.

- What - in the literal sense of the word and in its true essence - is the kingdom of heaven about which Jesus speaks?
- How could it be figuratively likened to a treasure hidden in a field, a precious pearl, a fishing net or young virgins waiting for their grooms?
- Is the kingdom of heaven a real, tangible location where God and all the blessed dwell?

To me, the concepts and the analogies expressed by Jesus regarding heaven were illogical and made no sense.

Does heaven really exist, or is it a mere figment of the imagination?

I concluded that so far Jesus neither succeeds in demonstrating the existence of God nor in revealing the kingdom of heaven.

Yet, my conclusion gave me no rest, and I decided to keep prodding along in my search, hoping that eventually all of the pieces of the puzzle would fit together and I would have my answers.

CHAPTER 30

JESUS COMFORTS HIS DISCIPLES

John, Chapter 14

4: "And where I go you know, and the way you know."

5: Thomas said to him, "Lord, we do not know where you are going, and how can we know the way?"

6: Jesus said to him, "I am the way, the truth, and the life. No one comes to the Father except through Me."

7: "If you had known Me, you would have known my Father also; and from now on you know Him and have seen Him."

8: Philip said to him, "Lord, show us the Father, and it is sufficient for us."

9: Jesus said to him, "Have I been with you so long, and yet you have not known Me, Philip? He who has seen Me has seen the Father; so how can you say, 'Show us the Father'?

10: "Do you not believe that I am in the Father and the Father in me? The words that I speak to you I do not speak on My own authority; but the Father who dwells in me does the works.

11: "Believe Me that I am in the Father and the Father in Me, or else believe Me for the sake of the works themselves.

12: "Most assuredly, I say to you, he who believes in Me, the works that I do he will do also; and greater works than these he will do..."

My take on all this:

Jesus begins to comfort His disciples, saying that soon He was going to leave them, and that they knew where He was going. In the fifth verse, Thomas calls Jesus' attention to the fact that the Apostles did not know His destination.

If they truly did not know where Jesus was going, how could they be expected to know the way?

In verse sixth, Jesus tells Thomas that He is *"…the way, the truth and the life" John 14:6.*

Nevertheless, the disciples did not understand what Jesus was saying.

This is confirmed in verse eighth, when Philip immediately disavows Jesus' assertions by simply saying, *"Lord, show us the Father and we will be satisfied" John 14:8*

Philip's statement demonstrates that the apostles thus far have neither understood Jesus' teachings nor who is His Father.

At this point, what I found most intriguing was Jesus' response to Philip in verses nine to twelve. Instead of explaining in simple fashion how, by seeing Him, the Apostles have already seen the Father, and thereby immediately satisfying Philip's request, Jesus avoids a direct response by rebuking Philip for not understanding His message after having been with Him for so long.

In the remaining verses, Jesus explains that whatever He said, taught, and did was engendered in Him through the Father God, who dwelt in Him, and not by Himself.

Then He urges the Apostles to acknowledge that He is in the Father and the Father in Him—if only because of the works He performs.

Finally, He adds that whoever believes in Him can do the same works He does and even greater ones.

*"Most assuredly, I say to you, he who believes in Me, the works that
I do he will do also; and greater works than these he will do..."*
John14:12

At this point, I must admit that just like Philip over 2,000 years ago, I
found it difficult to understand, and consequently to believe and accept,
what Jesus was saying.

CHAPTER 31

Jesus Promises the Assistance of the Holy Ghost - The Promise of the Holy Spirit The Love between Christ and His Followers - Jesus' Prayer

John, Chapter 14

15: "If you love Me, keep my commandments.

16: "And I will pray the Father, and He will give you another Helper, that He may abide with you forever -,

17: "the Spirit of truth, whom the world cannot receive, because it neither sees Him nor knows Him; but you know Him, for He dwells with you, and will be in you.

18: "I will not leave you orphans; I will come to you.

19: "A little while longer and the world will see Me no more, but you will see Me. Because I live, you will live also.

20: "At that day you will know that I am in my Father, and you in Me, and I in you.

21: "He who has My commandments and keeps them, it is who loves Me. And he who loves Me will be loved by My Father…"

22: Judas (not Iscariot) said to him, "Lord, how is it that you will manifest Yourself to us, and not to the world?"

23: Jesus answered and said to him, "If anyone loves Me, he will keep My word; and My Father will love him, and We will come to him and make Our home with him.

24: "He who does not love Me does not keep My words; and the word which you hear is not Mine but the Father's who sent Me."

After reading the above verses several times, I concluded that:

- Jesus' teachings, the *Word*, were not His, but of His Father God.
- It is important for the disciples to love Jesus and follow His commandments.
- If they would do that, the Father God would send them a new *Helper*, the *Spirit of Truth* that would abide with them forever.
- That whoever observes Jesus commandments and loves Jesus, will be loved by Jesus and His Father (God).
- How could be possible such thing?

At this point, what frustrated me the most was the fact that Jesus kept preaching over and over the same thing, without giving, in my opinion, a clear and tangible explanation of the following:

- **How could Jesus be in God and God in Jesus?**
- **How could the Apostles be in Jesus, and Jesus in the Apostles?**
- **How could Jesus and God be in the Apostles, and the Apostles in Jesus and God?**
- **How could it be possible that whoever loves Jesus and follows His commandments could be in God and in Jesus, and vice versa?**

"...I am in my Father, and you in me, and I in you." John14:20

John, Chapter 16
13: "However, when He, the Spirit of truth, has come, He will guide you into all truth; for He will not speak on His own *authority*, but whatever He hears He will speak; and He will tell you things to come."

In this verse, Jesus states that when the *Spirit of Truth* - which is to say the *Helper* - goes to the Apostles, it would lead them to the whole truth, disclosing the future, as well.

I was sensing that Jesus, indirectly, was explaining the process of how we learn the truth about things. I also was sensing that Jesus, without saying it, was explaining the meaning of clairvoyance and how it works.

"...and He will tell you things to come." John 16:13

At this point, I wondered what was the true essence of this *Helper* that the Father God was going to send to the Apostles to teach them everything they needed to know.

So I asked myself:

- **Were the terms** *Helper, Holy Spirit,* **and** *Spirit of truth* **different names used by Jesus to describe the same entity?**
- **Why, at times, did Jesus say that He would pray to God to send the Apostles the Holy Spirit, causing me to understand that the Holy Spirit is an entity living outside the human body, although at other times He said the Holy Spirit is actually inside?**
- **Is the Holy Spirit an entity living outside the human body that with the interception of Jesus' prayer is sent by God...or is it an entity that is an integral part of the body, that dwells in it at all the time?**
- **And if that were the case, would that mean that the Holy Spirit is inside and part of every human being who comes into this world?**
- **And, if it were, why aren't we all conscious of having the Holy Spirit within us?**

John, Chapter 15
7: "If you abide in Me, and My words abide in you, you will ask what you desire, and it shall be done for you."

How could that be, I asked myself?

John, Chapter15
12: "This is My commandment, that you love one another as I have loved you."

I noted in these verses that Jesus never tires of trying to instill in the minds and hearts of His disciples the great importance of expressing and manifesting their love.

- **Why, I asked myself, is it so important to manifest our love to others?**
- **Why does Jesus give love such prominence as to make it the core of His doctrine and teachings?**
- **What is, in its true essence, the sentiment of Love?**

John, Chapter 17
1: "....Father, the hour has come. Glorify Your Son, that Your Son also may glorify You,
2: "as You have given Him authority over all flesh, that He should give eternal life to as many as You have given Him.
3: "And this is eternal life, that they may know You, the only true God, and Jesus Christ whom You have sent.
5: "And now, O Father, glorify Me together with Yourself, with the glory which I had with You before the world was.
20: "I do not pray for these alone, but also for those who will believe in Me through their word;
21: "that they all may be one, as You, Father, are in Me, and I in You; that they also may be one in Us, that the world may believe that You sent Me.
22: "And the glory which You gave Me I have given them, that they may be one just as We are one:

23: "I in them, and You in Me; that they may be made perfect in one, and that the world may know that You have sent Me, and have loved them as You have loved Me."

As I was reading these verses, I had the fleeting sensation that I understood precisely what Jesus was saying. At the same time, the true significance of His message escaped me.

When He speaks to the Father, Jesus affirms that He has glorified God on earth by accomplishing what God the Father has entrusted Him to do, which is to give eternal life, not only to the Apostles, but to all those who would eventually believe in Him through the Apostles' words.

In this manner, all would coalesce into one entity - God with Jesus and vice versa, and all those who believed, with the Father and the Son.

Then Jesus says that eternal life amounts to knowing the Father, who is the only true God, and the Son whom God had sent: Jesus Christ.

Furthermore, Jesus prays to the Father to glorify Him with the same glory that He had in the presence of God before the world existed.

The above presented me with the following dilemma:

- **In what manner could Jesus the Son glorify God the Father, when supposedly were one entity?**
- **How could it be possible that all those who believed in Jesus' teachings would eventually be one with God and Jesus?**
- **In what way would the Word, or Jesus' teachings, make it possible to know both God and Jesus?**
- **What did** *to know* **God or Jesus mean?**
- **How would we know when we really know God and Jesus?**
- **In what way would this knowledge guarantee us eternal life?**
- **What does** *eternal life* **really signify?**
- **Why did Jesus, who was one with the Father, have to pray to God?**

- By praying to God, wasn't Jesus praying to himself?
- What reason did He have to pray to himself?
- What is the meaning of Jesus' prayer to the Father, asking him to *glorify the Son with the same glory Jesus enjoyed in the presence of God before the world existed?*
- If Jesus and the Father were really one, what would be the point of Jesus asking Himself, in essence, to be glorified with the same glory He already had before the Father prior to Creation?

CHAPTER 32

FORETELLING OF THE PASSION - THE TRAITOR REVEALED
JESUS PREDICTS THE DISCIPLES' DESERTION

Matthew, Chapter 16
21: From that time Jesus began to show to His disciples that He must go to Jerusalem, and suffer many things from the elders and chief priests and scribes, and be killed, and be raised the third day.
22: Then Peter took Him aside and began to rebuke Him, saying, "Far be it from You, Lord; this shall not happen to You!"
23: But he turned and said to Peter, "Get behind Me, Satan! You are an offense to Me, for you are not mindful of the things of God, but the things of men."

Matthew, Chapter 20
18: "Behold, we are going up to Jerusalem, and the Son of Man will be betrayed to the chief priests and to the scribes; and they will condemn Him to death,
19: "and deliver Him to the Gentiles to mock and to scourge and to crucify. And the third day He will rise again."

Matthew, Chapter 26
21: Now as they were eating, He said, "Assuredly, I say to you, one of you will betray Me."

23: He answered and said, "He who dipped *his* hand with Me in the dish will betray Me."
25: Then Judas, who was betraying Him, answered and said, "Rabbi, is it I?" He said to him, "You have said it."

Matthew, Chapter 26
30: And when they had sung a hymn, they went out to the Mount of Olives.
31: Then Jesus said to them, "All of you will be made to stumble because of Me this night, for it is written: 'I will strike the Shepherd, And the sheep of the flock will be scattered.'
32: "But after I have been raised, I will go before you to Galilee."
33: Peter answered and said to Him, "Even if all are made to stumble because of You, I will never be made to stumble."
34: Jesus said to him, "Assuredly, I say to you that this night, before the rooster crows, you will deny Me three times."
35: Peter said to Him, "Even if I have to die with You, I will not deny You!" And so said all the disciples.

The last two chapters show that Jesus possessed a highly evolved degree of clairvoyance. So much so that He was capable of predicting future events in their most minute detail. A case in point is how He predicts His anguish and martyrdom in Jerusalem through the intervention of the elders, the chief priests, and the scribes; and how He plans to rise from the dead on the third day and meet with the Apostles in Galilee.

He also predicts that Judas will betray Him with a kiss, that the Apostles will abandon Him, and Peter will deny him three times on the night of His capture.

Now, how was Jesus able to predict the future with such precision?

John, Chapter 16
13: "However, when He, the Spirit of truth, has come, He will guide you into all truth; for He will not speak on his own *authority*, but whatever He hears He will speak; and He will tell you things to come.

If I understood correctly, this also meant that anyone who receives or gets in touch with the *Spirit of Truth* could foresee the future or future events. In today's language, we may call this being *clairvoyant*.

Could this also be how fortunetellers predict the future?

At this point, the enigma, the mystery, to understand who is this *Spirit of Truth*, that allows us the perception and the prediction of future events, was not explained; consequently I remained in the dark, and in my ignorance.

CHAPTER 33

JESUS' CAPTURE - JESUS BEFORE PILATE

Matthew, Chapter 26

47: And while he was still speaking, behold, Judas, one of the twelve, with a great multitude with swords and clubs, came from the chief priests and elders of the people.

48: Now His betrayer had given them a sign, saying, "Whomever I kiss, He is the One; seize Him."

49: Immediately he went up to Jesus and said, "Greetings, Rabbi!" and kissed Him.

50: But Jesus said to him, "Friend, why have you come?" Then they came and laid hands on Jesus and took Him.

51: And suddenly, one of those who were with Jesus stretched out his hand and drew his sword, struck the servant of the high priest, and cut off his ear.

52: Then Jesus said to him, "Put your sword in its place, for all who take the sword will perish by the sword."

John, Chapter 18

10: Then Simon Peter, having a sword, drew it and struck the high priest's servant, and cut off his right ear. The servant's name was Malchus.

11: So Jesus said to Peter, "Put your sword into the sheath. Shall I not drink the cup which My Father has given Me?"

Matthew relates that while Jesus is speaking to the Apostles in the Garden of Gethsemane, Judas arrives on the scene leading a group of people armed with swords and staves sent by the elders and the chief priests. At the moment of Jesus' arrest, Simon Peter, draws his sword and strikes a servant of the high priest, cutting off his right ear. Seeing this, Jesus orders him to put his sword in place, urging him not to react with violence, since *"...All who take the sword will perish by the sword." Matthew 26:52*

- **What could Jesus mean by this statement?**
- **How, and by virtue of what law, does a person who uses the sword to wound or kill become sentenced to the same fate?**
- **Was there a law of retribution?**
- **Why didn't Jesus explain?**

John, Chapter 18
29: Pilate then went out to them and said, "What accusation do you bring against this man?"
30: They answered and said to him, "If He were not an evildoer, we would not have delivered Him up to you."
31: Then Pilate said to them, "You take Him and judge Him according to your law." Therefore the Jews said to him, "It is not lawful for us to put anyone to death,"
32: that the saying of Jesus might be fulfilled which He spoke, signifying by what death He would die.
33: Then Pilate entered the Praetorium again, called Jesus, and said to him, "Are you the King of the Jews?"
34: Jesus answered him, "Are you speaking for yourself about this, or did others tell you this concerning Me?"
35: Pilate answered, "Am I a Jew? Your own nation and the chief priests have delivered You to me. What have you done?"
36: Jesus answered, "My kingdom is not of this world. If My kingdom were of this world, My servants would fight, so that I should not be delivered to the Jews; but now My kingdom is not from here."

37: Pilate therefore said to him, "Are You a king then?" Jesus answered, "You say *rightly* that I am a king. For this cause I was born, and for this cause I have come into the world, that I should bear witness to the truth. Everyone who is of the truth hears My voice."

38: Pilate said to him, "What is truth?" And when he had said this, he went out again to the Jews, and said to them, "I find no fault in Him at all.

39: But you have a custom that I should release someone to you at the Passover. Do you therefore want me to release to you the King of the Jews?"

40: Then they all cried again, saying, "Not this Man, but Barabbas!" Barabbas was a robber.

John, Chapter 19

4: Pilate then went out again, and said to them, "Behold, I am bringing Him out to you, that you may know that I find no fault in Him."

5: Then Jesus came out, wearing the crown of thorns and the purple robe. And Pilate said to them, "Behold the Man!"

6: Therefore, when the chief priests and the officers saw Him, they cried out, saying "Crucify Him, crucify Him!" Pilate said to them, "You take Him and crucify Him, for I find no fault in Him."

7: The Jews answered him, "We have a law, and according to our law He ought to die, because He made Himself the Son of God."

8: Therefore, when Pilate heard that saying, he was the more afraid,

9: and went again into the Praetorium and said to Jesus, "Where are You from?" But Jesus gave him no answer.

10: Then Pilate said to him, "Are You not speaking to me? Do You not know that I have power to crucify You, and the power to release You?"

11: Jesus answered, "You could have no power at all against Me unless it had been given you from above. Therefore the one who delivered Me to you has the greater sin."

12: From then on Pilate sought to release Him, but the Jews cried out, saying "If you let this Man go, you are not Caesar's friend. Whoever makes himself a king speaks against Caesar."
15: But they cried out, "Away with Him, away with Him! Crucify Him!" Pilate said to them, "Shall I crucify your King?" The chief priests answered, "We have no king but Caesar."
16: Then he delivered Him to them to be crucified. So they took Jesus and led Him away.
17: And He, bearing His cross, went out to a place called the Place of a Skull, which is called in Hebrew, Golgotha,
18: where they crucified Him, and two others with Him, one on either side, and Jesus in the center.

In the preceding chapters, John relates that on the morning following Jesus' arrest, He is led from the house of Caiaphas, the chief priest, to the seat of the Roman magistrate, Pilate office - there to be judged and condemned. Pilate asks the Jews who conducted Jesus to him, what sort of crime Jesus has committed. They reply that He is a criminal who proclaims Himself king of the Jews and, worse yet, the Son of God.

According to Judaic law, anyone declaring himself the Son of God was guilty of a heinous crime, punishable by death. Hence, the Jews ask Pilate to judge Jesus and condemn Him to death. Noting that Jesus had committed no crimes under Roman law, Pilate doesn't want to get mixed up with the Jews' religious quarrels—perhaps for fear of antagonizing Jesus' followers and the attendant consequences. Therefore, he tells the Jews to judge Him themselves, according to their own law.

But they immediately retort that their own law prevents them from applying the death penalty, and that's why they brought Jesus to Pilate in the first place—to have Him condemned to death by Roman law. At that point, Pilate finds himself with his back to the wall and has no choice but to react. He calls Jesus inside the judgment hall and asks Him if the accusations the Jews bring against Him are true, and if He does indeed proclaim Himself the king of the Jews.

Jesus replies that His reign is not of this world, because were that the case, His followers would fight to keep Him from falling into the hands of the Jews.

Pilate therefore said to him, ...

"Are you a king then?" Jesus answered, "You say rightly that I am a king. For this cause I was born, and for this cause I have come into the world, that I should bear witness to the truth..." John 18:37

"Pilate said to him, "What is the truth"? John 18:38

...Jesus remains silent.

Why did Jesus not explain to Pilate what the *truth* is, and how He bore witness to that *"truth"*?

Convinced that Jesus has committed no crime, Pilate can find no reason to sentence him to death, so he goes outside the judgment hall, where the Jews await Jesus' sentencing, and tells them that he does not find the prisoner guilty, and as a result cannot condemn him. Upon hearing this, the Jews cry out that Jesus should be condemned to death.

It appears that Pilate does not want to take upon himself the responsibility of sentencing an innocent man; nor probably does he want to contradict the Jews for fear of an uprising. Since there exists a tradition allowing a condemned man his freedom on Passover, Pilate gives the Jews a choice between freeing Jesus, or freeing a prisoner who was in the Romans jail, by the name of Barabbas, yielding his responsibility to the Jews and literally washing his hands of the matter.

Given the choice, the Jews choose to grant Barabbas his freedom, leaving Jesus in the hands of the Romans to be led to the hill called Golgotha, where He is put to death on the cross in the company of two other prisoners.

Mark, Chapter 15
42: Now when evening had come, because it was the Preparation Day, that is, the day before the Sabbath,
43: Joseph of Arimathea, a prominent council member, who was himself waiting for the kingdom of God, coming and taking courage, went in to Pilate and asked for the body of Jesus.
44: Pilate marveled that He was already dead; and summoning the centurion, he asked him if He had been dead for some time.
45: So when he found out from the centurion, he granted the body to Joseph.
46: Then he bought fine linen, took Him down, and wrapped Him in the linen. And he laid Him in a tomb which had been hewn out of the rock, and rolled a stone against the door of the tomb.

In the above verses, we have the assurance that Jesus died and was laid in the tomb.

CHAPTER 34

*JESUS' RESURRECTION - JESUS APPEARS
TO MARY MAGDALENE -
JESUS APPEARS TWICE TO THE APOSTLES*

Mark, Chapter 16

1: Now when the Sabbath was past, Mary Magdalene, Mary the mother of James, and Salome bought spices, that they might come and anoint him.

2: Very early in the morning, on the first day of the week, they came to the tomb when the sun had risen.

3: And they said among themselves, "Who will roll away the stone from the door of the tomb for us?"

4: But when they looked up, they saw that the stone had been rolled away - for it was very large.

5: And entering the tomb, they saw a young man clothed in a long white robe sitting on the right side; and they were alarmed.

6: But he said to them, "Do not be alarmed. You seek Jesus of Nazareth, who was crucified. He is risen! He is not here. See the place where they laid Him.

7: "But go, tell His disciples - and Peter - that He is going before you into Galilee; there you will see Him, as He had said to you."

John, Chapter 20

1: Now on the first day of the week Mary Magdalene went to the tomb early, while it was still dark, and saw that the stone had been taken away from the tomb.

2: Then she ran, and came to Simon Peter, and to the other disciple, whom Jesus loved, and said to them, "They have taken away the Lord out of the tomb, and we do not know where they have laid Him."

3: Peter therefore went out, and the other disciple, and were going to the tomb.

4: So they both ran together, and the other disciple outran Peter and came to the tomb first.

5: And he, stooping down and looking in, saw the linen cloths lying there; yet he did not go in.

6: Then Simon Peter came, following him, and went into the tomb; and he saw the linen cloths lying there,

7: and the handkerchief that had been around His head, not lying with the linen cloths, but folded together in a place by itself.

8: Then the other disciple, who came to the tomb first, went in also; and he saw and believed.

10: Then the disciples went away again to their own homes.

11: But Mary stood outside by the tomb weeping, and as she wept she stooped down and looked into the tomb.

12: And she saw two angels in white sitting, one at the head and the other at the feet, where the body of Jesus had lain.

13: Then they said to her, "Woman, why are you weeping?" She said to them, "Because they have taken away my Lord, and I do not know where they have laid him."

14: Now when she had said this, she turned round and saw Jesus standing there, and did not know that it was Jesus.

15: Jesus said to her, "Woman, why are you weeping? Whom are you seeking?" She supposing Him to be the gardener, said to Him, "Sir, if You have carried Him away, tell me where You have laid Him, and I will take Him away."

16: Jesus said to her, "Mary!" She turned and said to Him "Rabboni!" (which is to say, "Teacher")

17: Jesus said to her, "Do not cling to Me, for I have not yet ascended to My Father; but go to My brethren and say to them, 'I am ascending to My Father and your Father, and to My God and your God.'"

18: Mary Magdalene came and told the disciples that she had seen the Lord, and that He had spoken these things to her.

As I read the verses of the two preceding chapters, I noted that the sequences of events following Jesus' death are related differently in each Gospel. Mark states that Mary Magdalene went to the sepulcher accompanied by Mary, the mother of James and Salome. Upon reaching Jesus' sepulcher, they notice that the stone covering its entrance has been moved, and when they enter the tomb, they see a young man dressed in white, who informs them that Jesus is no longer there because He is raised. Then the young man tells them to go to Jesus' disciples and inform them that Jesus will precede them into Galilee, as promised.

John, on the other hand, reports that Mary Magdalene goes to the sepulcher alone before daybreak, and finds the stone in front of the tomb entrance removed. So, she runs to Simon Peter and to the other disciple whom Jesus loves telling them that Jesus has been taken away to an undisclosed location. Peter and the other disciple then run to the sepulcher, where they go inside and see the burial clothes and the napkin from Jesus' head lying in a different spot. When the disciples leave, Mary Magdalene remains outside the tomb, crying. Looking into the sepulcher, she sees two angels dressed in white, one sitting at the head and the other at the feet of where Jesus' body had been. They ask Mary why she is crying, and she replies it is because Jesus' body is missing.

Soon thereafter, she turns around and sees Jesus, but doesn't recognize Him. He asks her why she is crying. Thinking she was speaking to the gardener, she asks Him if He took the body away, and, if so, where could she find it. But when Jesus calls her by name, she recognizes Him and cries out: "Rabboni."

Jesus tells her not to detain Him because He has not yet ascended to the Father and asks her to go tell the disciples that He is about to ascend to His Father and their Father, His God and their God. Mary immediately runs to tell the disciples that she has seen Jesus and relates what He said to her.

I asked myself:

- **Why do Mark and John report the occurrence differently?**
- **How could we be sure, behind any reasonable doubt that Jesus truly resurrected from the death?**

John, Chapter 20
19: Then, the same day at evening, being the first day of the week, when the doors were shut where the disciples were assembled, for fear of the Jews, Jesus came and stood in midst, and said to them, "Peace be with you."
20: When He had said this, He showed them His hands and His side. Then the disciples were glad when they saw the Lord.
21: So Jesus said to them again, "Peace to you! As the Father has sent Me, I also send you."
22: And when He had said this, He breathed on them, and said to them, "Receive the Holy Spirit."
23: "If you forgive the sins of any, they are forgiven them; if you re- tain the sins of any, they are retained."
24: Now Thomas, called the Twin, one of the twelve, was not with them when Jesus came.

25: The other disciples therefore said to him, "We have seen the Lord." So he said to them, "Unless I see in His hands the print of the nails, and put my finger into the print of the nails, and place my hand into His side, I will not believe."
26: And after eight days His disciples were again inside, and Thomas with them. Jesus came, the doors being shut, and stood in the midst, and said, "Peace to you!"
27: Then he said to Thomas, "Reach your finger here, and look at My hands; and reach your hand here, and put it into My side. Do not be unbelieving, but believing."
28: And Thomas answered and said to Him, "My Lord and my God!"
29: Jesus said to him, "Thomas, because you have seen Me, you have believed. Blessed are those who have not seen and yet have believed."

In this chapter, John relates that on the evening of the same day - the first day of the week and the same one on which Jesus appears to Mary Magdalene - Jesus also appears before the disciples and says:

"Peace be with you" John 20:19.

Then He shows them His hands and ribs to identify Himself, adding that just as the Father has sent Him, so will He send them now. Soon after, he breathes on them and says:

"Receive the Holy Spirit" John 20:22.

He goes on to say that if they—the disciples—were to forgive someone's sins, the sins would be canceled; and if not, the wrongdoer would be left uncleansed of his misdeeds.

Thomas, one of the twelve Apostles, is missing from the assembly, but when he returns, the others tell him they have seen Jesus. He says that unless he sees with his own eyes the signs of the crucifixion on Jesus' body he will not believe.

Eight days later, as the disciples are assembled with their doors shut - this time with Thomas present - Jesus appears again and bids them peace. To give Thomas the proof he needs, he says:

"...Reach your finger here, and look at my hands; and reach your hand, and put it into my side; do not be unbelieving, but believing."
John20:27

Thomas answers, "My Lord and my God!" John20:28

Jesus responds, "Thomas, because you have seen Me, you have believed. Blessed are those who have not seen and yet have believed."
John20:29

After a lot of reflecting, I asked myself:

- **How could Jesus walk into the room with closed doors?**
- **How could He give them the Holy Spirit, when supposedly, the Holy Spirit was already within them?**

"Or do you not know that your body is the temple of the Holy Spirit who is in you, whom you have from God, and you are not your own?"
Paul, I Corinthians 6:19

- **Who is in reality the *Holy Spirit*, *and what is the nature of His essence?***
- **What is the relationship between *God* and *Holy Spirit*?**
- **How could the disciples forgive sins?**

CHAPTER 35

THE APOSTLES' MISSION

Mark, Chapter 16

15: And He said to them, "Go into all the world and preach the gospel to every creature.

16: "He who believes and is baptized will be saved; but he who does not believe will be condemned.

17: "And these signs will follow those who believe: In My name they will cast out demons; they will speak with new tongues;

18: "they will take up serpents; and if they drink anything deadly, it will by no means hurt them; they will lay hands on the sick, and they will recover."

Summing up, I noted that up to the end Jesus never tires of teaching His disciples that all those who believe in His doctrine, even those who have not personally witnessed His works…

"Blessed are those who have not seen and yet have believe." John20:29

…will be able to:

- **Chase away devils;**
- **Speak new tongues;**

- **Handle serpents;**
- **Drink toxic substances without being poisoned;**
- **And place their hands on the sick and heal them.**

Until the end of His mission - at least, from my perspective - Jesus never truly explains what He means by *believe*, and in what way by *believing* one could acquire His powers.

I found it difficult to accept the notion that by simply believing or having a strong faith in the divinity of Christ, anyone could acquire the powers that Jesus appeared to possess.

My assessment would seem to be reinforced by the fact that over the course of centuries, millions upon millions of people, including virtually all the leaders of various Christian religious groups, have affirmed and continue to affirm that they believe.

But, how many of these millions during their lifetimes have acquired the power to match the works of Jesus Christ?

In our time, only two names come to mind:

Padre Pio of Pietralcina, Italy and **Brother Andrew of Montreal, Canada.**

These two people, whom the Catholic Church has canonized as saints, while living, at certain moments in their lives, were targeted by complaints, criticism, and retribution - not by non - believers, but by their superiors and their Church.

How could all this be explained?

It was the reality of these facts through which I was able to conclude that the simple belief in Jesus' teachings was not sufficient in itself to gain access to His powers.

After completing my research on the Gospels at what I considered the most logical and important points of Jesus teachings, His death and His resurrection, I had to ask myself:

- **Had I discovered the mechanism of my healing experiences?**
- **Had I finally understood who is, in His very essence and form, that Being we refer to as God?**
- **In all sincerity and honesty, no!**

In other words, after having scrutinized the Gospels, I found myself at exactly the same point at which I began my study.

The questions that had plagued me since childhood that I had hoped to shed some light remained immersed in the darkness of a deep, apparently unfathomable enigma.

What could I do?

Instinctively, I began to pray with more intensity. Soon after that, from the voice of my heart I perceived to continue to pray, and in due time, I would find the answers to my questions.

Comforted by this perception, I continued my life the best I could.

CHAPTER 36
Sale of the R.V. Park
Birth of Journey of a Healer

While the turmoil of my spiritual life continued, my children were focused on how income could be increased from the R.V. Park as well as the golf course.

After much research, Pino, Nino and Paolo Jr. found out the hotel industry in Twentynine Palms was very prosperous.

Based on these findings, they believed that if we could install some small manufactured units called *Park Models* in our R.V. Park that we could rent daily, weekly and monthly, just like a hotel, our income not only would increase, but would remain steady throughout the year.

I liked the idea, so we tried it. It was the right thing to do. Finally, after many sacrifices and uncertainties, our financial future looked very bright and secure, and we were all very happy.

In 1998, Pino got married, but one year after divorced. This episode brought a lot of grief into our hearts.

After long reflection, Pino, hoping to rebuild a new life, moved to San Diego. He went to work for a large urban development company, where he was able to acquire a lot of experience in large-scale urban planning and development. He truly enjoyed his new job.

These new conditions brought new joy to his life. Pina and I were very happy for him.

Soon after Pino moved to San Diego, one evening while having dinner, Nino and Paolo Jr. told us with hesitation and in a very diplomatic way that working for the R.V. Park and the golf course was not what they wanted to do for the rest of their lives. Pina and I explained to them that soon we were going to go into semiretirement and that we were going to give everything to them, so they could enjoy the fruit of all our sacrifices.

They said that the R.V. Park and the golf course were our dreams, not theirs, that they were very happy to have helped us to make our dreams come true, but that was not what they wanted.

For Pina and I, that was a shock. We always thought the R.V. Park and the Golf Course was going to stay in the family for the rest of our lives. After we reflected for a while, Pina and I decided to sell everything. First, we sold the R.V. Park.

After the transaction, waiting to sell the Golf Course, we went to live in villa # 25, one of the two cottages in the R.V. Park of which we retained ownership.

One late afternoon while Pina was outside cleaning the driveway, Bill Stock, a good friend of ours and long-time resident of the R.V. Park, came to our cottage, and asked Pina if I was home.

Pina called me. We shook hands, and with a big smile he asked me what I was doing.

Before I could reply, he turned his head and looked toward the west and said, *"What a beautiful sunset!"*

Pina and I looked in the direction indicated by Bill. A few clouds, white, dark and black, surrounded the sun, which was about to go down behind the mountains. The rays of the sun going through those clouds made a spectacle of lights that I had never, in all my life, witnessed before. The view was magnificent!

While I stared transfixed by that fantastic vision, Bill suggested I take some pictures. I grabbed my digital camera and started shooting. A few minutes later, that marvelous spectacle was gone.

Soon after, I invited Bill in for a cup of coffee. Politely, he declined my invitation, saying he had something to do. He wished us a good evening and then left.

After his departure, Pina and I stayed there, trying to analyze Bill's visit. It seemed like the only purpose for him coming to our house was to bring to our attention that beautiful sunset and to make sure that I took pictures of it. The entire encounter was very strange. I saved those pictures in my computer and forgot about the event.

A few months later, while visiting my friend Dr. Robert Harmon at his clinic in Bermuda Dunes, California, he asked me if I had already chosen the name for my book. I promptly answered no.

Dr. Harmon began to reflect for a few seconds, and then he said, "Paolo, I think you should call it *Journey of a Healer*."

I said the title would not be appropriate. He asked me why. I explained that the title would mislead people, making them think I was the healer, while we both knew the healer was God.

He told me he didn't agree with me. Then he said he was aware the actual healing was performed by the intervention of God, but he was also aware that God doesn't answer everyone's prayer, but He was answering my prayers.

"Paolo, if we keep that in consideration, I believe you are also part of the healing process. So it would be okay to call your manuscript *Journey of a Healer*." Not very convinced by his words, I promised I would think about it.

Then I thanked him kindly for his effort to try to help me, and I went home.

While driving, I asked the voice of heart if I should name the book *Journey of a Healer*. Immediately, a great feeling of peace, joy and harmony filled all my being. In that moment I knew it was the right name to give my manuscript. Thus was born *Journey of a Healer*.

Nevertheless, my concern of misleading people remained on my mind. I hoped in time I would discover the reason why it was the right name to give.

After this resolution, because the manuscript was very long, I divided it into three volumes, each one representing a specific period of my life.

In the first volume, I narrate the early *struggles* of my life.

In the second volume, I talk about how some of my *healing experiences* occurred.

In the third volume, I narrate how I came to understand *Jesus' teachings*, and how I found the *answers* to all the questions I had been asking others and myself for most of my life.

Here are the names as they appear on the books:

- *Journey of a Healer—Volume I—The Struggle*
- *Journey of a Healer—Volume II—Healing Experiences*
- *Journey of a Healer—Volume III—Jesus' Teachings and Questions Answered*

CHAPTER 37

*Birth of Universal Center for Self-Enlightenment
And Self-Healing
Creation of the Logo for the Center
Creation of the Front and Back page
of "Journey of a Healer"
Pino and Rachel Get Married
More Chest Pain*

After I came to terms with the name of my manuscript, from the voice of my heart I perceived that I had to create a center through which I could share my findings and my experiences. At this point, I asked myself what I should name the new center.

After days of prayer, I was filled with a great sense of joy and peace. At the same time, from the voice of my heart, I perceived the name of the center should be:

> *"Universal Center
> for
> Self-Enlightenment
> and Self-Healing".*

At the same time, I perceived that the center had to have a logo. Not having any ideas for an appropriate logo, I began to pray.

One night while I was in deep prayer, I had a vision of a geographical globe with a blue background, surrounded by the name of the center.

At the center of the globe was the figure of a man, in deep meditation, radiating energy.

The energy was also portrayed by two intense rays of light, one at the man's forehead, and a more brilliant one, at the bottom of his heart.

At that vision, my heart leapt with joy.

LOGO OF THE CENTER

Although at the time I did not quite understand the meaning of the logo, I was sure it was the right logo for the center.

Now, to complete the book, the only important thing left to do was to design the front and back covers.

Although I tried very hard, I could not find anything that met the approval of the voice of my heart.

One night, unable to sleep, I got up and went to my computer desk. After I turned on the computer, instead of working on my manuscript, I looked at the pictures I had saved.

Every picture brought happy recollections of places and events of my life. I enjoyed them tremendously.

As I scrolled the pictures on, the photo of the sunset I had taken approximately a year before from the front of my cottage in Twentynine Palms appeared.

The photo was magnificent.

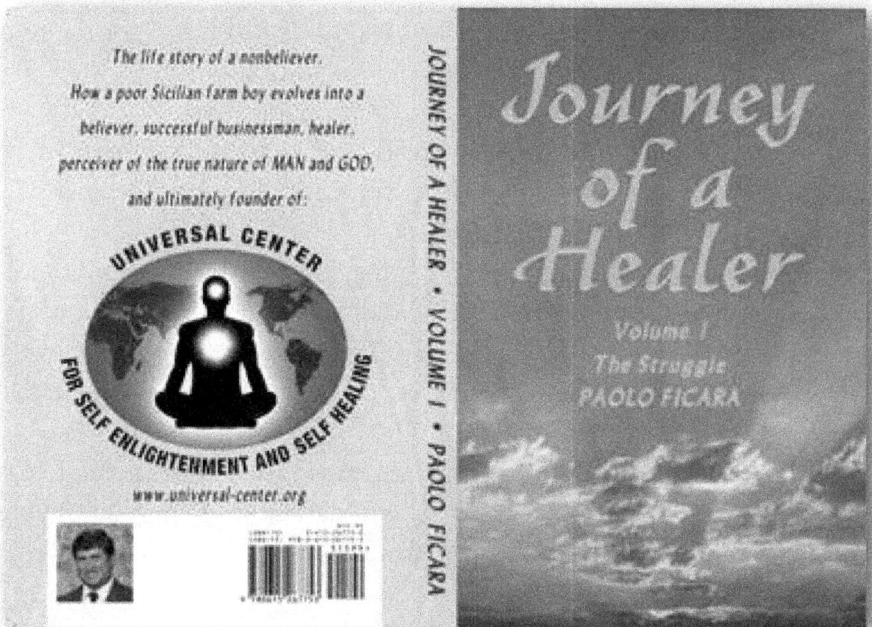

As I admired that marvelous image, from the voice of my heart I perceived that picture was going to be the front cover of my book.

At the same time, I perceived that for the back cover, I had to use the logo created for the center.

I had the sensation that all the pieces came together, and the only thing left to do before we could present the manuscript to the public was to finish the final editing.

I was as happy as I could be.

Meanwhile, our son Pino met a beautiful young girl named Rachel. After they dated for a while, they married on March 9, 2008.

The ceremony was held in San Diego, in the presence of many relatives and friends that came from near and far.

Rachel and Pino were very, very happy, and so were we, Pina and I, and Jan and David, Rachel's parents, as well as the invited guests.

It was a day we will remember and cherish in our hearts for the rest of our lives.

On March 1, 2008, one week before Rachel and Pino got married, I experienced the same symptoms I had on the morning of September 25, 2000: chest pain and gas in my stomach.

Concerned, I phoned a friend of mine, Dr. Stuart Barton, who, after hearing my symptoms, told me he didn't think I was having a heart attack, but he recommended that I go immediately to the Eisenhower Medical Center Emergency Room, located in the city of Rancho Mirage, California.

After the tests, they told me my heart was fine, but I suffered from acid reflux, and that I had nothing to worry about. They gave me some medicine that made me go to the bathroom. Once I passed the gas, I was fine.

CHAPTER 38

SALE OF THE GOLF COURSE AND RETURN TO JOSHUA TREE, OUR PROMISED LAND

In 2007, we sold the golf course. After that, Nino and Paolo Jr. went into the sales and installation of manufactured homes while still helping me in the paving company.

Now that we had no more interest in living at Twentynine Palms, Pina and I decided to relocate to Yucca Valley to be closer to our children.

After we looked at several houses, we put an offer on a house in the Western Hills area, in the town of Yucca Valley. The house was located near Paolo Jr's residence and had a nice view of the town, but needed some remodeling to fit our needs. We had two weeks to consider. During this period, we could withdraw our offer without penalty. Although potentially the house seemed to have what we wanted, I didn't feel comfortable with the deal, and I felt confused. Constantly I thought to our empty house in Joshua Tree. From the voice of my heart, I perceived that we were making the wrong move and that it was best for us to return to our house in Joshua Tree. Because Pina wanted to live near the children, I didn't say anything; I did not want to spoil her joy.

The day before the contract would become binding, I couldn't sleep. I knew we were making a mistake. In the morning, Pina noticed I was nervous, so she asked me if something was bothering me. I thought it was the right occasion to tell Pina my feelings. I asked her if she was sure about our move to Yucca Valley. She turned around, giving me the shoulder treatment, and didn't answer my question. After a few seconds, I asked the question again. At this point, she slowly turned around and looked into my eyes. She asked if I wanted to know the truth. Yes, I answered. She took a big breath and calmly said she didn't like that house and wanted to move back to our house in Joshua Tree.

I said I felt the same way; we immediately called our real estate agent and told him that we were withdrawing our offer. Then we called our children and told them what we had decided.

Since we had moved to Twentynine Palms, we had neglected to do any type of maintenance to our house. We felt it was necessary to do some repair and improvements to bring it to the standard we wanted.

Nino and Paolo Jr. took responsibility for the work, which they completed during the first week of December 2008. One week later, the fifteenth, we moved in. That was a wonderful and a memorable day. Finally, after sixteen years, we were back to what we always called home. The feeling was incredible.

That day, I felt a cycle of my life had ended and a new one had begun.

Deep in my heart, I felt urgency to finish writing my autobiography. For that reason, I promised to dedicate more time to it.

CHAPTER 39

MOTHER PASSES AWAY

Around May 2008, a few weeks after Pino and Rachel got married, I noticed that my mother had begun to forget things.

My brothers and I took her to the family doctor. After the visit, he said she had begun to suffer dementia, and that she was going to get progressively worse.

I became scared and depressed; I remembered my father's long illness and his suffering. I didn't want her to undergo the same pain and suffering.

As time passed, her condition worsened. My brothers and I agreed she was not able to live by herself any longer, and that she needed help. Gioacchino and Rosa, his wife, who were living right across the street from her, convinced Mother to live with them. Her health began to deteriorate rapidly to the point that she no longer had control of her bodily functions. It was hard to see her in this condition, but I accepted her fate peacefully, praying to God not to let her suffer too much.

Approximately seven months after she moved to Gioacchino and Rosa's house, the evening of February 22, 2009, at approximately eleven-thirty, surrounded by the love of all her family, she passed away.

The thought of not having her around anymore filled my heart with sadness. I knew I was going to miss her a lot.

In that sad moment, what comforted me the most was the under-standing that death is only a change of form. I strongly believe that the Spirit, the soul of a person, goes on and continues to live. This thought gave me peace, and the hope that one day I will be reunited with her and my father.

Rosa Ficara, Paolo's Mother
Yucca Valley, Ca. 2005

Paolo - Rosa Ficara (Mother) - Brother Gioacchino
Yucca Valley, Ca. 2009

CHAPTER 40

Nino and Jaime Get Married -
Publication of Journey of a Healer Volume I -
More Chest Pain and Open Heart Surgery

In the first part of April 2009, Nino and Jaime, his beautiful sweetheart from high school, decided to get married. The date was set for September 26, 2009, in Yucca Valley.

The ceremony was beautiful, and we were honored by the presence of many relatives and friends. We were all very happy to see Jamie and Nino begin their married life and to go on to fulfill the dreams of their lives.

On September 28, 2009, with the help of my friend Professor Greg Gilbert, we presented to the public at Copper Mountain College (our local community college), the first volume of my autobiography.

Finally, after almost twenty-seven years from the day I began to write it and after many nights and countless hours at my desk and at my computer, the first part of my life-long dream became reality. I was overwhelmed with joy.

On September 19, one week before Jamie and Nino's wedding, I suffered a repeat of what had happened on March 1, 2008, the week before Rachel and Pino were married: chest pain and gas in my stomach.

This time I didn't go to the hospital for a checkup convinced that once I passed the gas from my stomach I would be fine. In fact, soon after I went to the bathroom, I was perfectly fine.

It happened again, on a Saturday morning a few days after Nino and Jamie's wedding, while I was working in Yucca Valley. This time I was concerned.

On the following Monday, I went to see my friend Dr. Robert Harmon, who after the exanimation told me my heart was fine. He also told me there was the possibility that the source of my chest pains was an ulcer in my stomach. However, to be sure and for peace of mind, he told me to go to Eisenhower Medical Center for a check-up. After the test, I went back to my friend's clinic, waiting for the results from the hospital. About an hour later, the hospital faxed the results: my heart was fine. Instead of feeling relived at the news, I felt concerned.

I questioned the doctor about the most accurate way to find out if I had any blockage in my arteries. He told me it was a procedure called *Angiogram.*

I asked where I could go to get it done. He told me that, that type of procedure, was performed only by a cardiologist. He continued saying that he knew a very good cardiologist by the name Dr. Melvin Gonzalez, whose office was nearby in Eisenhower Medical Center. I asked him if he could schedule an appointment for me because I wanted that procedure done. The appointment was set for the following Monday, October 18, at ten o clock.

When Pina and I got to Dr. Gonzalez's office, the receptionist asked me about the nature of my problems. I said that I needed an angiogram. Surprised by my request, she asked what made me think I needed an angiogram. I said I had to find out for sure if there were any blockages in my coronary arteries.

Smiling, she said that I had to discuss that with the doctor, and then asked us to follow her to one of the examination rooms.

A few minutes later, the doctor came in, a nice-looking man in his fifties whose expression showed a lot of self-confidence. From the voice of my heart, I perceived that I had the right doctor. After we shook hands, he asked me what was bothering me.

I told him I had been experiencing pain in my chest and that I was very concerned. For that reason, I wanted an angiogram. I wanted to be sure I didn't have any obstructed coronary arteries.

With a big smile on his face, he told me that before he would perform the angiogram, he needed to do an E.K.G. If this test was positive and showed some problems with my heart, he would do a stress test, and then if this confirmed I had some problems, he would do an echocardiogram, and if this test were positive, then he would do the angiogram.

I told him his reasoning made good sense. We began with the E.K.G.

This first test showed that my heart was working normally. The doctor was satisfied with the results, congratulated me and told me not to worry.

I told him I still wanted to take the stress test.

Surprised by my request, the doctor looked at me as to say, "I am the doctor, don't you trust me"? He asked me why. I said I didn't know, but something inside me was telling me I had to have that test done.

He said I didn't need it, but if that were what I wanted, he would do it.

Therefore, he scheduled the procedure for nine o'clock on Thursday morning, October 22, 2008.

During the test, the doctor and his assistant were very happy to see that I had no chest pain, no shortness of breath, no high blood pressure, and that my heartbeat was normal.

When we finished, he smiled and said, "I told you, your heart is fine and you have nothing to worry about."

Instead of feeling relieved, I continued to be concerned, so I asked if he could do the echocardiogram.

Reluctantly, he agreed to my request and scheduled me to have it done on Monday the 26, at 11:30 a.m.

After I finished with Dr. Gonzalez, I went to see my friend Dr. Harmon.

He was pleased to learn that both tests were negative, and suggested I see a specialist to check my stomach. He thought my problems could have originated from an ulcer. I told him that was a good idea.

His secretary scheduled an appointment with the specialist for Monday the 26, at 8 a.m.

When I arrived on Monday morning at the doctor's office, the secretary informed me that the doctor was not there because he had to go to the hospital to assist some other patients.

Disappointed by the inconvenience, I left. As I was walking to my car, I felt mild chest pain with an accumulation of gas in my stomach. By the time I arrived where I had parked my car, the pains were much stronger.

Not knowing what to do, I decided to go to see my cardiologist, Dr. Gonzales, whose office was not far from where I was.

By the time I arrived at Dr. Gonzalez's office, my chest pain had become unbearable.

When the receptionist saw me, she reminded me that my appointment was for 11.30. I explained that I had chest pain.

She took me immediately into one of the examination rooms, and soon thereafter Dr. Gonzales arrived. He performed an E.K.G. and took my blood pressure. Strange to say, everything looked good. The doctor was perplexed.

Then he asked me on a scale 1 to 10, how strong my pains were. I answered 11 or 12. I did exaggerate a bit, but it got his attention. He became serious, and then he left, telling me he would be right back. About five minutes later, he came back and said he had arranged for me to be admitted at the hospital and he was going to perform an angiogram immediately.

Then he asked me if I was able to drive by myself to the hospital, which was located only a few hundreds yard away, or if I needed help. I replied that I could drive.

As soon I got in my car, I thought of calling Pina, but was afraid she would over-react. I called Paolo Jr. and Nino instead.

Alarmed by the news, they asked me if I was okay.

Calmly and smiling, I assured them I was fine.

They told me they were going to pick up their mom and would come immediately. Within an hour, they were at the hospital. Later in the day, Pino and Rachel also came from San Diego.

By 10 a.m., I was in my room, where they prepared me for the test.

By noon, I was in the operating room. They gave me a local anesthetic, and then performed the test.

The findings were shocking. I had four blockages: three arteries were blocked 95%, while the fourth was 70%.

Afterwards I was taken to my room, where Pina, Nino and Paolo Jr. waited.

A few minutes later, Dr. Gonzalez came and told me that surgery was a necessity. Pina, Nino and Paolo Jr.'s faces paled, and I could feel their fear and concern. In an attempt to make them relax, I told Pina and the boys not to worry, that everything was going to be fine; then smiling, I cracked a few jokes.

That evening my brothers and some of their children, along with many friends, came to see me at the hospital. It was overwhelming to see so great a display of love.

The next day, Tuesday the 27, the doctors did all the necessary tests to make sure I could go through the surgery safely. On Wednesday the 28 of September 2008, at 1:30 p.m., Dr. Wilson performed the surgery.

The surgery was successful, and five days later, I went home. We were all delighted.

I prayed to God for an immediate recovery.

Although I prayed very hard, I was not able to get in touch with the voice of my heart. Consequently, I wasn't able to experience a miraculous recovery like some of the people I've prayed for as narrated in *Journey of a Healer Volume II*. I was concerned and confused.

CHAPTER 41

Brother Gioacchino Passes On

It was July 31, 2011, an early Sunday afternoon, when the phone rang. I answered: it was my oldest son Pino.

"Hi, Dad. How are you?"

"I am doing fine. How are you doing?"

"I am doing not too good."

"Why?"

After a relatively long pause, he said, "Dad, I have sad news for you."

"What is it?"

After another long pause, he said, "I just talked to my cousin Carmela, and she told me that early this morning, Uncle Gioacchino went to the emergency room and was diagnostic with terminal cancer on the liver." He paused. "They gave him two weeks to live."

In hearing those words, deep in my heart, I felt a great sense of fear. "Are you kidding me? It can't be. It's got to be a mistake."

"Dad," he said, his voice quivering. "There is no mistake."

I was petrified. Pina and I rushed to the hospital.

When we got out of the elevator, we found all my brother's children, Rosettina, Carmela, Marianna, and Jacquelyn. After they hugged us, they began to cry.

"Don't cry," I said. "We're going to pray to the good Lord and your daddy is going to get well." We walked toward his room.

We found him calmly lying in bed, with no apparent discomfort.

I asked in Italian: *Come ti senti?* (How are you?)

Smiling, he answered: *Ho un po' di dolore alla stomaco, ma a parte questo, mi sento bene.* (I have some pain in my stomach, but other than that, I am fine.)

After a while, I asked: *Ti piacerebbe pregare con me?* (Would you like to pray with me?)

Calmly, he looked at me with a sense of joy and hope, and then he said: *Si, mi piacerebbe pregare con te.* (Yes, I would love to pray with you.) Then he motioned for me to sit down near him.

After I sat down, I closed my eyes and silently, I began to pray.

But I was too agitated to concentrate on my praying. And, as if that was not enough, the nurses continuously interrupted us.

We decided to continue praying the next morning, hoping it would be quieter.

Pina and I stayed there until the evening, and then we went home, promising him that I would be back early in the morning.

That night I couldn't sleep; I couldn't believe the news about my brother was reality. It seemed like a bad dream.

The next morning, as soon, I got to the hospital, we began to pray. Although I was trying hard, I was still too emotional and I couldn't relax. Consequently, I was not able to get in touch with the voice of my heart, and Gioacchino did not perceive anything.

That evening, when I went home, I spent most of the night praying God to help me detach myself from my emotions, to answer my prayers, and to help Gioacchino.

The next morning, Tuesday, August 2, 2011, as I was driving to the hospital, I felt more relaxed. After we began to pray, energy began to flow through my right hand. After a while, I asked Gioacchino if he was feeling anything. He told me that he felt warm all over his body. Then he said that the heat was stronger in his abdomen; that he was no longer in pain; and he was feeling good. We continued to pray.

At approximately 11:30, the nurse, brought his lunch, so we stopped praying. After he finished his lunch, accompanied by Rosa, his wife, he went for a walk. It seemed that he was doing extremely well. We continued to pray in the afternoon, with the same apparent results: no pain.

Wednesday morning, August 3, 2011, when I got to the hospital, Rosa, Gioacchino's wife, - told me that in the course of the night, the pain came back, and to make him feel comfortable, the nurse gave him some pain medicines.

We began to pray.

After about twenty minutes, Gioacchino told me that he was feeling warm again, and that the pains were gone. We prayed for about three hours, and then we continued for another two hours in the afternoon.

Thursday morning, August 4, Gioacchino informed me that again in the middle of the night, the pain came back and that he had to take pain medicines. In my previous experiences, when a person felt the heat and his health improved, the improvements were permanent.

I couldn't understand why, a few hours after we stopped praying, the pains were coming back. I was very concerned.

Friday, August 5, was exactly the same. That afternoon, the doctor came in the room, and in the presence of Gioacchino, Rosa, all their children and me, he said that we were facing an almost hopeless case and suggested chemotherapy as a last resort. He said that if we would agree, they would begin the treatment the following Tuesday, August 9, as an outpatient, and that the next day, Saturday, August 5, Gioacchino could go home.

I explained to the doctor that while praying, Gioacchino's pain faded, and for that reason, before the beginning of the chemotherapy, we'd like them to do some x-rays to see if there was any change in the condition of Gioacchino's liver.

He said no. I asked why.

He said he didn't think the insurance company would pay for the cost of them, since he didn't believe it was a necessary test. Of course, what he was alluding to without actually saying it was that he didn't believe that our prayer could have had any impact on Gioacchino's condition.

I became upset. Rosa and their children wept silently.

While all this was going on, Gioacchino watched everyone with an expression on his face that didn't show any fear. To the contrary, the expression on his face was very calm, tranquil and peaceful, while his eyes radiated with all the love he held for all of us. It seemed as though he had no concerns whatsoever, as if the patient we spoke about wasn't him, but someone else.

I wondered how he could be so calm. While I was thinking that, from the voice of my heart, I perceived that Gioacchino was well aware of his condition, but his love for all us was so great, that he was more concerned about us than himself. He didn't want us to suffer, or be concerned.

One more time, my brother Gioacchino, the person I'd always looked up to, was showing us an incredible display of mental power and love.

While I was immersed in these thoughts, Gioacchino looking to all us, and smiling said: "Why are you crying? I'm not dead yet,". "Don't worry. Tomorrow I'll go home, I'll eat more, and in no time, I will be fine." His calm conviction made us all smile, which made him glow with joy.

Sunday morning, at his house, we prayed from approximately 8:30 to until 11:30: He was pain free.

Then he got up from his bed and started to walk around the house. While he was walking, Rosa prepared some Italian minestrone. Gioacchino ate a big bowl of it. He looked really good, which gave us hope.

We continued to pray some more in the afternoon. In the evening, when I left his house, I told him that I would be back the next morning at about seven o'clock.

The next morning, at about ten minutes to six, while I was taking my shower, the phone rang. Immense fear filled me. .

Pina answered the phone. She came in and told me that Rosa was crying because Gioacchino was not able to get up from bed - he couldn't stand up.

Immediately I dried myself and went to their house. When I got there, I couldn't believe my eyes. My brother could hardly move.

I couldn't believe that in less than twelve hours he could have made such a drastic change for the worst. In that moment from the voice of my heart, I perceived that he was not going to make it. I felt desperate!

When we asked him how he was feeling, he always answered, "I am fine." He never spoke one word of discomfort or fear.

In the afternoon, when we tried to talk to him, he became unresponsive. It was obvious his body was shutting down and he was preparing for the passing.

In those sad moments, the one thing I wasn't able to understand was his apparent improvement first, followed by his worsening.

Why were his improvements not permanent? Why? Why?

Although I do believe the soul doesn't die and that so-called death is just a change of form, it was very difficult and painful in not being able to help him, and to see him slowly go.

At 1:15 in the morning of Tuesday, August 9, 2011, my brother Gioacchino, surrounded by the love of his wife, his children with their spouses, his grandchildren, as well as the love of my family and the love of our brother Ignazio and his family, he passed away.

The person I had worked with and dreamed with throughout my life was gone.

In that moment, I felt a part of my life left with him.

The doctor's prognosis was wrong. He didn't live fourteen days as predicted; he barely made it nine days.

The night before his funeral, I wrote the following eulogy to read during his service. But when the time came to do so, I wasn't able to do it. I was too sad. So I asked my son Pino to do it for me.

Here are the last words that I dedicated to my brother Gioacchino:

What can I say about my brother Gioacchino?

I can begin by saying that his love for his family was immense.

That his family was the most important thing in his life, to whom he dedicated all his time and efforts, and to whom, without hesitation, he gave all he had.

I can say that he was truly an extraordinary human being from every point of view. I know it, because we spent all our lives dreaming and working together, and nobody knew him better than me.

For me, it was blessing from God to have had a brother like him.

I am proud to say, with all the sincerity that I can express in my heart and without hesitation, that he was truly my greatest hero.

He was the person that – through - example, not words - was able to instill in my mind and in my heart unselfish love.

Although someone looking from the outside could get a different perception, he was the one who, for most of my life, I looked to for inspiration, and who inspired me.

I loved him for his simplicity, altruism and his constant desire to make a difference in somebody's life.

I am very grateful to his wife Rosa and to his children Rosa, Carmela, Maria Anna, Jacquelyn, and to my wife Pina and to my children, for having allowed me to spend the last eight days of his life with him, to pray with him and to prove to each other that our love was above what at times could have been our differences.

Those last moments that we spent together, I will cherish and keep with me for the rest of my life.

I wish I could have done more for you, my dear brother, but seemed that the good Lord had a different plan. So we humbly accept His will.

Goodbye, my dear brother.

Thank you for all the love that you always had for me and all the things that you did for me.

Dear brother, I am going to love you always with all my heart, and you will always have a special place in my heart.

I hope that one day we will be together again, in the company of our dear parents, in a place where the suffering and the struggle of human life doesn't exist. I bless you and I wish you to rest in peace.

Your beloved brother Paolo.

Rosa & Gioacchino Ficara

Princess Cruise
Miami, Florida 2005
Gioacchino Ficara
Princess Cruise
Miami, Florida 2005

My niece Carmela Ficara Robinson, Gioacchino's second daughter, wrote the following eulogy:

Gioacchino Ficara, my father.

He had many names: Papa, Grandpa, Padrino, Zio Jack, and Yekie. He also had many special characteristics: strong, hard-working, encouraging, patient, fun, giving, jokester, honorable, a teacher, and a one of a kind man.

My father shared with me the first step of wisdom, which is silence, and the second, which is listening.

The one thing about my dad that everyone knew was that he was a man of few words, except when it came to soccer or Indy car racing, and every once in a while he would mention some drama on *All My Children* or *One Life to Live*.

A funny story about my father is, he was very hard of hearing. As we told a story and asked some questions, he nodded as if he understood. Then we'd ask him to explain what was said, and he would smile, shrug his shoulders, and say, "I don't know," and we would laugh.

He was the only Italian that hated tomatoes, but loved to plant them.

He loved the ocean, but didn't know how to swim.

Would age every year, but always said he was eighteen.

Be extremely exhausted, but would never say no to someone in need.

He loved my mother so much, and showed her as he helped her every evening as he washed the dishes. At times my mother would say, "Leave them alone Jack, I will do them tomorrow" and he would always reply, "It's okay, I need to wash my hands."

He would bring her coffee in bed every morning.

He would rub her legs when she felt pain. He never complained and always wanted to keep peace in his life.

One of the proudest moments of his life was when he had his first grandchild. So happy that he finally had a boy. Poor guy, had to deal with four daughters. And now Brenden Gioacchino Robinson lives on to have many traits of his grandfather. He not only has his name, but he looks like him. He has his walk, his smile, his personality, and I thank you.

The one thing that annoyed my mother that will now be missed was the way my father chomped his food while he ate. However, it still lives on through his youngest daughter Jacqueline and his grandson Brenden, and so we thank you guys for that.

He loved to dance with my mom and we loved to watch her lead. I know he loved his walks with my mom as his hand was always resting on her shoulder. They made beautiful pizzas in their beautiful pizza oven. They fed many chickens and collected many fresh eggs.

Even though my father made many friends and partied with all of them, and made many memories, he was a homebody and his best friend was my mother. I know he will protect her from above as we mourn for him. In life we shall find many men who are great or good, but very few men who are great and good, which my father was. I am so sad that he is gone, but glad to have given him to loving arms of the angels above.

Daddy, you are my hero!

CHAPTER 42
REVELATION OF THE TRUE NATURE OF GOD

Going back to the time that followed the reading of the Gospels, I need to say that during that time, my thoughts were constantly focused on God.

I couldn't help but anticipate the day I would finally penetrate the mystery of His existence, knowing it would be the happiest day of my life.

Thus, I went on praying and hoping for something to happen.

The responses to my questions finally came out, but, as I mentioned in the introduction, in a gradual, strange, unexpected fashion.

In the following pages, I shall share all my experiences with the reader.

However, before relating what went on, I want to explain that although my experiences are described faithfully and truthfully, I have to say that I abbreviated them and that the time span of their occurrence was considerably longer than it would appear in my narration.

Another point I would like to clarify is how I ultimately came to perceive the answers to my lifelong questions.

Here is the procedure that I used:

- Whenever I wanted to know something, or I wanted something, I would formulate the idea in my mind, in the form of thought;

- Then, I would put that idea in writing the simplest, shortest, a clearest possible;
- After that I would sedan in a very comfortable chair, or in my bed, with my spine perfectly strait.
- Then, I would close my eyes, and begin to focus all my attention to that part of my being previously identified as *the voice of my heart.*
- After that, with sincerity, humility, and expectation, I begin to say slowly, over and over, and over, without stopping, -- for at least one hour at the time, -- the content of my writings (prayer).

As the time goes by, I try to intensify my effort, and my plea, to the maximum of my ability.

When finally, I do get totally connected with *the voice of my heart,* I feel like, all my being is immersed in an ocean of bless, peace, harmony and joy, impossible to describe or express with words.

When that happens, I know that the object of my prayer has been granted.

This is what I call true prayer.

If for whatever reason I don't get the expected results, I don't' get discouraged, to the contrary I would intensify my effort, and I will try again, and again, and again, without tiring, until I will get what I want.

Always remember, the secrete to success, is to be perseverant and to never give up, regardless of how long may take: one our, one day, one week, one month, one year or even several years.

The reason I'm clarifying all these details is because I want the reader to know and to understand very clearly, the process whereby my experiences took place over the years, albeit not without considerable effort and perseverance.

Should readers decide to undertake the same spiritual path and not immediately achieve the desired results, I advise them not to give up, but to keep trying.

Just as it was for me, Jesus, the Saints, and other Holy Men of the Christian religion—as well as for all the Saints and Holy Men of other faiths, including Judaism, Islam, Buddhism, and Hinduism - the goal of understanding God's true nature is attainable.

However, to reach that goal, one must be endowed by an unshakeable and sincere desire to want to know the truth, free of ulterior motives or personal agendas.

For those desirous of taking the journey, be aware there is an arduous road ahead, fraught with multitudes of stumbling blocks - but with rewards at the end that are no less than extraordinary.

Another thing that I would like to clarify with the reader is the view that I grown to have of God.

To me, God is not an individual, with a specific form and entity, who lives in some place of the universe, as commonly believed.

To me, *God is the Energy comprised into every atom existing in the universe*, which gives form and life to the body and the spirit of man, as well as to all creation.

It is for this reason that when I do address myself to God, I am not addressing myself to an entity that resides outside the sphere of my being, but I address myself to the Energy that is the essence of my being.

This Energy, that in the course of my narration I call also *Creative Power Within*, whose focal point is located between the diaphragm and the rib cage of our body, who most of time is felt unconsciously, but can be felt consciously during deep prayer and meditation, is responsible for all our perceptions, as well as for all our experiences, good and bad.

I know, that at first glance it is hard to believe that what I am saying is the *truth*.

But I can assure you, that if you are going to continue to read and begin to live and to practice my findings, you too are going to have the fortune and the blessing not only to understand the *truth*, but also to experience the *truth*, and with it, experience things that commonly are called *miracles or supernatural*.

Now let us begin…

The period of my life that followed my reading of the Gospels was characterized by an ever-growing, almost compulsive desire to grasp the mysteries of God's existence; so much so, that one day while I was working, I became so tense and nervous that I had to stop.

While trying to relax, I told myself that I would go on praying relentlessly and with the utmost intensity until God saw fit to make Himself known to me.

That evening, after I retired to my bedroom, I made up the following prayer:

> *"My God, I'm sure that You are aware of the desire gripping my heart at this very moment and that You already know how much I'm suffering. I am asking You therefore, with all the strength my heart and mind can muster, to appear and speak to me."*

For about ten days, I continued repeating this prayer several times a day, as well as every evening before going to sleep.

While praying one evening, I felt my words sink to the deepest point of the voice of my heart. From that same place, I felt as I had so many times in the past, a great sense of peace and harmony that slowly spread throughout my being.

After being pervaded with this beautiful sensation for about forty-five minutes, I perceived deep in my heart - with a touch of reprehension - that I shouldn't keep pounding on the same issue. For, as I had already been given to understand, God couldn't appear to me - for the simple reason that He had no specific shape or form through which he could manifest Himself.

Upon perceiving this message, I felt a great sense of shame, which fortunately did not last long. I took heart, and proceeded with the following prayer:

> *"My God, I understand that You can't appear to me, as You have no form; but will You at least let me perceive how You express Yourself?"*

Having repeated the above appeal for a few days, one evening after praying for about an hour and getting ready to go to bed, I perceived from the voice of my heart the following:

> **"My son, I do express Myself through all Creation."**

After perceiving that, I asked:

> "What does that mean - that You 'express Yourself through all Creation'?"
> **"It means that I, God, can be found in all the elements constituting the whole of Creation."**

Next, I asked:

> "What does it mean that You, God, *'can be found in all things that make up Creation?"*

The response was immediate:

> **"Exactly what you perceived: that I, God, am found in all the things you see and in all the things you don't."**

I wondered, in that case, whether God could also exist in the body of every human being. Therefore, I asked:

"My God, if You are to be found throughout Creation, does that mean You also reside within the human body?"
The reply was, **"Yes."**

I then participated in the following question-and-answer dialogue with God through the process I have already explained. I posed the questions and God allowed me to perceive the answers.

"What relation is there between You and me?"
"Unity."

"What do You mean by *'Unity*?"
"That I am a part of you; I'm the essence of your being and the Life of your life."

Having perceived the above, I couldn't help feeling stunned at how the complex mystery of God and man's existence was unfolding before my senses and my eyes, wondering how anything like what I had just discerned could ever be possible. After a short break, I resumed the process.

"What do You mean when You say You are *the essence of my being*?"
"That all the particles in your body are made up by my essence, and that you and I are one being."

"What do You mean when You say that You are the *'Life of my life*?"
"That I am the one who gives Life to your life."

"How can that be possible I asked?"

Immediately after, I felt a break in my connection with the voice of my heart. From that moment on, I could no longer perceive anything. Following a short pause, I decided to touch on another subject, and asked:

"My God, who is responsible for all my healing experiences?"
"I am."

"Who is responsible for everything I have experienced in life?"
"I am."

"How can such a thing be possible?"

Once again, I could get no reply. After praying for a while without receiving a response, I asked:

"My God, what is, in its true essence, the voice of my heart?"
"It is I, God, within you."

It is impossible to express in words what I felt at that moment.

- **Was it really possible that what I had always thought to be the voice of my heart was in reality God?**
- **Could God actually dwell deep in my heart, and could He and I in fact be one and the same?**

As I mulled over these ideas, the following new considerations came to mind:

- **If what I had perceived mirrored reality, why is it that I was not aware of it?**
- **How could I explain my inability to resolve the problems that had pursued me all my life, and which at times left me feeling desperate and powerless?**
- **Why couldn't I steadfastly manifest the same strength, joy, and all the various characteristics we imagine God to possess?**

As this brain-wracking process continued, I slowly became aware that instead of being happy and gratified - as I should have been in reaction to the positive outcome of my search—I was becoming nervous and confused.

Probing my frame of mind, I realized - after taking into account my inability to properly assess the data received - that the nervous tension and state of confusion were due mainly to my uncertainty about whether or not the things I had been allowed to perceive really represented the *"Truth"* - the same *"Truth"* in which I had been in fervent pursuit.

Then, I asked myself:

- **Why was I finding it so difficult to believe and accept what I had perceived?**
- **Could it be that unconsciously I was waiting for someone to materialize before my eyes, saying, "Here I am. I'm God - and to prove that I'm God I'll perform some miracles for you?"**

Hoping to shade some light on my dilemma, I formulated the following question:

"My God, since You can't show Yourself, as You have no real form as such, could You possibly let me perceive the true essence of Your being?"

After approximately half an hour of repeating those words, from the voice of my heart I perceived:

"My son, the true essence of my Being is "Energy"."

Upon further analyzing this perception, I remained unable to fathom in what way the essence of God could possibly be Energy.

Thus, I formulated this new prayer:

"My God, I'm sure You're aware of my inability to understand the things You allow me to perceive. It is precisely for this reason that I pray to You humbly and with the utmost sincerity to help me understand through example, or through a manner more in keeping with my intellectual make-up, how Your essence can possibly be defined as Energy."

I repeated this prayer continuously, day and night.

One evening while praying, my mind envisioned the Ribera of my childhood. I used all my willpower to divert my thoughts from those memories of bygone years, which were seriously distracting me from my prayer. However, a very strange thing happened: the more I tried to turn away from them, the more I felt a need and desire to recollect those past events.

After grappling for some time with this internal struggle - noticing meanwhile that despite all my efforts I couldn't succeed in dispelling the extraneous thoughts from my mind - I finally gave up and let my imagination roam freely, at that moment, my entire being filled with a great feeling of peace and joy.

Many memories surfaced:

- **My mother's malady induced by the three conjurers' spell;**
- **My decision to help my father and brother in the fields;**
- **The extraordinary coincidence of Mr. Carmelo's inability to sell us the mechanic's overalls, which put an end to my mechanic apprenticeship;**
- **My friend Enzo Tortorici's illness, and my subsequent visit with him on which occasion he informed me that a new school was opening in town and suggested that I should attend it; that move, as the reader might remember, changed the whole course of my life.**

My thoughts wandered further to:

- **My first days of class in Sciacca;**
- **To my schoolmates, my teachers, the subjects I studied at the time, and finally to my chemistry teacher, Mr. Licata.**

I remembered with great joy his kind nature and the esteem in which I held him, both because he was a competent teacher and a good man.

I recalled the first time he spoke to us about *Atom*. That lecture has remained engraved in my memory and my heart up to this day, and I am sure it will remain there as long as I live.

Even now, when I consider that in reality the *Atom* - the essence of which is *Energy* - comprises the building blocks of the universe, it staggers my imagination. I deem myself fortunate and blessed to have had the opportunity to acquire this knowledge.

I don't recall exactly how long I remained immersed in this contemplation. What I remember very vividly, however, is that when I came out of it, I automatically recalled what I had perceived from the Voice of my Heart:

"The Essence of God is Energy."

At that moment, I wondered whether there was a relationship between the energy existing in the atoms and the energy making up the essence of God.

Unable to reach a satisfactory conclusion, I pleaded for God's help:

"My God, I entreat You to let me perceive without a shadow of a doubt if there is a relationship between the energy found in the atoms and the Energy making up the essence of Your nature."

Approximately twenty minutes later, I felt the usual sense of relaxation and peace that precedes a perception, and then it began:

"My son, I'm pleased that despite the hardships you have faced, you never got discouraged and never abandoned your resolve to know the truth, always keeping alive, as you did, the hope that one day you would be given the privilege of understanding what is My true nature and the mystery apparently enshrouding it.

"I want you to know that the making of the energy that is found in the atoms, in reality, is My Energy.

"That's why, when you asked Me to appear - that is, to materialize before you - I let you perceive that I couldn't. After all, in what shape and form could I appear to you without deceiving you of My true nature?

"For this same reason, no one in the world can claim to have directly seen Me.

"If you would like, you can see Me and you can find Me in everything making up the entire universe, because the entire universe is made with the essence of My nature: My Energy."

In that very moment, a familiar expression came to mind, the significance and meaning of which had eluded me until then:

God is in Heaven, on Earth, and Everywhere.

Not until that moment had, I realized the truth and eloquence of those words.

After that perception, I asked:

> "My God, I understand the fact that I should see You in every-thing existing in the Universe, but how in a practical way can I get in touch with You?"
> **"The way you always have: through prayer."**

> "My God, I also understand that I can find You in whatever ex-ists in the Universe, but this concept is so immense that I have a hard time understanding how I can find You among all creation. Is there a specific place or more practical way I can search for You and find You?"
> **"Yes, My son."**

> "Where is this place"?
> **"Within you."**

> "Where within me?"
> **"In the voice of your heart."**

At this perception, once more, I was in complete shock. Finally, after a lifetime of suffering, dreaming, and wishing, I was able to discover and understand God's nature, the essence of His being and where He abides.

My joy was indescribable.

CHAPTER 43

REVELATION OF THE WAY GOD OPERATES

U nfortunately, as is often the case with me, this state of bliss was not meant to last forever. On the morning of September 11, 2001, while working with my two sons, Pino and Nino, and my workers at the golf course, getting it ready for sowing the winter grass, we heard the news about the terrorist attacks on the New York Trade Center and the Pentagon.

That event, which engendered an enormous wave of violence throughout the world that even now has yet to abate, brought back to my mind those issues I had incessantly asked myself and others since childhood and to which I have yet to find the answers:

- **How could God allow the occurrence of such horrible events that wreak fear, terror, bewilderment, death, and destruction to the minds and bodies of innocent human beings?**
- **What benefits did humanity reap from these infamous deeds?**
- **Could this barrage of violence ever be stopped?**

The general sense of euphoria affecting me during that period had given rise in my mind to the notion of seeking God's intervention in this all-too-human mix-up of war and terror, asking Him to put a stop to all the senseless violence occurring in every corner of the globe.

I created the following prayer:

"My God, I entreat You fervently and with all the strength that is in me to put an end to the violence which at this moment is spreading throughout the world."

After repeating this plea for about thirty minutes, from the depths of my heart I perceived the following:

"My son, I understand your pain, your sorrow, and your desire. Nevertheless, you must know, or at least attempt to understand, that I do not have direct control or power over the events that are troubling the world, and that it's impossible for me to intervene directly to change the course of those events."

In all sincerity, I wasn't expecting to perceive that kind of message; as a result, I was left shocked, deluded, and confused. I found it impossible to accept what I had just perceived.

- **How was it possible that God, the creator of the universe, who I believed has unlimited power, let me perceive that He didn't have direct control or power over the events that are troubling our society, and that He couldn't intervene directly to change the course of those events?**
- **If He couldn't, then who could?**

So I asked:

"My God if You can't, then who can?"
"Man himself, My son."

This perception left me very perplexed, to say the least.

After much pondering, I became aware that it was true that I now understood who God is, where He is to be found, and the essence of

His nature. However, another important element of His aspect still eluded me:

THE WAY GOD OPERATES.

Consequently, I made up the following prayer:

> *"My God, I pray You with all the sincerity that I can express in my heart, to help me understand why You can't intervene in a direct way to help us with the problems existing in the world, and how this privilege is reserved for man himself. I will never stop pleading with You until You see fit to answer my plea."*

One evening, after several days of reciting this simple prayer for an hour at a time, while praying, I perceived the following message:

> **"My son, I'm pleased that your quest hasn't simply concluded with the discovery of who I am and how I express Myself, but that you have persevered instead to understand the apparent mystery concerning the way I operate.**

> **"Before I let you perceive why I cannot help, first, you most fully and clearly understand what is the makeup of the essence of My nature.**

> **"As you already know, the essence of My nature is Energy.**

> **"What you still do not know is that My Energy is omnipresent, and is infused with the essence of My Will, Mind and My Creative Power, whose function is:**

- The Will to keep the Mind in motion;
- The Mind, as you already know, to create in the form of thoughts whatever is the desire of the Will;
- The Creative Power—which is infused with the Omnipotence and the Omniscience of My essence— to manifest and materialize whatever the Mind creates in the form of thoughts;
- "Will, Mind and Creative Power, although are and represent three different elements and aspects of My nature, are bonded together in a such way that they work in unison as one entity, and one cannot perform and operate without the cooperation of the other two;
- "They are the makeup of the Trinity of My nature."

After this perception, I asked:

"My God, can You help me to understand the meaning of *Omnipresent, Omniscience* and *Omnipotent,* and what task does each one of them fulfill?"

Here is what I perceived:

- "*Omnipresent,* means that it is found in everything that exists in the universe;
- "I already explained it to you when I let you perceive that the building blocks that constitute all creation in the entire universe are the atoms, whose essence is Energy, My Energy. It has the task to give form and life to all creation;
- "*Omniscience,* means all-knowing, knowing everything there is to know about all the apparent mysteries of the creation. It

has the task to teach to everyone the truth about everything that exists in the universe;

- *"Omnipotent,* means that it can perform any conceivable task. It has the function to manifest whatever the mind creates and conceives in the form of thoughts.

"My son, the essence of My nature is Energy, and I do express Myself through the body of every person that comes into the world, to whom I give form and life, and with whom I become one entity.

"The reason why I allowed you to perceive that I am powerless and not able to help you directly in your plea is because in being one with man, it is the will and the mind of man who has total control over the Omnipotence of My Creative Power within.

"Consequently, it is the will of man who is responsible for all the events happening in the world--good and bad--and it is the will of man who has the power to stop or change the course of any or all the catastrophic events that are happening."

In perceiving all the above, I was in total shock.

After this perception, I was curious to know if the Omnipotence of the Creative Power within has other functions besides the one to exteriorize and materialize whatever is created and conceived by the will and mind of man in the form of thoughts.

I asked:

"My God, are there other functions that the Omnipotence of Your Creative Power within man is involved in?"
"Yes, My son."

"Can you allow me to perceive what they are, my God?"

- **"To give to all the *Atoms* existing in the universe the capability to combine between them, and to exchange their electrons and protons;**
- **To supervise the proliferation and multiplication of molecules and cells;**
- **And to regulate and coordinate endlessly all the cycles of all life—from beginning to end, from conception to fulfillment—giving life the ability to procreate and perpetuate itself indefinitely."**

I was amazed!

Nevertheless, after a few days, I had more questions, so I asked:

"My God, You did allow me to perceive that man is the expression and manifestation of Your Energy, and that he is endowed with the same Divine attributes that You possess.

- If that is the truth, why are so few people aware of this truth?
- Why, more often than not, does man feel to be *powerless, weak,* and *miserable*?
- Why are some people pervaded by a *palpable madness*, crowned by *evil* and *ill will*?
- My God, could You let me perceive and demonstrate without ambiguity that everything You have allowed me to perceive represents the truth?

Here is the response to my questions:

"My son, as you already know, the essence of My nature is Energy.

"What you don't know yet is that the essence of My Energy is Absolute Perfection and Ultimate Harmony, and that in the pure state, has no form.

"The life cycle began when I decided to externalize My Essence by means of Creation.

"In the beginning, humans were conscious of their divine nature, of the divine nature of all Creation, and that they are all interconnected.

"For that reason, they loved one another and they respected every living and not living thing existing in the universe.

"Consequently, their lives were blessed and filled continuously with joy, peace and harmony.

"Man's problems arose when he began to erroneously identify himself and everything else in the Creation as individuals.

"This new way of conceiving the reality of existence slowly and progressively made man lose awareness of his true identity, essence and nature, as well as awareness of the true identity, essence and nature of all creation.

"My son, it is precisely from the loss of this awareness that all of man's misfortunes come into being—misfortunes that often transform his life into a truly living hell.

"Everything you learned in the past concerning the role and function of thoughts—including their similarity to seeds—is true.

"The invisible part of man's being—the Omnipotence and the Omniscience of My Creative Power—that is responsible for the manifestation of what is conceived in the form of thoughts—and whose function was likened to the function of the soil in relation to the seeds—is also true.

"My son, it is precisely the mismanagement—by the will of man——of the creativity of the mind that let man fall into an immense, deep and dark pit without apparent escape.

"It is also the same mismanagement that prevents man from seeing and understanding the origin of his problems, how to overcome them, and how to regain his lost sense of security, joy, peace and harmony.

"Now, engulfed in all this mess and not knowing how to get out of it, he (man) began to think and to believe that his lost security and happiness could be reacquired through the possession of material things: the more he possessed the greater would be his sense of security, and more gratifying and durable his happiness would become.

"It is this belief that gave birth to the concept of *possession*, to the concept of *power,* and to the *ego* and *egoism* in man—the *monsters* responsible for the mischief of hatred within the human race, and their apparent inevitable suffering.

"After man noticed that material things, money and power were only illusory and not were giving him the sense of security and happiness that he was searching, he began to develop the conception that I am an individual, living in some place in the sky, from where I control everyone's lives.

"He also began to think and believe that I get upset, that I am a vengeful being, and that when they do not behave properly, I punish them severely and make them suffer.

"These beliefs made man fear Me, and made man think that I need to be appeased and pleased.

"Consequently, man developed and performed all kinds of different rituals.

"Time and history are proving that the performances of rituals are inefficacious, worthless, and a waste of time.

"My son, I do not get tired of letting you perceive that it is the will of man and his mind, with the cooperation of the Omnipotence of My Divine Creative Power that dwells within, that has the power to stop or change the course of those actions that create turmoil, pain and insecurity in the world and in everyone's lives.

"But man, can't do that until:

- He understands clearly his true nature and essence, as well as the true nature and essence of his fellow man, and of all creation;
- He learns that *hate* brings *hate*, *wars* bring only more *wars*, and with those wars come poverty, misery, fear, unhappiness and destruction;
- And he learns that it is the expression of unconditional *love* to all creation that allows him to experience true *happiness* and that brings lasting *peace* among the people of the world."

In examining the above perceptions, I clearly understood why God could not respond to my plea, and why He could not interfere in people's lives to restore peace and harmony among them, and why that privilege belongs only to man.

At the same time, I had the confirmation that what I had learned in the past represented the truth, and I was happy to be reassured that we have total control over our lives and our destiny.

My heart was bubbling with joy.

CHAPTER 44

GOD'S ROLE IN MAN'S LIFE

A few days after receiving the above perceptions and still animated by a state of euphoria, I addressed the following question to God:

> "My God, why don't You teach all these things to every man in the world, just like You have done with me, so that everyone can understand and believe?"

Just as I was posing that question, I perceived the following:

> **"Why is it that after all the things I have made you perceive, you still persist in thinking that I am an individual, capable of giving lessons at will?"**

Surprised by the reproach I asked:

> "My God, what are You trying to say?"
> **"My son, what I am telling you is that notwithstanding the mental and spiritual progress you have made, it seems like you still have no idea about My real nature and the role I play**

in the intricate labyrinth of life. In fact, if you did, you would not be asking these questions, as you would have discerned that I cannot directly teach anything to anyone."

After this perception, I said:

"My God, why can't You teach directly to anyone?"
"For the same reasons that I cannot interfere directly with man's experiences."

"On who rests the power to do so?"
"The Omniscience of My Creative Power Within, the only true teacher of Mankind."

After I reflected for a while on the above perceptions, to make sure that I would not misunderstand what I perceived, I asked:

"My God, could You give me a practical example, more in keeping with the level of my mental and spiritual capability and development, so that I might be able to understand without any ambiguity or doubts?"

Here is the response:

"My son, the essence of My nature is made by My Will, Mind and Creative Power."

"The Will and the Mind represent the creative branch of My nature, while the Creative Power—whose components are the Omnipotence and the Omniscience of My essence—represent the executive branch."

"As you already know, mankind is the expression and manifestation of My essence, My Energy; consequently he is endowed with the same traits that I have: *Will, Mind* and *Creative Power.*"

"My son, to make it easier for you to understand, first you need to reply to the following questions:
"Where is located the top soil in relation to the earth?"
"My God," I replied, "what does the top soil of the earth has to do with what I would like to know?"

"My son, just answer the question and in time you will find out."

Knowing that I would be proved wrong, I answered the question.

"On the first eight to ten inches of the crest of the earth."
"Well said, My son."

"From now on, we refer to it just as soil and not top soil. Now, what is the main function of the soil?"
"To provide the environment for the seeds that are sown in it to carry out and manifest the nature of their makeup and fulfill the purpose of their mission, which is to germinate, to grow and to produce fruits, and seeds so they can procreate themselves."

"If you go into the woods, My son, could you describe what would you see?"
"Mostly wild trees, wild plants and weeds that grow together in confusion, without any order."

"Why are they growing in confusion and without any order?
"Because there is nobody who cares and who controls them."

"If you visit a farm land instead, what are you going to see?"
"Selected and specific cultivations of plants."

"Who is responsible for this?"
"The farmer, per se Man."

"How can the farmer (man) accomplish that?"
"Through the power of his free will to choose."

"To the eyes of the soil, are there good seeds or bad seeds?"
"No."

"Could the soil, at its own discretion, let some seeds grow and others not?"
"No."

"Could the soil, at any given time, make grow something without seeds?"
After I did reflected for a few seconds, I replied, "No."

"Are you sure, My son?"
After I reflected again, I replied, "Yes, I am sure."

"Could you explain why, without the seed, the soil is not capable of making anything grow?"

Although the answer seemed to be easy and obvious, it took me several days of thinking and reflecting before I could come up with what I thought was the most appropriate answer.

"Because, my God, in the universal play of Your creation, You assigned each one of them to perform and carry out a unique and specific job, and one cannot perform the job of the other one.

"The job of the soil, as I said before, is to provide the conditions to assist the seeds in carrying out the cycle of their life.

"The job of the seeds is to carry within them the essence of their species, so they can perpetuate their existence to the infinite. Soil and seeds, they need each other to fulfill the job that You entrusted them to do."

"Are you sure, My son?"
After I reflected for a few minutes, I replied, "Yes, my God, I'm sure."

"My son, in your opinion, can we get tomato plants from orange seeds, or vice versa?"
"No, my God."

"Can we get almond plants from broccoli seeds, or vice versa?"
"No," I answered without hesitation.

"Why?"
"Because, as I said before, each seed can only reproduce and exhibit the essence and the characteristics of its nature. So from tomato seeds we are going to get tomato plants, from almond seeds we are going to get almond plants, from broccoli seeds we are going to get broccoli plants, and so on…"

"Once more: Are you sure of that?"
"Yes, my God, I am very sure."

"My son, do you understand the reason I asked you to answer all these questions?"
After giving the matter some thought and failing to see the connection with what I wanted to know, I replied, "No, my God."

Immediately after, I perceived the following:

- "**My son, the** *Plants* **represent man's** *Will* **and** *Mind;*
- "**The** *Seeds* **represent the** *Thoughts* **of man;**
- "**The** *Soil* **represents the** *Omnipotence of My Creative Power* **dwelling in man.**

"**As the** *job* **of the** *Soil* **is to allow and assist the seeds that end up in it to germinate, to grow and to produce fruits and seeds;** "**Likewise, the** *job* **(role) of the** *Omnipotence* **of** *My Creative Power within man* **is to manifest and make tangible in man's life everything that has been conceived by his will and mind in the form of thoughts/seeds, regardless of their nature and purpose."**

"**As the soil has no** *Discriminating Power* **over the seeds, and gives equal opportunity and assistance to all the seeds, re-gardless whether to the eyes of man they may be good or bad;** "**Likewise, the** *Omnipotence* **of** *My Creative Power that dwells within man* **has no** *Discriminating Power* **over the thoughts/ seeds to be processed, so it assists equally the enfolding of good thoughts/seeds as well the enfolding of the bad thoughts/ seeds, allowing to manifest in man's life in the form of experi-ences the essence of their nature—good or bad."**

"**As the** *Free Will* **of the farmer (man) has the power to choose the seeds to be sown in the soil;** "**Likewise, the** *Free Will* **of man has the power to choose the type of thoughts/seeds to be sown in the** *Omnipotence* **and the** *Omniscience* **of** *My Creative Power dwelling in his own being."*

"**As the** *soil* **is not able to make grow anything without the seeds;**

"Likewise *My Creative Power dwelling in man* is not able to make anything happen without the thoughts/seeds."

"As the *types* of *seeds* that are sown in the soil by the will of the farmer (man) determine the kinds of plants that will grow in the soil;
"Likewise, the *essence of the thoughts/seeds*——conceived by the will and mind of man, that consciously or unconsciously, directly or indirectly, are broadcasted and are sown into My Creative Power that dwells in man—determines the experiences in man's life."

"My son, can you imagine for a moment the sort of chaos resulting between man and nature if the soil had the power to determine which plants should grow and which should not?"

"Can you imagine man's bewilderment if, after having sown tomato seeds, he were to see thorn bushes grow in their place, simply because the soil opted to grow them instead of the tomatoes?"

"Can you also imagine for a moment the chaos resulting in man's life if the Omnipotence of My Creative Power had the capability to ignore man's direction and to manifest in man's life the opposite of what he wanted?"

"My son, the reason I made you perceive that I can't teach mankind directly is because the Omniscience of My Creative Power responds only to the desires expressed by the will of man in the form of thoughts/seeds—just like the Omnipotence of My Creative Power does."

"The mechanics of your own experiences, My son, demonstrate the truth of the above statements. My answers to you were always preceded by your request in the form of prayers."

"If you recall, before you went to work at James Bay, you asked yourself—in reality, you were asking the Omniscience of My Creative Power within you—if you should go to work at James Bay or not. On that occasion, I let you perceive my answer in the form of *peace* for *yes* and *fear* for *no*."

"Then, while working at James Bay, the conversations with your co-worker and roommate about the occult and the mysteries of life rekindled your lifelong desire to know and to understand.

"Unconsciously at first and consciously later, you began to create and broadcast to the Omniscience of My Creative Power within you thoughts/seeds expressing the desire to understand the apparent mystery of creation.

"It is exactly this action that spurred the Omniscience of My Creative Power within you to let you perceive the object of your desires and inquiries."

"What you have been learning over the course of your life is a direct consequence of what you have created and conceived in the form of thoughts/seeds."

"In the light of this truth, I am hoping that now you understand why I let you perceive that the Omniscience of My Creative Power by itself is not capable of teaching anything to anyone."

At this point, I felt that I had finally grasped in it fullness the essence and the role of God, the essence and the role of man, and the mechanism of how they work together.

I was super happy.

~

But, as I was savoring this joy, I recalled the words of the lady healer from Marsala, who said my mother's illness, had been conjured by the will of three women.

Therefore, I asked myself:

- **Do voodoo, sorcerers, black magic and all the mysterious sciences of the occult truly exist, or are they just a figment of man's imagination?**
- **If they exist, does that mean the Omnipotence of our Creative Power Within can be influenced by other people's thoughts, causing us to go through undesired, unknown, and unexpected experiences?**
- **Does that also mean we aren't always in total control of our lives and destinies?**
- **Isn't this notion diametrically opposed to everything I've learned until now?**

Unable to find satisfactory explanations to my queries, I asked:

"My God, *voodoo, sorcerers* and *black magic*—do they really exist?"
"Yes, My son, they do exist."

After this perception, I asked:

"My God, if they exist, would that mean Your Creative Power that dwells in me, and that dwells in every human being, can be influenced by thoughts generated in the minds of other people, causing us to go through undesired, unknown, and unexpected experiences?"
"Yes, My son."

"Does that mean we're not always in total control of our lives?"
"Yes, My son."

After this perception, I asked:

"My God, why first did You allow me to perceive that we have total control over our lives and destiny, and afterwards You let me perceive that the Omnipotence of the Creative Power within can be influenced by the thoughts/seeds created by other people? Don't You think the two contradict themselves?"
"No, My son."

"My God, how could such a thing be possible? I think the contradiction is clear and indisputable!"
"My son, you are right. At first glance, it seems like there is a contradiction.
"But I will explain to you why in reality there is not."

"As you already know, when man thinks, he conceives thoughts that are instantaneously transmitted to the Omnipotence, and the Omniscience of My Creative Power within."

"**What you still don't know is that the instant thoughts are conceived, they are not only broadcasted to the** *Omnipotence* **and the** *Omniscience* **of** *My Creative Power within,* **but are also broadcast** *throughout the ether*—**or** *infinite space*—**from which they can be** *consciously* **or** *unconsciously* **intercepted and perceived by any other human being.**"

"**The person who intercept those messages will** *consciously* **or** *unconsciously* **transmit them to the Omnipotence and to the Omniscience of My Creative Power that dwells in him, which in turn, as you already know, will manifest them in his life in the form of whatever experiences were conceived in those thoughts.**"

Upon perceiving the above, I asked:

"My God, how can something like that be possible?"

Soon after, I perceived:

"**My son at the moment, you are still not sufficiently spiritually developed to perceive the true significance of the message.**"

The awareness of my inadequacy caused me to focus all my attention on the depths of my being wherein the voice of my heart lies. Just as if I were looking someone straight in the eye, I said: "My God, I'm aware that I may not yet be capable of understanding the meaning of Your mysteries. It is with that in mind that I am asking You with humility and sincerity to fulfill my need to know, being confident that if You so wish, You can easily find a way of letting me understand what I can't understand."

One evening, after a few days of constantly repeating this prayer, I felt pervaded by that familiar peace, after which I perceived the following:

> **"My son, I know that your desire to know the mysteries of My Divine Nature is deep-seated and sincerely prompted by a longing to discover the truth. Since it's impossible for your *human nature*—which is limited—to understand My *Divine Nature*—which is *unlimited*—I shall simplify the subject matter through the use of examples, allowing you to participate in a dialogue that will continue until you have understood the truth."**

Soon after this revelation, deep from the voice of my heart I perceived the following question:

> **"My son, what is *telepathy?*"**

Even though I already knew what the word meant, before replying, I checked the dictionary to find the most appropriate definition.

"*Telepathy:*

- Transference of thoughts or ideas from one mind to the mind of another human being without speaking.
- Perceptions of a distant occurrence without the use of mechanical or electronic devices.
- Foreboding or sensation on the part of an individual of something occurring a distance away."

From the voice of my heart, I perceived:

> **"That is the right definition, My son."**

Soon after, I perceived the following question:

"Have you ever had a telepathic experience?"
Without even thinking about it, I responded, "Yes."

As far as I was concerned, telepathy is a common phenomenon that every human being experiences nearly every day.

Soon after, I sensed the following question:

"Do you know how telepathy works?"
Not being exactly sure about the answer, I replied, "No."

Immediately following that, I perceived the following question:

"What do you know about radio transmitters and radio receivers?"
"Radio transmitters and receivers are devices that transmit and receive sounds, allowing the communication between people from a distance.

**"My son, your answer regarding the function of radio is correct.
"Now, you must understand that man works similar to a radio receiver and a radio transmitter.
"When someone thinks, the essence of his ideas are simultaneously transmitted to the *Omnipotence* and the *Omniscience of My Creative Power that dwells in him*, and into space as well, where they can be perceived by the invisible antennas of other human beings who will subsequently transmit them to the Omnipotence and the Omniscience of My Creative Power that dwells in them."**

"My God, how can that ever happen?"

"My son, as you know, science and technology have demonstrated that sounds and images can be projected into space through special equipment such as an antenna and can be picked up at a distance by other antennae. Think of cellular telephone and TV stations; fax machines, the Internet and so on. It's practically impossible for the average human mind to fathom what goes on in infinite space, away from the human eye."

"Now I want to ask you something else.

"When you turn on the TV, how many programs appear on the screen?"
I promptly replied, "One."

But, failing to understand why I was being deluged by all these questions, I asked: "My God, what does this entire conversation have to do with what I want to know?"
I immediately perceived the following:

"My son, be patient, and in due time I will make you understand what you want to know."

Comforted by the reply, I calmed down.

Soon thereafter, I perceived the following question:

"My son, can you explain why, with all the TV programs floating in space, you can see only one program at a time on your screen, and not two or three or more?"

I replied:

"My God, You must forgive my ignorance, since I have never studied such matters and therefore don't know the details involved in broadcasting. What I do know is that each program is telecast through a specific channel and can be seen only when the TV is synchronized with the channel broadcasting the program we want to see."

After the above reply, I soon perceived the following question:

"When you turn on the TV, who decides what program should appear on your screen?"
"I do," I replied.

"How?"
"By setting the TV to the channel transmitting the program I want to see," I replied.

The perception went on:

"My son, can the TV, at its own discretion change the channel and force a person to watch a program that he is not interested in watching?"
"No."

"Why not?"
"Because the television's function is to relay the program, not to choose the program to show."

"Who has the privilege to make that choice?"
"The person who watches the TV."

"My son, are you sure about what you're saying?"

Without even thinking about it and without the slightest hesitation, I replied,

"Yes, I'm sure."

"My son," continued the voice, "I want you always to remember what you have stated, as it will be extremely useful in making you understand what I'm about to let you perceive at this point.

"As the various radio/TV programs are projected into space by special antennae and intercepted by other antennae;
"In the same way the thoughts conceived by the will and mind of man are broadcasted into space with his unseen antenna and intercepted by the unseen antennae of others.

"As the various radio/TV programs travel in predetermined, unseen channels to man's eyes;
"In the same way the thoughts created by the will and the mind of man and broadcasted by his unseen antenna, travel through special predetermined unseen channels that are determined by the nature of man's thoughts and emotions."

"My God," I said, "Can You be more specific?"
"My son, the instant any idea is conceived in the mind of an individual, it is automatically impregnated with the type of energy that expresses the essence of the thought of that idea. The nature of the energy expressing the thoughts determines the channel through which it will travel."

"As I made you perceive earlier, man—in his own right—is a radio transmitter as well as a radio receiver.
"Consequently, he is constantly and continuously synchronized to a specific channel, which is determined by the emotions expressing the nature of his thoughts."

"Therefore, if he thinks about negative issues, he automatically becomes synchronized with those channels conveying negative thoughts.
"If, instead, he thinks of positive matters, he is automatically synchronized with those channels that convey positive impulses."

"Hence, it is vitally important to constantly monitor the nature of one's thoughts and emotions."

"Ignorance of this law is the source of man's chronic problems."

"Going back to the sickness of your mother orchestrated by the three women, I can tell you, those women did an evil thing.
"But if your mother had not been synchronized with the channels conveying negative thoughts, she would never, I say never, have intercepted the essence of the three women's *destructive, malevolent thoughts,* and consequently she would not have gotten sick."

"The opposite process took place when your father and you took your mother to the healer in Marsala. In that case, as in the previous one, her receptiveness and synchronization to the healer made the Omnipotence of My Creative Power dwelling in your mother manifest the intention expressed in the healer's prayer. Thus, she was cured of her illness."

Then the perception continued:

"Do you remember when, hoping your company wouldn't send you to James Bay, you made up the story—which you then told to your supervisor—that Pina had a fibroma?"
"Yes."

"Do you remember, subsequently, as she was giving birth to your son Nino, the doctor discovered she really did have a uterine tumor?"
"Yes."

"What made that happen was that at the moment you were conceiving those thoughts, Pina was synchronized on the same channel as you. Consequently, unconsciously, Pina perceived and transmitted to the Omnipotence of My Creative Power dwelling in her what you had conceived with your mind.
"In due time, she manifested the nature of your creation, two fibroma, one big and one little one. As you remember, the big one was removed at the moment of your son's birth, and the little one the doctor left alone."

"It was thanks to your awareness of the function of man's thoughts that you were ultimately able to broadcast healing thoughts to Pina. This time, she consciously intercepted your healing message, allowing the fibroma to vanish."

"The work was carried out both times by the Omnipotence of My Creative Power that dwelled in her. The first time she intercepted the suggestion to create the fibroma, while the second time she intercepted the suggestion to let it vanish."

"Do you remember when, after the financial disaster of Winnipeg, you often felt as though you were being stung by millions of small needles, which made you feel sick and caused you to suffer terribly?"
"Yes," I answered.

"During that specific time of your life, you were constantly synchronized with channels carrying negative thoughts. Consequently, the perception of that negative Energy made you quiver and feel sick."

"Then there was the gentleman in Ottawa who gave you the talisman and advised you that whenever you were feeling ill, all you had to do to feel better, was to touch the talisman and pray to Me."

"As you followed the man's advice and touched the talisman and prayed to Me, believing we were going to protect you, you felt as though you were surrounded by a swarm of raging wasps. Soon thereafter, as you continued to touch the talisman and to pray, your irritation and bewilderment gave way to a sensation of harmony, peace, and well-being."

"The sensation of being surrounded by a swarm of raging wasps was caused by the clash between negative energy and positive energy while you were switching channels."

"Both the negative perception, preceded by ill feelings, and the positive perception followed by feelings of harmony, peace and well-being, were the result of your will's choices."

"First, unconsciously, your will synchronized you to the negative channels, while later——consciously—your will switched channels and synchronized you to the positive channels."

"The talisman, at any giving time, had nothing to do with, and had no power over what you were experiencing."

"Unconsciously and consciously, your experiences were the result of the choice of your will."

Having received the above perceptions, I felt pervaded by a new joy I had never before experienced.

Finally, after an entire life of suffering, waiting and seeking, I understood there was no such a thing as destiny or fate.

In the reality of life, we, and we alone, more unconsciously then consciously, are responsible for all our experiences—*good* or *bad* as they may be—and that so-called *Hell, Purgatory,* and *Paradise* exist only inside our own being and not outside the sphere of our existence.

The *key* that opens the doors of these mysteries lies within our awareness and understanding of our true nature—the true nature and essence of all creation—how they are synchronize together, and the way they work in unison."

CHAPTER 45
PROCREATION AND REINCARNATION

A few days after perceiving the above message, I found other new questions arising in my mind.

I asked myself:

- **If sickness is originated by the negative thoughts/seeds created by the cooperation of the will, mind and the Omnipotence of the Creative Power within, how do we explain that many infants—who have not yet developed the capacity to control and use their will or the creativity of their mind to influence the Omnipotence of the Creative Power within—are born sick?**
- **What is the source of their diseases and other related problems?**
- **Who decides who will be born in good health and who will be born sick?**
- **Why do newborns have varying levels of intelligence and different personalities?**
- **Who determines their degree of intelligence and the nature of their distinguishing physical traits?**

After reflecting on these issues with no forthcoming enlightenment, I composed the following prayer, which I repeated several times daily.

"My God, You who are in me, part of me and life of my life, You who are the universal source of knowledge, capable of providing any explanation, I pray You allow me to perceive the answers to all my questions and to tear aside the apparent veil of mystery enveloping them."

After having prayed for a long while, attempting at the same time to keep synchronized with the depth of my being—from the Voice of my Heart— I perceived the following:

"My son, as you already know, the mind constantly creates thoughts/seeds which, in turn, are automatically broadcasted to My Creative Power that dwells in man, where they are stored, waiting to be processed and manifested according to the nature of their essence."

"At the moment of so-called death, the Creative Power that dwells in man is fully liberated from the body, taking with her all the unfolded thoughts/seeds."

"At this point, if the thoughts/seeds stored in the Creative Power are all positive and express Divine harmony, the energy making that Creative Power will automatically and instantly integrate with My infinite pure Energy that permeates the entire universe, becoming one with it."
"A practical example would be rainwater, which, once it joins the sea, becomes one with it."

"If, instead, some of the thoughts/seeds stored in the Creative Power are still impregnated with negativity, the Creative Power will not be able to integrate with My pure Energy.
"A practical example is the mixing of oil and water."

After receiving the above perception, I asked:

"My God, if the Creative Power that still contains negative thoughts/seeds cannot be integrated with Your pure Energy, what will become of it? Will it remain forever separated from You?"
"No, My son."

"So when can that Creative Power join You and become one with Your Energy?"
"After it frees itself from all the negative thoughts/seeds."

"My God, considering that the body is already deceased, how is that accomplished?"
"By reincarnating in a newborn baby."

"How can the Creative Power of a deceased person be integrated with that of a newborn infant?"
"My son, the process can only be understood by people whose spiritual evolution has reached the highest level; never the less, I will give you a glance of what is happening."

"It is very important to remember that the Creation, including the human body, is the continuous expression of the essence of My Energy, which is repeated over and over."

"As you know, the conception of life occurs through the consummation of the sexual act between a male and a female. You also know that during the act of intercourse, the male partner produces sperm and deposits it inside the woman's vagina, where it passes through to the uterus and attempts to penetrate an egg produced by the woman's body."

"During this process, the Creative Power of the male impregnates the newly created sperm cell with the following:
"The nature of all the traits of his personality, of his intelligence, of his psychological traits, of his character, of his disposition, of his cultural preferences, of the physical aspects of his health condition, and with the essence of the traits of all the unexpressed and unfolded thoughts/seeds that are stored in his Creative Power.
"In the same fashion, the Creative Power of the female impregnates her egg's cells."

"At the moment of the conception, the Energy making the sperm's cells and the Energy making the egg's cells, with a process that at this moment you are not able to understand, will attract from the ether the Energy of the Creative Power of a previously departed being with the same affinity."

"The integration of those three different entities of Energies will give birth to a new creature that will reflect and express all the physical traits—such as health or sickness, color of skin, etc.—and all the non-physical traits, such as personality, intelligence, character, cultural preferences, etc., as well as all the unfolded and unexpressed essence of the thoughts/seeds (which will be unfolded in the course of its life) of the three entities that participated in its creation."

"Part of the purpose of all this is to lead the new creature:

- First to the understanding of its true nature, My true nature, the true nature of the Creation, and to the relationship that associates them;

- **And second, to the purification of its Creative Power, so at the moment of its trespass (death), it can be integrated and reunited to My Divine Energy for eternity."**

At this point, I was able to understand the reasons why children are born healthy or sick, why they have different tendencies and different intelligences, and why they have unique personalities.

What remained unclear was the proper and most effective method to ensure a rapid and permanent purification of an individual's Creative Power.

CHAPTER 46

The Way that Leads to the Purification of the Creative Power Within

After debating with myself for a relatively long period of time in what would be the best, the fastest and the most appropriate way for an individual to free himself permanently from all negative thoughts/seeds that he had inherited, I asked the question to the Omniscience of My Creative Power.

Here is the response:

> "My son, before an individual is able to learn, understand and follow a method through which he can free himself permanently from all the negative thoughts/seeds he inherited in his Creative Power, he must become aware of:
>
> - His true nature and essence;
> - My true nature and essence;
> - The relationship existing between us;
> - The function of his mind;
> - The function of the Omnipotence and Omniscience of My Creative Power that dwells in him;

- The interaction existing between will, mind and Creative Power;
- And finally, he must become aware of the importance and the function of prayer.

"Only after learning all these concepts, and only after he has learned to integrate them continuously in the daily living of his life, will man be able to choke, or kill, all the negative thoughts/seeds stored in his Creative Power before they begin the process of their enfoldment and manifestation, liberating himself from the painful experiences they can cause."

After this perception, I asked:

"My God, although what You have allowed me to perceive in this moment seems to be very clear, I have to confess that I have difficulty in understanding how, in a practical way, we can choke all the negative thoughts/seeds in the Creative Power and consequently avoid the corresponding negative experiences. For that reason, I implore You to have mercy on my intellect and be more specific."

"My son, the answer to your question is through prayer."

"My God, prayer is a very vague word. Could You please give me more details?"

"My son, in this case, prayer refers to letting the will and mind of man continuously create only positive thoughts/seeds.

"The positive thoughts/seeds are more powerful than the negative thoughts/seeds.

"Consequently, once they reach the Creative Power within and begin the process of their enfoldment, they neutralize, choke and kill the enfoldment of the negative thoughts/seeds, freeing and making pure the individual."

"My God, could You give me a practical example?"

"The sterilization of the soil through fumigation is a perfect example, My son.

"The poisoned fumes created in the course of fumigation kill the germination power of all the seeds in the soil, freeing the soil of the danger of being infested by unwanted bad plants.

"In the same way the positive thoughts/seeds neutralize the negative thoughts/seeds, freeing man from their danger."

CHAPTER 47
REVELATION OF MAN'S TRUE ESSENCE

In analyzing the perceptions about reincarnation, I became confused and filled with doubt. I had been taught that every human being is unique, is eternal and his identity (his soul, spirit) cannot be destroyed or duplicated.

After a long debate with myself, and not being able to dissipate my doubts, I formulated the following question:

> "My God, if the Energy that makes the Creative Power of every human being is unique, how can it be integrated with the Energy of the Creative Power of another entity?
> Wouldn't this process make him or her lose his/her previous essence and identity?"
> **"No, My son."**

Unable to understand how the Energy of an individual if integrated (melded) with the energy of another Creative Power could manage to keep its identity, I asked:

> "My God, how is that possible?"

After a while, I perceived the following:

"My son, once more I remind you that it is not easy for your mind that is controlled by human limitation to understand the complexity of My Divine Nature. But in trying to satisfy your desire, I will engage you again in a conversation that will help you understand."

"My son, of what are made the oceans, the seas, the lakes and the rivers?"
"Water," I answered.

"Is the water important for the survival of man, of animals and of plants?
"Yes, my God. Not just important, it is essential."

"Why?"
"Because water is the main component that constitutes the body of the cells that make all the tissues and the organs of every living thing in the universe."

"What is the chemical formula of the water?"
"H_2O."

"In your opinion, while water participates in the make-up of the cells of all those different things that we find in various forms and shapes throughout the universe, does its chemical formula, H_2O, ever undergo structural changes?"
Having mulled that over in conjunction with all I had learned about chemistry in school, I answered: "No."

"In what forms does water manifest itself?"
"Solid, liquid and vapor."

"What process does water go through?"

After reflecting for a while, I answered:

"My God, under the influence of heat, water evaporates into the atmosphere. When its temperature decreases, water vapor condenses and returns to liquid form, producing rain, or under sufficiently cold conditions, snow or hail."

"Could we say that regardless of its form—vapor, liquid or solid (ice, snow, etc.)—the structure of the chemical formula of the water remains the same: H_2O?"
"Yes, My God."

"What is the cycle to which water is subjected in regard to the creation?"
"My God, water is subjected to two processes: assimilation and elimination. In the process of assimilation, water comprises the cells of the majority of all living things in the universe.
In the process of elimination, water is freed from the cells of the living things and returns to its original source—bodies of water and the atmosphere—thus, beginning a new cycle.
"In either case, the structure and the composition of the molecule will always remain the same: H_2O."

After that, I perceived the following:

"My son, the immense mass of water of the seas, lakes and rivers symbolizes My infinite pure Divine Energy that pervade in the entire universe."

"A single molecule of water represents the Energy comprising in every atom that exists in the universe."

"As the water, during the complex course of its journey, never loses the identity or its chemical structure (H_2O);
"Likewise the essence of My Energy that participates in the making of every atom never loses the essence of its identity while participating to the making of all the things existing in the universe."

"It is very important that you understand and remember that the essence of your nature is not the body through which you express and identify yourself as Paolo Ficara.
"The true nature of your essence is the essence of My Energy that makes the atoms that compose the molecules of the tissues of all the organs of your body."

"As the molecule of water, during its journey in participating to the expression of this dream-world of Mine, never loses the essence of its identity;
"Likewise the Energy making the Creative Power comprised in the atoms, in the course of its journey, never loses the essence of its identity."

"As a molecule of water can be absorbed by any living entity (today it can be part of a human body, but tomorrow the same molecule of water can be found in a plant or in a fruit or in a vegetable, and yet another time it can be found in a cell comprising animal tissue, and so on);
"In the same fashion, the Energy of My Creative Power flouting into space can be attracted by any living entity, becoming part of that entity and becoming part of this dream-world of Mine that is the creation."

"Today it could be found in a cell making the tissue of a human body, while tomorrow it could be found in a cell comprising the tissue of an animal or a plant or a fruit or a vegetable, etc.

" But regardless where it is, it never loses the essence of its identity."

In analyzing the above perceptions, I replied:

"My God, doesn't what You have just allowed me to perceive in this moment, demonstrate that we don't have a true and a permanent identity, and that we are in a constant change"?

"No, My son."

"How is that My God? Can You explain?"

"My son, you still have difficulty in understanding and consequently accepting the fact that you are not the body with which you are expressing yourself in this specific moment, but the energy that is making the atoms that are making the cells of the tissues of your body."

"My God, if what You have allowed me to perceive is true, how does one explain that from time to time entities from the past, like Jesus, the Virgin Mary, other saints, and even some of our departed ones, materialize and have been seen with their original aspect and form?

"If they were already part of a new entity, how can they come to us and materialize before us with the same form they had once?"

"Once more, you are forgetting the fact that the essence of those entities is Energy, My Energy."

"When a human being is praying to Me and sees Me in the form of Jesus, I will go to him with Jesus' form."

"If he sees Me in the form of Buddha, I will go to him with Buddha's form."

"If he sees me in the form of one of his family's departed, then I will go to him with the specific form of that departed one."

"I always manifest Myself the way they see Me."

"But regardless how they see Me and how I will manifest to them, what never changes is one thing: The essence of My Divine Energy."

Having perceived and comprehended the above message, I was over-whelmed by an indescribable joy.

For the first time in my life, I felt I had clearly and fully understood—as well as accepted unconditionally—that our true essence and nature is not the body through which we express ourselves, but the Energy that creates the atoms that make the molecules of every tissue that make up the organs of our bodies.

CHAPTER 48
Benefit of Pain and Suffering

After a few days of enjoying my newfound enlightenment, I began to think intensely on the subject of pain and suffering, attempting to understand the reason for their existence and to fathom why they are often considered necessary and even beneficial.

While such perspectives have validity, I refused to accept the theory that man could derive any significant benefit from grief and affliction.

I reflected on the problem for quite some time and, taken up by my resolve to answer all the queries that were vexing me, I wrote the following prayer, which I recited whenever possible:

> *"My God, You who are in me, who are part of me and are the life of my life, I thank You with all the sincerity I can summon for having always guided and enlightened me. Now, My God, I pray You to let me perceive in what way pain and sorrow can profit humanity."*

One day as I was praying and driving at the same time, I perceived the following:

> **"My son, the reason you cannot catch sight of the benefits brought on by pain and suffering lies in your inability to**

make an objective in-depth analysis of those experiences to which you refer as being painful.

"I can assure you, My son, that pain and suffering are the only two elements capable of igniting in man's will the desire to react to life's adversities. This process will gradually awaken in him the desire to understand the real meaning of life—the true essence of his nature as well as the true essence of the nature of all Creation.

"The formulation in the form of thoughts/seeds of the essence of those desires is the beginning of the path that leads to understanding, acceptance and Enlightenment."

"To demonstrate to you the truth of My assertions, I will examine for you some of your most painful experiences and pinpoint the repercussions they had in determining and shaping the course of your life."

"It began with your enrolment at the school run by Catholic sisters, which you attended from kindergarten to the third grade. During that period, under the nuns' watchful eyes, you and the other children were exposed on a daily basis to the teachings and deeds of Jesus, and to the stories of the Holy Trinity, and Adam and Eve. They also thought God's great love for mankind and the belief in an Omnipresent, Omniscient, and Omnipotent Creator: God."

"Since you didn't understand what the nuns were trying to teach, you asked them to explain how the Father (God), the Son (Jesus), and the Holy Spirit—while being three distinct persons—could also be one single being."

"If you recall, you also asked them to give you more details about the Adam and Eve story. On how their disobedience could make God lose the light of reason—so much so that He chased them out of Eden, condemning them and their off-spring to eternal pain and suffering."

"According to the nuns, thousands—or even millions—of years after this episode, God repented for His severity, tried to make amends by sending to earth His only begotten son, Jesus—who, as part of the Holy Trinity could be construed as none other than God Himself—to institute the sacrament of baptism, to suffer like a common mortal and to be killed on the cross like a criminal."

"According to the nuns' narration, through His baptism and death on the cross, God, under the semblance of Jesus, freed humanity from the slavery of Adam and Eve's original sin, redeeming man and allowing him eternal life."

"My son, if you recall, despite your youth, you instinctively refused to accept the nuns' teachings, using a logical argument to demonstrate their explanations were full of contradictions."

"In fact, what your young mind couldn't manage to understand and consequently accept was that if God had truly been Omniscient—that is, capable of knowing past, present, and future— He should have known that:

- Adam and Eve's personality traits were not strong enough to withstand temptation;
- They would have disobeyed his commands;
- He would have been provoked to anger;
- He would have cast them out of paradise; they would live forever in misery and pain;

- He would later regret His action; He would have come to earth in the form of Jesus;
- He would have suffered like any mortal;
- He would have been crucified.

"Furthermore, notwithstanding His materialization in the form of Jesus and His sacrifice on the cross, which were meant to bring redemption and freedom to mankind, you noticed that man, is still confronted with a never-ending number of problems, that make him suffer continuously."

"My son, you used to wonder why God, if He had been truly Omniscient, didn't know what was going to occur before it did, and why He made such drastic decisions in the first place."

"You also used to ask yourself why, if God were truly Omnipotent, He didn't endow Adam and Eve with sufficient fortitude to withstand his order; that way, they wouldn't have sinned, inciting Him to throw them out of paradise and condemning humanity to pain, suffering and death."

"My son, if you remember, the questions you asked the nuns made them uncomfortable. Not knowing what to answer, they told you to be quiet and not ask so many questions.
"Their inability to give you the right explanations—a move that would have satisfied your hunger for knowledge—caused you to suffer terribly."

"It was precisely this pain that awakened in you the desire to learn My true identity, where I can be found, and, above all, the reasons for My mysterious way of governing the universe—which at times seems to your reasoning inconsistent, contradictory and devoid of logic."

"Having said that, My son, it's time to remember that you were born soon after the end of World War II, a time when most Italian families, included your own, lived in poverty.
"In the hope of improving the family's economic conditions, your father managed to buy a plot of land. In so doing, however, he incurred a heavy debt, which, due to high interest rates and the poor harvests that followed, plunged your family into dire financial straits. Because of this, you had to be transferred from parochial to public school."

"Given the resultant worry and stress of your childhood, you thought seriously about a better and more comfortable future for all your family members."

"Then, the mysterious circumstance of your mother's illness caused by the three women and followed by the miraculous cure affected by the old healer in Marsala intensified your desire to understand My mysteries and My rule over creation."

"My son, the events I have just reminded you of are the milestones that eventually determined the course of your life."

After considerable reflection on what I had just perceived, I was not able to understand fully the importance of those experiences.

A few days of vacillation passed before I decided to ask for God's help and made up the following prayer:

"My God, I'm sure that at the present moment You're well aware of the thoughts that are troubling me. Please enlighten

me as to why the events of my childhood are the milestones that determined the course of my life."

The response wasn't long in coming. I soon perceived the following:

"My son, the frustration derived from your inability to understand the nature of My essence, combined with the financial insecurity of your family, were the chief elements that induced your young mind first to want to find the answers to My apparent mysteries, and second to want to build for yourself and your family a more secure financial environmental."

"The creation by your will and mind of these two resolutions, in the form of thoughts/seeds, are the foundations upon which, unconsciously, you built all your future experiences."

"Just as in building any structure, you have to begin with a strong foundation;
"Likewise in order for your wishes come true, you first needed a good education."

"During the course of your elementary studies and in the two years following, you were not a hard-working pupil, and you came to the conclusion that you lacked the intellect to be a good student."

"The Omniscience of My Creative Power that dwells in you, was aware that to realize your goals, you needed a good education that you were not able to get if you stayed within the environmental in which you were. You needed a change."

"Without you being aware of it, the Omniscience of My Creative Power that dwells within you inspired the school principal to transfer you and your friend Enzo Tortorici from the all-boys class to the mixed morning session.

"The Omniscience of My Creative Power knew that your fear of embarrassing yourself in front of young girls would force you to study with greater concentration and commitment, allowing you to become a good student, as proved after."

"My God, why was I transferred with my friend Enzo Tortorici and not someone else?"

"Because Enzo was one of the most brilliant pupils in your class and would inspire you to emulate him."

"Thanks to your efforts, by the end of the first quarter of the school year, you showed a considerable improvement over your usual academic performance."

"This change for the better made you understand that you had the ability to be a good student and the reason you had not excelled before was due to your lack of application and effort."

"This newfound awareness of your academic capabilities also generated in you a great fondness for books.

"Now, despite the fact that you were perfectly aware that your parents didn't have the financial means to let your studies continue, you fantasized that somehow and someway circumstances would pave the way for the continuation and eventual completion of your studies.

"It was with this conviction in mind that occasionally, instead of spending the allowance your mother gave you to have fun with your friends on Sundays, you invested in lottery tickets; but you never won.

"At the end of the school year, you went to work as a mechanic's apprentice.

"In spite of the harsh reality of those circumstances, you never gave up hope and instinctively continued to dream of being seated at your desk in the Sciacca Technical Institute."

"Then your mother got sick, and the doctors were unable to help her.

"The case seemed desperate and hopeless.

"Your aunt suggested a consultation with the old healer in Marsala, who not only cured your mother, but explained the origin and nature of her disease: three women had plotted to cast a spell on her."

"The burden of your mother's malady fulfilled in your life two objectives: a desire to understand the mystery surrounding those events; and an intensified desire for financial security in the future."

"But to fulfill those objectives, a good education was a must.

"The Omniscience of My Creative Power that dwells within you was aware of that and once more, created the right conditions to get you back to school.

"Thus, Mr. Carmelo's unavailability on the day you intended to buy the mechanic's overalls was not in the least fortuitous; neither was your friend Enzo Tortorici's illness.

"The information that Enzo gave you when you went to see him—the opening of a private school and his suggestion that you ask your father to allow you to enroll—and the idea of your brother Gioacchino going to work in Germany in order to help to pay for your tuition—all worked together to help you reach your goals."

"Then there was the experience you had with Enzo Vella when you were studying for the admission exams to the Technical Institute.

"On that occasion, due to the advice of friends of yours—pupils of Mr. Misuraca, the teacher who was going to examine you—you decided to skip the chapter that was talking about the anatomy of the human body, because the teacher had not covered it during the school year.

"Thinking that you would not undergo questioning on that subject, you both skimmed through the chapter.

"Instinctively you began to feel that you had made a mistake.

"In spite of that perception, you still chose not to study the material and, as a consequence, you began to feel so anxious and nervous that you couldn't concentrate on studying your other subjects.

"Finally, you explained to Enzo how you felt, and he suggested you go back and study the chapter.

"You did, and the nervousness subsided."

"The above experience had two purposes: the first was to keep you on track in the pursuance of your goals; the second to make you reflect, thus generating within you the desire to know whether or not someone was trying to warn you of approaching danger signs.

"My son, your nervousness was caused by the Omniscience of My Creative Power that dwells in you that was already aware of the first question the teacher was going to ask you.

"Had you not followed the Omniscience of My Creative Power's advice, your examination results would have been very poor, resulting in failure.

"As a consequence of that scenario, your father—given his precarious financial condition—would not have been able to let you repeat the school year, and the course of your life would have gone in a different direction."

"Then, there was the sorrow caused by your first love experience with your friend's sister.

"This was an extremely important milestone in your life, as it produced within you the desire to understand the workings of human behavior, and particularly, why people are so often engaged in a process of mistrust, mutual maltreatment, and self-destruction.

"Had the girl decided to accept your love, your life would have certainly taken a different turn, precluding the fulfillment of your aspirations."

"Your first trip to Germany and the revelation of the poor living and working conditions of your brother Gioacchino, had the purpose of making you aware of the enormous, altruistic love your brother bore the family, prompting in you the resolution to do whatever it took to reunite the entire family at some future date and to provide them with a decent life, free of financial problems."

"Your experience with the girl you met soon after receiving your diploma resulted in your engagement and your subsequent immigration to Montreal.

"The pain and suffering you endured after breaking up with her served the purpose of tempering your inexperienced, sensitive, youthful nature.

"This chain of events kept you on the path that would eventually bring you to the fulfillment of your goals."

~૭

"After you broke your engagement with your fiancé in Montreal, the girl who had been your first love wrote to you from Sicily, giving you the impression that she was willing to start a relationship with you.

"That had a specific purpose for your life.

"Although you were forced to make an extremely painful decision by not pursuing that relationship, the outcome reinforced your character and kept you on the road that in time would take you to the realization of your dreams."

~૭

"The Quebec government's call for you to enroll in a French language course proved extremely important, as it resulted in a decisive turn in your life.

"It was precisely while attending that evening class that you met Miss Pina, the girl who became your friend, your wife, your lover and your lifelong companion, and who followed you everywhere with infinite love and without complaint.

"She turned out to be the rock upon which you could always lean with great assurance, never fearing its collapse.

"She has been your best friend, both in the best of times and in the worst; she has always understood you, helped, advised and inspired you, given you all that she could without the slightest reservation and asking nothing in return but your love."

~~~

"The disastrous earthquake in Sicily in early 1968—destroying entire towns and families—turned out to be the event that made it possible for your family to be reunited in Waterbury, Connecticut—finally making your dream a reality."

~~~

"The litigation between your father and his cousin who refused to return the land in accordance with their agreement and your father's negative reaction to that situation were at the root of his eventual terminal disease, which proved an important turning point in your own spiritual growth."

~~~

"The Calgary adventure, a few months after you and Pina were married, seemed like a major fiasco, but nonetheless had huge positive consequences: it strengthened your love for your family, and made you understand that you did not have yet the strength, needed for the heavy burden of running a business."

~

"Although, you were perfectly aware of that and you needed to bring some change into your life, you didn't know how to do it.

"To achieve that, you still needed to go through a lot of pain, sorrow, fear and deep psychological depression, which you later experienced through your father's incurable disease and ensuing death, your Uncle Lillo's greedy behavior, the disastrous Winnipeg experience, and the unwarranted criticism from your friends and relatives after your return from Winnipeg to Montreal.

"All those vicissitudes to which you reacted with what little strength you had left in you, toughened and helped to strengthen your character and made you resolve to stay on the road you had chosen until you attained your goals."

~

"The meeting with the 99-year old clairvoyant, who in a clear and simple way explained the financial disaster of the Winnipeg adventure and advised you to change job as soon as you were given the opportunity, was also a very important event.

"It heightened your curiosity and your desire to understand, and prepared and helped you to make the right decisions later.

~

"It was your disastrous financial situation that made you resolve to go to work at James Bay.

"Pina's pleading not to be left alone with your little son in Montreal without the necessities for survival forced you to confront the dilemma of either going to James Bay to earn desperately needed money, or stay with her in Montreal and confront together that critical period of your life.

"Your love and desire to please Pina induced you to invent the lie about Pina's tumor as an excuse for not going to James Bay."

~

"Now, My son, we will analyze the extraordinary importance of the events of that special and unique period of your life.

"The fear of making another mistake—a contingency that would have destroyed you psychologically—caused you to instinctively ask yourself many times whether or not to go to James Bay.

"During the course of this inner struggle, as you recall, you sensed that when you felt disposed towards going to James Bay, deep in your heart you felt peaceful and relaxed, but when you questioned yourself about staying in Montreal, you were overwhelmed by fear, nervousness and anxiety.

"Then, came the recollection of the words of the old clairvoyant, who approximately one month earlier had told you to change job when the opportunity presented itself."

"In the throes of fear and indecision, you questioned whether this was the opportunity to which the old clairvoyant referred. When you were asking yourself if it was the right opportunity, deep in your heart, you felt peaceful and relaxed, but when you asked to wait for another opportunity, you felt fear, nervousness and anxiety.

"As you were trying to evaluate your circumstances, your boss called you aside, making it very clear that if you didn't go to James Bay, the company manager would be forced to fire you.

"The fear of having to find another job was simply unbearable; so you decided to take the James Bay assignment.

"After that, you felt relieved."

"As proven by your future experiences, that extremely difficult decision was a major turning point of your life, and served as a launching pad for the discovery of three significant truths:

- The existence of what you then called *the voice of your heart;*
- The understanding that when you follow the *inspiration of the voice of the heart,* you never make a mistake;
- And the realization and awareness of the powerful role thoughts/seeds play in people's lives.

"Another extremely important outcome of your decision to go to James Bay was that you met a fellow worker there who was interested in the supernatural, and you spent frequent evenings together discussing the mysteries of the occult.

"Those brief and apparently insignificant conversations were to revive deep in your heart your nearly forgotten concern for Me (God), life, and all its apparent mysteries."

"The rekindling of this interest was instrumental in being directed by the Omniscience of My Creative Power dwelling in you to find and read that book explaining the importance of thoughts and their working mechanism."

"By making the decision to test out what you had learned, little by little, you came to understand and accept the idea that thoughts play a vital role in the unfolding of every human life."

"Accordingly, you began to pay very close attention to what you were thinking.
"You strove to hold only those positive thoughts that would help you realize your dreams, and you strove to dismiss or neutralize those that you knew would prove deleterious."

"After numerous trials, you had indisputable proof that the nature of your thoughts had been responsible for creating Pina's uterine tumor."

"In light of those experiences, you began to make a continuous effort to control the nature of the thoughts that polluted your mind, while at the same time you developed the practice of continuously questioning *the voice of your heart*—allowing you to follow your intuition rather than your reason."

"It was because of this that you decided to spend the money you earned at James Bay on a house in Montreal rather than saving it to begin a construction company at some future date.

"Thus, you began to overcome with greater ease the obstacles in your path and make progress economically as well as spiritually."

~

"You even began to believe that in Montreal you were finally in the right place at the right time and the time had come for your mother and brothers to move there and join you—allowing you to work and prosper together as you had always dreamed of doing.

"With that in mind, you advised your brother Ignazio, who wanted to become a lawyer, to enroll in law school in Montreal.

"You asked Gioacchino to apply to the Canadian consulate for an immigrant visa.

"Thus, you hoped that before the onset of fall, you would have succeeded in uniting your family."

~

"But things didn't work out as you had hoped.

"Gioacchino didn't obtain the Canadian visa, and Ignazio was not admitted to law school in Montreal.

"On top of it all, you made the great mistake of contracting an enormous job that you couldn't carry out."

~

"These seemingly disastrous events upset all your projects and left you in a state of deep psychological depression that made you doubt everything you had learned so far."

〜〜

"Then, as you were trying to understand why fate was working against you and your family, you suddenly remembered the old saying:

"Non tutti i Mali, Vengono per Nuocere
"Not all Ills in Life Come About to Cause Harm

"After long reflecting on the meaning of this saying, you decided that if the message it conveyed were true, all your experiences would ultimately work to your benefit.
"Because of this new perception and the unconditional acceptance of the message, you began to look at your problems with detachment, while at the same time firmly believing that those negative experiences in time would lead you to positive experiences and consequently to the fulfillment of your dreams."

〜〜

"This new way of thinking and believing made you intensify your efforts to pray for the object of your desires.
"These efforts helped you develop at the conscious level—no longer instinctively—the relationship you already had with what you called *the voice of your heart.*
"This development helped you meet your daily problems head-on, almost with a feeling of joy, confident that regardless

of how bad they seemed, you would draw from your daily trials and tribulations all the necessary experiences needed to reach your lifelong goals.

"No longer were you discouraged, nor subject to the deep states of depression you had previously experienced."

~

"As the facts were to demonstrate later on in your life, the chief aim of all those experiences was to reinforce and temper your character and your will, which were still very weak, and to engender in you a limitless trust in the *voice of your heart.*"

~

"This newfound conviction was to develop and increase the degree of communication between your mind and the voice of your heart, transforming the latter into your best friend and a refuge in which to find help, protection, and solace at any given moment."

~

"My son, having come to this awareness was one of the most important milestones in your life—for in the *voice of your heart* you found the perfect guide to help you attain your purpose in life and to turn your dreams into reality."

~

"All of the events in your life are the consequence of the thoughts/seeds that you created with your will and mind—unconsciously first and consciously afterwards—and that you fed to the Omniscience and the Omnipotence of My Creative Power that dwells in you, which ultimately shaped the course of your existence."

After all this, I asked:

"My God, what was the reason for going through all of these ups and downs in my life?

"Why didn't You allow me to find what I wanted in Ribera or in Montreal?"

"Because, at that time Ribera or Montréal was not the ideal place for you to fulfill your heart's desires.

"The Omniscience of My Creative Power that dwells in you was fully aware of that problem, and therefore set up the conditions that would take you through the experiences necessary to eventually achieve your goals."

"But why, my God, wasn't Ribera and Montreal the right places?"

"Because if the people who knew you there—relatives and friends—had become aware of your interest in phenomena outside of traditional Catholic teaching, through ignorance they sooner or later would have reached the erroneous conclusion that you were dealing with witchcraft, and consequently branded you and judged you harshly.

"Such conditions would have hampered the research that you needed to carry out.

"Consequently, the Omniscience of My Creative Power that dwells in you gradually guided you into leaving first Ribera and then Montreal and steered you towards Joshua Tree, that small town lost in the Southern California desert that eventually became your final home."

"Joshua Tree, provided you with the ideal environment in which to accomplish everything you have always wanted:

- Living close to your family;
- Creating a small construction company that would guarantee your family steady work and a decent standard of living;
- And a community of people who would help you grow spiritually so you could finally understand the apparent mysteries surrounding My nature."

After this perception, I asked:

"My God, what would have happened to me if I had not followed the guidance of the Omniscience of Your Creative Power that dwells in me?"
"You would have continued to be engulfed in your ignorance and you would have suffered more."

CHAPTER 49

REVELATION OF THE DIFFERENCE BETWEEN
HUMAN LOVE AND DIVINE LOVE

After the perceptions describe on the previous chapter, I was simply ecstatic.

But, as on many other past occasions, after a few days my rapture gave way to a new curiosity and more questions:

"Why is there in all living beings the innate, uncontrollable urge to procreate in spite of the inherent risks?"

Having reflected for a while and still unable to understand the reasoning, I made up the following prayer:

"My God, I'm sure that You already know what's troubling me.
"I entreat You, therefore, with humility and sincerity, to let me perceive why human beings—despite the certainty that giving birth to children is almost invariably accompanied by heavy self-sacrifice, significant responsibility and sometimes even misery—nonetheless continue to bring forth children into this world.

"And, if for whatever reason they're unable to bear children, they feel they have failed life's most essential and important mission."

After a few days of reciting this prayer, I perceived the following:

"Because it is during the process of procreation that man and all creation express and fulfill the fundamental essence of their nature and My nature."

"My God, what is the fundamental essence of Your nature?"
"Love, My son. Love."

"My God, in the past You have let me perceive that the essence of Your nature is Energy."
"Now You let me perceive that the fundamental essence of Your nature is Love.
"Are You Energy, or Love?"
"I am both, My son."

At this perception, I couldn't help but ask myself:

"If God has no form because His essence and nature is Energy, as I have been instructed to believe, how could His essence also be Love, which in reality is an individual feeling—or better yet, an emotion from an individual?"

As I reflected on the above, I perceived this:

"My son, before you begin to doubt the veracity of what you have just perceived, answer the following question:

What is love, according to your understanding?"

Thinking there was a simple answer to all of this, I replied without the slightest hesitation:

"My God, the word *love* expresses the feelings of happiness, goodwill and kindness that we experience under the influence of our emotions that we hold for the people who are dear to us: wives, husbands, children, parents, uncles, aunts, cousins, and friends."

"My son, what you have described, is the essence of the inner emotions of man. It can be defined as *human love*, and does not represent the essence of *true Love*."

At this perception I asked:

"My God, what is the difference *between human love* and *true love?*"

"*Human love*, as you rightly said, that is generated by the nature of man's thoughts, emotions and actions, is *conditional and changes continually according to his feelings.*

"I'll do such-and-such thing for you, if it is being returned in kind, and you do something for me.

"If you do nothing for me, the emotional attachment is disrupted, the relationship ceases to exist, the bond is broken, and the love between those peoples vanishes.

"*True love* instead, is the essence of My Divine Nature, is steadfast, it is *unconditional and never changes.*"

After this perception, I asked:

"My God, could You be more specific about what is *true love*, so I can understand?"

"My son, what are the sensations that you experience in the depths of your being, when you are deeply immersed in prayer

267

and you are in perfect tune with your inner being, with, in reality, is the voice of your heart?"

After a few moments of reflection, I answered, *"Harmony and peace."*

Soon after, I began to perceive the following:

"**My son, the essence of** *true love* **is quite different from what you have always been taught to believe** *is love.*
"**In reality,** *Love* **does not stand for what man feels toward others, but for what man feels deep within himself in the guise of** *Harmony* **and** *Peace.*"

"**My son, as I let you perceive before, the joy flowing from the emotions of man is subject to the continuous fluctuation of the individual's psychological and emotional state; it's inconstant and easily fades.**"

"**The harmony and the peace that is felt within a person's depths—which is perceived with greater intensity during prayer and deep meditation, as you already know—never changes. It is not subject to conditions, it is ever-present, and it embodies all my creations.**"

"**My son,** *True Love* **is** *Divine,* **is** *the Harmony* **existing in the Energy of all the atoms in the universe.**
"**Hence, the saying:**
"**I God, am** *Love,* **and all Creation is impregnated with the** *Infinity* **of** *My Divine Love.*
"**Can also be said: I God,** *am Harmony,* **and all Creation is impregnated with the** *Infinity* **of** *My Divine Harmony.*"

"My son, when man is able to perceive consciously the *Harmony* and the *Peace* of My essence and his essence;

"When man consciously is able to engulf himself in *My Harmony* and *Peace*;

"And when man is able to manifest that *Harmony* and that *Peace* to every living creature, to every living thing and to all creation itself, without asking and expecting anything in return;

"Only then can man say that he is in *Love* and that he *Loves*."

At that point, I felt that I understood that *True Love (Divine Love)*, in its very essence is not an *emotion*, as we typically think and believe, but is the *Harmony* that is found in the Energy of which we are all a part.

CHAPTER 50
JESUS, WITNESS OF THE TRUTH

As time went by, I wondered if my perceptions were really reflecting the truth or if they were the fruits of my imagination.

In hope of shedding some light, I formulated the following prayer:

"My God, I firmly believe that everything You are making me perceive is the absolute truth, but as You can see, my weakness makes me wonder. On account of that, I humbly ask You with all my strength, with my entire mind, and with all my heart, to let me perceive if there are other people who have acquired the knowledge of the truth who could serve as witnesses."

Here is the response to my prayer:

"My son, there are many people who have acquired the knowledge of the truth **in the past as well as in the present— more than you can think and imagine—who could serve as witnesses for the** eternal truths **I have made you perceive."**

"However, since the majority of humanity still lives in ignorance and is incapable of understanding, most of these

people, in order to avoid being misunderstood, criticized, or, for that matter, even persecuted—have opted to lead their lives in quiet seclusion."

"Some of those who have perceived the truth have been identified and celebrated as saints or prophets."

"Today, one of the most prominent and revered of these men is the one who is known by the name of Jesus."

"Jesus, after having perceived the very same truths that I let you perceive, and after he had mastered and integrated them into His life, He had the courage and determination to share and profess His knowledge. In spite of knowing very well, that the religious leaders of the time not only would reject Him and His teachings, but would crucify Him as if He were a dangerous criminal."

"His doctrine, teachings and miracles are the most clear and eloquent witness that everything I have made you perceive is the absolute truth."

Upon having the above perception, I remembered the *ambiguity and the mystery* I felt when I'd read of the teachings and works of Jesus.

I soon had this perception:

"My son, it's about time you realized there are *neither ambiguities nor mysteries* about what Jesus preached and the works he performed."

"My God," I replied, "what kept me from perceiving and understanding His message?"

"My son, what prevented you from perceiving Jesus' message was mainly due to the following facts:

- My Creative Power dwelling within you was and still is filled with many negative thoughts/seeds;
- While you were reading the Gospels, you were emotionally agitated and excited;
- And most of all, you erroneously tried to discern the message of the Gospels using logic and reason."

"What do You mean my God? Can You be more explicit?"
"My son, I remind you that man is made of *visible* and *invisible* parts.
"The *visible* are represented by the different organs of the body;
"While the *invisible* are represented by My will, My mind and by the Omnipotence and the Omniscience of My Creative Power within man."

"You know that each part of his body, accomplishes a specific task that has been assigned to it by My Divine Will and that task is not interchangeable."

"For example, the feet and legs, whose function is to allow man to walk, cannot perform the function of the mouth, whose primary task it is to chew food and articulate sounds."

"The lungs, whose function is to allow breathing, cannot take over the role of the heart, whose task it is to keep the blood circulating throughout the body.
And so forth."

"Similarly, the will and the mind, which, as you already know, have the task of creating the thoughts/seeds, *cannot* perform the task of the Omnipotence and of the Omniscience of My Creative Power within man, whose task is to manifest in man's life whatever his will and mind create in the form of thoughts/seeds, and to provide him with knowledge about all that exists in the universe."

"One of the two things that prevented you from understanding Jesus' message was that during that period, you were excited.
"Your excitement stirred all the negative thoughts/seeds in My Creative Power within you, blurring the connection between your mind and the Omniscience of My Creative Power within you.
"The other thing was that you tried to perceive Jesus' message using the reasoning of your mind.
"In doing so, you tried to make your mind perform a task that is not part of its role.

"If you had remained calm and allowed your mind to do the job My Divine Will assigned it to do, you would have stayed in tune with the Omniscience of my Creative Power—as you often had in the past— you would have properly perceived Jesus' message."

"My God, to make sure that I am not misinterpreting Your message, can You give me a practical example?"
"My son, if we get a clean glass and fill it with pure water, are you going to be able to see through it?"
"Yes, my God."

"**Now, if we, intentionally or unintentionally, add mud to the water in the glass and stir it with a spoon, mixing the mud with the water, what would happen?**"
"The water would become cloudy and would lose its purity and clarity."

"**At that point would you be able to see through the water?**"
"No, my God."

"**Now, My son, would it be possible at this point to restore the water in the glass to its original transparency and purity?**"
"Yes, my God."

"**How?**"
"By no longer stirring the water, so the muddy concoction can settle to the bottom of the glass."

"**For how long would the water maintain its clarity?**"
"Its clarity would endure as long as the mud is not allowed, intentionally or otherwise, to mix again with the water."

"**Could we conclude, then, that the water's clarity or transparency is only temporary?**"
"Yes, my God."

"**What should be done to permanently restore its original purity?**"
"The water and the mud should be separated."

"**How can we achieve that?**"
"By filtering or distilling the water. Either one of these processes would reinstate purity and clarity to the water and restore its transparency for good."

"My son, are you sure about that?"
"Yes, my God."

"My son, the *glass* represents your body.
"The *water* represents the Omnipotence and the Omniscience of My Creative Power dwelling in you.
"The *mud* represents the sum of your negative thoughts/ seeds.
"The *spoon* represents your will and mind, which control your emotions."

"As the mud and water blended by the spoon makes the water murky and reduces its transparency;
"Likewise, the negative thoughts/seeds stored in My Creative Power within you, under the influence of your uncontrolled emotional actions, makes the connection murkier and diminishes the communication between your will and mind and the Omniscience of My Creative Power within you."

"As the spoon's action makes the water murkier and more difficult to see through;
"In the same fashion, negative emotions stir the negative thoughts/seeds in My Creative Power within, obstructing the connection between the will and mind and the Omniscience of My Creative Power within you, preventing the perception and comprehension of the objects of your desire."

After perceiving the above, I said, "My God, what should I do to improve these conditions?"
"You should purify and free My Creative Power that dwells in you of all negative thoughts/seeds."

"How can I do that?"

"My son, as to restore to the water its original purity and clarity, you first must let it rest, then filter and possibly distill it;

"In the same manner, to free My Creative Power dwelling in you of the negative thoughts/seeds that consciously or unconsciously you have planted in it, you must:

- Calm down;
- Bring your emotions under control;
- Continue to pray as you have done in the past;
- Integrate and live what I have made you perceive."

"How long will it take to free myself?"

"That depends on the intensity of your desire, on the eagerness with which you apply yourself, and on the time you dedicate to prayer and meditation every day."

CHAPTER 51
PERCEPTION OF JESUS' TEACHINGS' TRUE MESSAGE

Following the perceptions described in the previous chapter, I felt an increase in my desire to understand the message of Jesus' doctrine. With great expectations I formulated the following prayer:

> *"My God, I pray You with all my heart, mind and will to allow me to perceive the true message of Jesus' teachings and works;*
> *"I thank You, because I know without any doubts, that in this moment, You are listening my prayer;*
> *"I also thank You, because I truly believe that in time, You will grant me the object of my desires."*

With humility and zeal, and with all my attention focused on the deepest spot of my heart, the seat of the Omniscience of the Creative Power within, I began to say the above prayer whenever I could.

It took me several years, a lot of perseverance, and many sacrifices before I could perceive what I wanted to know.

One night as I was praying, I perceived the following:

> **"My son, before I let you perceive the objects of your desire, it's important that you know and understand that Jesus never wrote down what he believed and professed.**

"What is known about His life and works has been handed down mostly by the writings attributed to John, Matthew, Mark, Luke, and Paul.

"Over the centuries, these writings have gone through many transcriptions, translations, and adaptations. Consequently, they do not reflect precisely, word-for-word, the terms and expressions that Jesus used during the course of His life."

"You can see the truth of this by reading and comparing the old and new versions of the King James Gospels, as well as when you read and compare bibles from different authors and translators.

"Although the meaning and the message stays the same, the wording is considerably different from one to another.

"Thus, My son, in order to grasp the true message of Jesus' teachings, you cannot rely on current biblical literature and its literal interpretation, but rather you must catch the true essence and spirit of His thoughts.

"If you stay in tune with the Omniscience of My Creative Power within you, and if you will ask Me specific questions about Jesus and His teachings, I will let you perceive the right answers, and finally you can understand the true core of His doctrine and His works."

After this perception, the first thing that came to my mind to ask was about the beginning of the Gospel attributed to John, which at the time of my research I could not understand at all.

So I asked:

"My God, what is the message of John, chapter one, verses one through verse eighteen" I then recited the verses.

"My son, to make things easier for you to understand the message of those verses, we will exam them individually. "We begin with verse one."

"In the beginning was the Word, and the Word was with God, and the Word was God." John 1:1
"This verse attests that in the beginning of time, before I created the universe, there was only Me, God."

"All things were made through Him; and without Him nothing was made that was made." John 1:3
"This verse bears witness and confirms that all things in the universe were made and created by and through Me. It also attests that everything that exists is the expression and manifestation of My essence."

"In Him was life, and the life was the light of men." John 1:4
"This verse witnesses that I, God, am life, and that My life is light, which also is the life and the light of men. It attests that I, God, express Myself through man, and that man is the expression of My essence."

"And the Word became flesh, and dwelt among us." John 1:14
"This confirms that I, God (the Word), manifest Myself in the form of man (flesh), who is the expression and manifestation of My essence and nature: the Light."

"That was the true Light, which gives light to every man coming into the world." John 1:9
"Herein it is reconfirmed, My son, that Jesus, the true light, was the manifestation and expression of My Light (Energy)— the same Light (Energy) that brightens and gives form and

life to every man that comes into the world. This verse confirms as well once more, that Jesus and all mankind are the manifestation of My Divine essence: The Light (Energy)."

"And the light shined in darkness, and the darkness did not comprehend it." John 1:5
"This is a confirmation that I, God, which is to say the Light (Energy), shines (Manifests) through the body of man, who, due to his own ignorance—the darkness—is not aware that his essence is the manifestation of My Divine Essence.
"This unawareness leaves him oblivious to his own real identity."

"He was in the world, and the world was made by Him, and the world did not know Him." John 1:10
"He came to his own, and his own did not receive Him." John 1:11
"These verses repeat and bear witness that despite the fact that My essence, the Light (Energy), is the essence that gives life and form to all creation, as well to the body of man, and that the body of man is My home, man, due to his ignorance, is unable to see, understand and accept the truth about Me and him, that we are one and the same."

"But as many as received Him, to them He gave the right to become children of God." John 1:12
"My son, this verse witnesses and attests that whoever believes in Jesus' teachings, accepts them, and most importantly, incorporates them into his daily life, will become aware of his true nature and essence.
"At that point, man will realize that he is the expression and manifestation of My Essence and of My Light (Energy), and that he and I are one and the same.

"This awareness will allow man once again to identify himself as My expression and part of My essence, and man will began to use consciously and wisely the Omnipotence and the Omniscience of My Divine Creative Power dwelling in him, making him experience things that the common person calls miracles or supernatural."

"Which were born, not of blood, nor of the will of the flesh, nor of the will of man, but of God..." John 1:13
"This confirms that in reality man is not the bi-product of man *"...not of blood..."* but is the bi-product of My Divine Light (Energy), as I let you previously perceive."

"And of his fullness we have all received, and grace for grace." John 1:16
"This verse attests that the spiritual understanding (Enlightenment), acquired by Jesus *"...and of his fullness ..."* has inspired and helped mankind for the good." *"...we have all received ... grace for grace".*

"For the law was given through Moses, but grace and truth came through Jesus Christ." John 1:17
"This confirms that Moses and the Ten Commandments established the law—the roadmap to follow—but the application and the demonstration of the working of the law, and the benefits that man can receive from their application, was performed and demonstrated by Jesus."

"...but grace and truth came through Jesus...." John 1:17
"No one has seen God at any time. The only begotten Son, who is in the bosom of the Father, he hath declared him." John 1:18
"... and we beheld his glory..." John 1:14

"These verses bear witness to the following:

- "That what I made you perceive some time ago is the truth: that no one can say they have seen Me face-to-face, because as you already know, I do not have a specific form with which I can be identified;
- "That Jesus was aware of the oneness existing between Me and Him, as well as with mankind and all creation.
- "That Jesus, in showing the ability to heal the sick, resurrect the dead, walk upon the waters, still the winds and storms, change water into wine, multiply bread and fish, and curse and cause to die the fig tree, etc., provided the evidence of what man can do when he is aware of his true nature and identity, and when he is tune with the Omnipotence and the Omniscience of My Creative Power."

Soon after I had this perception, I perceived the following question:

"My son, can you express in your own words the essence of the message I made you perceive?"

After reflecting for a while, I answered:

- "That in the beginning, before the existence of Creation, only the essence of Your nature existed;
- That the essence of Your nature is Light, (Energy);
- And that the entire universe and all the various forms of life including man are the manifestation and expression of the essence of Your nature: the Light (Energy)."

"Well said My son!"
"Now, before we continue, it is important that you answer a few questions..."

"What is the essence of My true nature?"
"Energy, my God."

"How do I express Myself?"
"Through all Creation."

"What does science say about Creation?"
"According to science, Creation is comprised of a mass of particles called molecules, constituted by atoms that are made up of electrons, protons and neutrons, and defined as Energy."

"In your opinion, are there any substantial differences between what is attested to in John, what I have made you perceive, and what is affirmed and demonstrated by science?"
After reflecting for a while, I answered:
"No, my God."

"Could you explain why there is no difference?"
"Because, my God, the nature of the Light spoken by John, the Energy about which You spoke to me, and the essence of Energy according to science is exactly the same thing."

"Could one say that I, God, am Light, Energy and that all Creation is the expression of My essence and is an intrinsic part of My being, which is to say of My Light (Energy)?"
"Yes, my God."

Then I continued and asked:

"My God, why did Jesus curse the fig tree and make it die?"
*"Now in the morning, as He returned to the city, He was hungry."
Matthew 21:18*
*"And seeing a fig tree by the road, He came to it and found nothing
on it but leaves, and said to it, "Let no fruit grow on you ever again."
Immediately the fig tree withered away." Matthew 21:19*
*"And when the disciples saw it, they marveled, saying, "How did the
fig tree wither away so soon?" Matthew 21:20*
*"So Jesus answered and said to them, "Assuredly, I say to you, if you
have faith and do not doubt, you will not only do what was done to
the fig tree, but also if you say to this mountain, 'Be removed and be
cast into the sea,' it will be done." Matthew 21:21*
*"And whatever things you ask in prayer, believing, you will receive."
Matthew 21:22*

～෨

*"Now the next day, when they had come out from Bethany, He was
hungry." Mark 11:12*
*"And seeing from afar a fig tree having leaves, He went to see if
perhaps He would find something on it. When He came to it, He
found nothing but leaves, for it was not the season for figs." Mark
11:13*
*"In response Jesus said to it, "Let no one eat fruit from you ever
again." Mark 11:14*
*"Now in the morning, as they passed by, they saw the fig tree dried
up from the roots." Mark 11:20*
*"And Peter, remembering, said to Him, "Rabbi, look! The fig tree
which You cursed has withered away." Mark 11:21*
*"So Jesus answered and said to them, "Have faith in God. Mark
11:22*

"For assuredly, I say to you, whoever says to this mountain, 'Be removed and be cast into the sea,' and does not doubt in his heart, but believes that those things he says will be done, he will have whatever he says." Mark 11:23

"Therefore I say to you, whatever things you ask when you pray, believe that you receive them, and you will have them." Mark 11:24

"To prove to His disciples and to mankind that whatever they believe without doubting is going to happen.

"And to prove that the Omnipotence of My Creative Power that dwells in man does not have the power to choice, and does not distinguish the difference between what man thinks is right or wrong."

"In different words, My Creative Power does not have the capability to act on its own.

"It simply has the task to manifest in man's life whatever his will and his mind conceives and creates in the form of thoughts/seeds."

"That is true whether the essences of the thoughts/seeds are expressed to heal people, change water into wine, and multiply fish and bread;

"Or make a tree die, start hostility among people, and start wars between countries."

$\sim\!\!\!\sim$

My God, why did Jesus command his disciples not to take money in exchange for the services they rendered to others and taught them it was not important to accumulate treasures on earth?

"Heal the sick, cleanse the lepers, raise the dead, cast out demons. Freely you have received, freely give." Matthew 10:8

"Do not lay up for yourselves treasures on earth,…" Matthew 6:19
"Because Jesus knew that money and wealth on earth represent the false hope of mankind."

"Money and wealth only give the illusion of meeting man's needs and desires for security, happiness, peace and joy;
"Money and wealth do not lead to understanding the Truth;
"That truth that sets man free of the bondage of his ignorance and limitations."

"Another reason that Jesus asked His disciples not to take money is that He knew if they accepted money for their services, they would have been swayed into leading a materialistic existence, with the consequences that you already know."

"You learned the truth of this precept a long time ago—when you entertained the notion of getting paid for your prayers and healing services."

Upon receiving this perception, the memory of that experience—now remote and painful—resurfaced, allowing me to finally understand the moral behind the time I contemplated charging a fee for my prayers.

After this perception, I asked:

"My God, if what You just allowed me to perceive is true, why do the majority of people—including so-called religious ones and ones who play a prominent role in religious groups seems to ignore this principle?"

Soon after, I perceived:

"Because they never fully and truly understood the teachings of their Masters, as well as what is My true nature, what is their true nature, how We are bonded together, and what is the purpose of life."

"My son, I remind you that after man lost awareness of his true nature and essence, he began to experience all kind of problems that were making his life a living hell."

"Not knowing how to overcome his problems, he began to think and believe that his lost security, joy, peace, and harmony could be acquired by the acquisition and possession of material goods and by the acquisition of power and influence over other people—and that the more he acquired, the greater would be his security and happiness."

"It is precisely because of this belief that the majority of people throughout the ages and up to the present days are dedicating their lives, their time, their energies, and their talents to the accumulation of money and physical assets."

"This illusion, My son, represents man's greatest tragedy!"

After this perception, I asked what Jesus meant when He said:

"… it is easier for a camel to go through the eye of a needle than for a rich man to enter the kingdom of God." Matthew 19:24

"This message is allegoric, and symbolizes that it's very hard for a person who is rich in material things to detach himself from his riches and undertake the Spiritual Path that leads to My kingdom—The Kingdom of God—where money, wealth and material possessions don't mean a thing."

My God, what did Jesus mean when He said:

"But I say to you that for every idle word men may speak, they will give account of it…" Matthew 12:36
"For by your words you will be justified, and by your words you will be condemned." Matthew 12:37
"My son, in verse thirty-six, although in a different way and with different words, Jesus is talking and explaining the function and the working of the will, and of the mind in relation to the working of the Omnipotence of My Creative Power within man.

"That every thought, *"idle word…"* good or bad, that man conceive, *"men may speak…"* in time he is going to deal with it in the form of experience *"they will give account of it…"*.

"The way he is going to deal with is explained in verse thirty-seven, where He said:
"For by your words you will be justified, and by your words you will be condemned." Matthew 12:37

"That simply means that good thoughts/seeds will make you have good experiences—*"by your words you will be justified"*—while bad or negative thoughts/seeds will make you have bad experiences— *"by your words you will be condemned."*

~

My God, what did Jesus mean when He said:

"Assuredly, I say to you, you will by no means get out of there till you have paid the last penny." Matthew 5:26

"That man will not be able to find and experience true joy and peace, and be reunited to Me and experience My Divine Love, until he frees himself from all the negative thoughts/ seeds stored in My Creative Power that dwells in him."

~

My God, why did Jesus say:

"You have heard that it was said to those of old, 'You shall not commit adultery." Matthew 5:27

"But I say to you that whoever looks at a woman to lust for her has already committed adultery with her in his heart…" Matthew 5:28

"Because Jesus knew the moment a person conceives the thought to lust another person, he/she transmits those thoughts/seeds to the Omnipotence of My Creative Power within, with the consequence that in time that person will be led to commit adultery."

~

My God, what Jesus mean when He said:

"Do not think that I came to destroy the law or the prophets. I did not come to destroy but to fulfill ..." Matthew 5:17
"That Jesus did not come to establish a new law or a new religion, but to teach, demonstrate and prove to the world the meaning and the working of the existing law professed by the Prophets."

My God, why did Jesus teach:

"In this manner, therefore, pray: Our Father in heaven ..." Matthew 6:9
"Could You let me perceive in which way You are our Father?"
"My son, you already know that all creation is the manifestation of My essence, of My energy. There is no difference in affirming that creation is the manifestation and expression of My essence and in saying that I am the Father of the creation. It is for this reason that Jesus refers to Me as the Father."

My God, what did Jesus mean when He said:

"For if you forgive men their trespasses, your heavenly Father will also forgive you." Matthew 6:14
"But if you do not forgive men their trespasses, neither will your Father forgive your trespasses." Matthew 6:15

"My son, in the above verses, although in a different way, Jesus is teaching the function of the Omnipotence of My Creative Power—the heavenly Father—dwelling in man, whose function, as you know, is to manifest whatever the will and the mind of man create in the form of thoughts/seeds.

"As you know, when man forgives, he creates thoughts of love.

"Consequently, the Omnipotence of My Creative Power dwelling in him is going to let him experience good things.

"On the contrary, if man does not forgive, he creates thoughts expressing hate.

"Consequently, the Omnipotence of my Creative Power dwelling in him is going to let him experience bad things.

"It is specifically for this reason that Jesus taught to forgive and to love—to prevent man from having bad experiences and suffer."

My God, what did Jesus mean when He said:

"I and My Father are one." John 10:30
"…believe the works, that you may know and believe that the Father is in Me, and I in Him." John 10:38
"The message of the first verse is the same as the one I allowed you to perceive in the course of your search, that man is the expression and manifestation of the essence of My nature, the

Energy, the Light; that he is an integral part of My Being; that he is one with Me in the same fashion that the all creation is one with Me.

"The demonstration that the first verse express the truth is confirmed and proved by the performance of Jesus' Miracles *"... the works..."*, through the action of the Omnipotence of My Creative Power within Jesus."
"... that you may know and believe that the Father is in Me, and I in Him". John 10:38

◦~~∘

My God, in the following verse, Jesus said:

"And as you go, preach, saying, "The kingdom of heaven is at hand." Matthew 10:7
"My God, what is *"The kingdom of heaven"* in its true form, and how is it *"at hand"*?"
"My son, *"The kingdom of heaven"* is the essence of My nature that abides within man, and it is *"at hand"* because it is within man himself, it is part of man, it is part of his make up."

◦~~∘

My God, what is it the meaning and the message of the following verses:

*"Do you not know that your bodies are members of the Christ?" **1** Corinthians 6:15*
*"Do you not know that you are the temple of God and that the Spirit of God dwells in you?" **1** Corinthians 3:16*

"Or do you not know that your body is the temple of the Holy Spirit who is in you, whom you have from God, and you are not your own?"
1 Corinthians 6:19

"My son, the three above verses, although with different words and in a different way, are stating the *truth* about Me and Man, that you already know.

"In Verse fifteen of Chapter six, the Apostle Paul states that the body of man is part of Me, made with the essence of My nature, My Energy.

"Verse sixteen of Chapter three states that the body of every man, although appearing to have a unique form, is the manifestation of My essence, is part of My nature, and is one with Me.

"Verse nineteen of Chapter six states that the body of man is the residence—or the temple—of Me—the Holy Spirit—and man is not his own because his body and his being is a by-product of the essence of My nature, My Energy.'"

After this perception, I asked:

My God, is there any tangible difference between You, and what is reported in the Bible with the names of *Holy Spirit*, the *Christ*, and the *Father within?*"

"No, My son. They are all synonyms, words, and names created by man to identify Me and to identify the essence of My nature.

"To the above list, you can add *The Creative Power Within* and *The Voice of the Heart."*

My God, why did Jesus say to the woman who had been bleeding for twelve years…

> *"Be of good cheer, daughter; your faith has made you well."* Matthew 9:22

"And to the blind man:

> *"Go your way; your faith has made you well."* Mark 10:52
> "How did merely *faith* heal the woman and the blind man?"
> **"My son, as you already know, the healing of any malady is performed by the Omnipotence of My Creative Power within.**
> **"You also know that what triggers the Omnipotence of My Creative Power to take action is unshakable** *belief* **or** *faith.*
>
> **"The reason why Jesus said to the woman and to the blind man** *your faith has made you well,* **is that in those specific occasions, the Omnipotence' of My Creative Power had been triggered, not because of the will of Jesus, but because of the will—the belief and faith—of the woman and of the blind man."**
> *"If only I may touch His garment I shall be made well."* Matthew 9:21
> *"What do you want Me to do for you?" … The blind man said to Him, "Rabboni, that I may receive my sight."* Mark 10:51

~⁊

My God, what is the most important element needed to experience the so-called Miracles?"

"Unconditional belief that what is asked is going to happen, My son."

"My God, how can we prove that?"
"By reading attentively the portion of the Scriptures that talks about Jesus' works."

"Now Martha said to Jesus, "Lord, if you had been here, my brother would not have died." John 11:21
"But even now I know that whatever You ask of God, God will give You."
John 11:22

"And Peter answered Him and said, "Lord, if it is You, command me to come to You on the water." Matthew 14:28
"He said, "Come." And when Peter had come down out of the boat, he walked on the water to go to Jesus." Matthew 14:2

"While He spoke these things to them, behold, a ruler came and worshiped Him, saying, "My daughter has just died, but come and lay Your hand on her and she will live." Matthew 9:18

"Now when Jesus had entered Capernaum, a centurion came to Him, pleading with Him," Matthew 8:5
"saying, Lord, my servant is lying at home paralyzed, dreadfully tormented." Matthew 8:6
And Jesus said to him, "I will come and heal him." Matthew 8:7
"The centurion answered and said, "Lord, I am not worthy that You should come under my roof. But only speak a word, and my servant will be healed." Matthew 8:8
"My son, Martha, Peter, the Ruler, and the Centurion, they all truly believed, and had total trust and confidence that Jesus had the power to do what they asked Him to do.
"At the same time, Jesus truly knew and believed without any doubt that whatever He asked to the Omnipotence of My Creative Power within Him would happen.

"Unconditional believe and trust, without doubt, is what it takes to experience the so-called 'Miracles."

~⁀

My God, why did Jesus say to the scribes that there was no difference between affirming:

"For which is easier, to say, 'Your sins are forgiven you,' or to say 'Arise and walk?" Matthew 9:5
"Because He knew that the Omnipotence of My Creative Power within man manifests always only the intended meaning that man gives to the words.
"If the intended meaning of the words composing two different sentences are expressing the same thing, the results will be the same."

~⁀

My God, what did Jesus mean when He said:

"I am the way, the truth, and the life." John 14:6
"That it is by the following His path *the way,* **and living His teaching** *the truth,* **that leads man to Me:** *The life."*

~⁀

My God, what did Jesus mean when He said to Nicodemus:

"Most assuredly, I say to you, unless one is born again, he cannot see the kingdom of God." John 3:3

"That until and unless man abandons the path of selfishness, of hate, of revenge, and of lust, and undertake the path of unselfishness, of love, of forgiveness, and of spirituality *born again*, he cannot feel *see* the joy, the peace, and the harmony of My Divine nature and My Divine Love, the *kingdom of God.*"

My God, what is Jesus' message in the following verse?

"No one has ascended to heaven but He who came down from heaven, that is, the Son of Man who is in heaven." John 3:13
"My son, to understand the message of the above verse, it is important that you understand that *the heaven* mentioned by Jesus is not a physical place located somewhere in the universe, but in this case, *heaven* symbolizes the nature of My essence, the Energy.
"Jesus' message is that every person *the Son of Man* who comes into the world *He who came down from heaven* after he completes his journey on earth, goes back *ascends* to the source of his origin, goes back to Me *The Heaven*, of which he always has been a part, and from where he descended."

My God, why did Jesus say:

"For God did not send His Son into the world to condemn the world, but that the world through Him be saved." John 3:17
"That Jesus did not come into the world to judge and punish people. He came to teach the path that leads to the understanding of My nature, their nature, how we work in unison and how we are connected.

"The understanding of the above truth frees people from the bondage of their ignorance, and allow them to free themselves from all the negative thoughts/seeds that are still in My Creative Power within them, so at the moment of their trespass, they will be able to be reunited with Me, *the Salvation, the Life.*"

~

My God, what did Jesus mean when He said:

"I am the living bread which came down from heaven. If anyone eats of this bread, he will live forever." John 6:51
"That His teachings *the living bread* **are from Me** *the heaven* **and that whoever practices and lives** *eats* **Jesus' teachings, will be reunited to Me for ever** *will live forever."*

~

My God, why did Jesus say:

"Do not judge according to appearance, but judge with righteous judgment." John 7:24
"Because He knew that more often than not, people don't use common sense *righteous* **when making a judgment."**

~

My God, what is Jesus' message on the following verse?

"While you have the light, believe in the light, that you may become sons of the light." John 12:36

"**Jesus** *the light* **exhorted people to believe and accept His teachings because He knew that it is by the accepting and the living of His teachings** *believe in the light* **that people would be led to understand the truth of who I am, of who they are, and of how we are connected together. Through this, people can free themselves of all the negative thoughts/seeds still abiding in My Creative Power within them, so at the moment of their trespass, they can become part of Me and part of My essence** *sons of the light.*"

After the above perceptions, I asked:

My God, why was Jesus teaching to forgive, to renounce hatred and revenge, not to quarrel, not to be haughty, and to pray for those who persecuted us—and to love our enemy and so on?"
"But I tell you not to resist an evil person. But whoever slaps you on your right cheek, turn the other to him also." Matthew 5:39
"You have heard that it was said, "You shall love your neighbor and hate your enemy," Matthew 5:43
"But I say to you, love your enemies, bless those who curse you, do good to those who spitefully use you and persecute you." Matthew 5:44
"**Because He knew that man's happiness and unhappiness as well his good experiences and his negative experiences are linked to the nature of his thoughts/seeds created by his will and mind.**"

"**Because Jesus knew that reacting in a negative way to the negative action of another person creates more negative thoughts/seeds, and with them more negative experiences and sufferings into their life.**
"**Instead, if they would react in a positive way to anyone who tries to harm them…**

"But I tell you not to resist an evil person. But whoever slaps you on your right cheek, turn the other to him also." Matthew 5:39
"...You shall love your neighbor and hate your enemy," Matthew 5:43
"but I say to you, love your enemies, bless those who curse you, do good to those who spitefully use you and persecute you." Matthew 5:44
... **they would create positive and good thoughts/seeds, bringing into their life positive and good experiences."**

"It is for this reason that Jesus taught to *Love* **all the time—family members and friends as well as enemies—because it is through the expression of** *Love* **that the Omnipotence of My Creative Power within man creates the conditions that lead man to experience true joy, happiness, and success."**

"Jesus, although in a different way, and with different terms taught the same thing that I taught you in the course of your search:

- **The mechanics, the functions and the impacts that thoughts/seeds have on man's life;**
- **To make him aware that his thoughts are responsible for all the experiences of his life."**

⁓

My God, what did Jesus mean when He said:

"Most assuredly, I say to you, he who hears My word and believes in Him who sent Me has everlasting life, and shall not come into judgment, but has passed from death into life." John 5:24

"My son, the message of the above verse is that whoever in the course of his life accepts and lives Jesus' teachings, knowing and believing that those teachings are My teachings, will free himself from all the negative thoughts/seeds existing in My Creative Power within him.

"Consequently, at the moment of his trespass *death,* he will join the infinity of My essence, My Energy, the *everlasting life -- but has passed from death into life.*"

My God, why did Jesus say:

"...Whoever drinks of this water will thirst again," John 4:13
"but whoever drinks of the water that I shall give him will never thirst. But the water that I shall give him will become in him a fountain of water springing up into everlasting life." John 4:14
"My son, in this case *water* is figurative for *knowledge.* The message is that whoever continues to live in ignorance will continue to crave new experiences and new things that he thinks will make him happy."

"To the contrary, whoever accepts and lives by Jesus' teachings *whoever drinks of the water that I shall give him* will experience My Divine joy, My Divine peace and My Divine harmony—in other words, he will experience My Divine Love, and his craving for new experiences and new things will be quenched forever."

My God, why did Jesus say:

"Judge not, that you be not judged. For with what judgment you judge," Matthew 7:1
"you will be judged; and with the measure you use, it will be measured back to you." Matthew 7:2
"Therefore, whatever you want men to do to you do also to them, for this is the Law and the Prophets." Matthew 7:12
"My son, the reason Jesus instructs not to judge and to treat people well *Therefore, whatever you want men to do to you do also to them* **is because He was aware of the working of the Omnipotence of My Creative Power within man, in relation with the working of the will and mind of man.**
"Jesus knew that for every word that man says, and for every action that he takes *"the measure you use",* **there is a reaction— the experiencing of what has been created in the form of thoughts/seeds and deeds** *it will be the measured back to you."*

"Jesus knew that man's experiences are the bi-product of whatever he creates and conceives in the form of thoughts/ seeds and actions, good or bad *With the measure you use, it will be measured back to you.* **It is for these specific reasons that He exhorted people do only good** *whatever you want men to do to you do also to them."*

~⁀

My God, what did Jesus mean when He said:

"Ask and it will be given to you; seek, and you will find; knock, and it will be opened to you." Matthew 7:7

"For everyone who asks receives, and he who seeks finds, and to him who knocks it will be opened." Matthew 7:8

"That for man to get what he wants, he needs to act and put forth the necessary effort *ask, seek, knock,* **and then the Omnipotence and the Omniscience of My Creative Power that dwells in him will manifest and materialize in his life the object of his desires.**

"One more time with different terminology, Jesus is teaching the interaction, the mechanics and the function of the Will and the Mind of man in relation with the Omnipotence and the Omniscience of My Creative Power that dwells in man."

My God, why did Jesus teach that the best place to pray is a quiet and secluded place and not in a church or temple in the company of other people, as suggested by most religious leaders?

"But you, when you pray, go into your room, and when you have shut your door, pray to your Father who is in the secret place; and your Father who sees in secret will reward you openly." Matthew 6:6

"Because He knew that when a person participates in a religious function—in a church or in large public place, in the company of many other people—the rituals imposed by the religious leaders most often do not allow people to create thoughts/seeds of what they desire and want.

"If a person does not create anything in the form of thoughts/ seeds, the Omnipotence and the Omniscience of My Creative Power within, that, as you know, have the task of processing what is created by the will and the mind, has nothing to process and consequently nothing to manifest."

"For this reason, the time spent in the church becomes sterile and unproductive."

"Instead, if a person goes to a quiet and secluded place and creates thoughts/seeds of whatever he desires and expresses them in the form of prayer, the *Father who is in the secret place*—the Omnipotence of My Creative Power that dwells in man's body—will exteriorize and manifest them – *and your Father who sees in secret will reward you openly.*"

∾

Why did Jesus teach that when we pray we should not use *many words in vain repetitions?*

> *"And when you pray, do not use vain repetitions as the heathen do. For they think that they will be heard for their many words." Matthew 6:7*
> "Because He knew that the Omnipotence and the Omniscience of My Creative Power within man, doesn't have the power to discern, and they work and act best when the thoughts-seed created and conceived by the will and the mind are concise, specific, simple and direct."

∾

My God, what did Jesus mean when He said:

> *"Therefore I say to you, do not worry about your life, what you will eat or what you will drink; nor about your body, what you will put on." Matthew, 6:25*
> *"But seek first the kingdom of God and His righteousness, and all these things shall be added to you." Matthew, 6:33*

"That the most important thing in man's life is not to be concerned about his material needs, but to be concerned about his spiritual needs."

"The search that leads to the understanding of the nature of My essence – *the kingdom of God* -- and the way I work – *His righteousness* -- should be man's most import task and purpose."

"As you know—because you have already experienced it—financial success is much easier to achieve when man works in unison with the law that governs My Divine principles.
"It is for this reason that Jesus preached to search for Me first and the way I work – the *kingdom of God and His righteousness*-- and financial success will come with it – *and all these things shall be added to you.*"

My God, what did Jesus mean when He said:

"Today this Scripture is fulfilled in your hearing." Luke 4:21
"That the prophecy of the scriptures announced in the Old Testament was fulfilled by Jesus' coming."

"My God, in what way did Jesus fulfill the prophecy?"
"By explaining the true meaning and message of the Scriptures, and by proving with His works that what He taught was indeed the truth."

My God, what did Jesus mean when He said:

"Now when He was asked by the Pharisees when the kingdom of God would come, He answered them and said, The kingdom of God does not come with observation;" Matthew 17:20
"Nor will they say, See here! Or See there! For indeed, the kingdom of God is within you." Luke 17:21

- **"That there is not, and doesn't exist, a place called heaven or paradise,…**

"The kingdom of God does not come with observation; nor will they say, See here! or See there!"
… **as taught by many religious leaders, and as commonly believed;**

- **"That I, God, am not an individual with a specific form, as believed by many peoples;**
- **"That I am, as you already know, the Energy in the atoms that make up the cells of all the tissues and organs of the body of every man living in the world;**
- **"That I am an intrinsic part of man's body, through which I express Myself;**
- **"And that indeed I dwell within him** – *For indeed, the kingdom of God is within you."*

~～

My God, what did Jesus mean when He said:

"Do not labor for the food which perishes, but for the food which endures to everlasting life." John 6:27

"That the most important thing in life is not the search *(labor)* to accumulate material wealth *(Do not labor for the food which perish)*,

"but the search *(labor)* for the understanding of My Divine nature.

"It is that understanding that leads man to eternal life *(the food which endures to everlasting life.)*"

~⸲

My God, what did Jesus mean when He said:

"For this cause I was born, and for this cause I have come into the world, that I should bear witness to the truth." John18:37
"That He came into the world to prove *witness* with His works and His teaching that the son of Man (humankind), is My Divine expression and manifestation and that we are one and the same *the truth*."

~⸲

My God, what did Jesus mean when He said:

"Thomas, because you have seen Me, you have believed. Blessed are those who have not seen and yet have believed." John 20:29
"That in the course of time, people who believe and live Jesus' teachings are going to experience the same benefits as the ones who witnessed His works."

~⸲

My God, what did Jesus mean when He said:

> *"And you shall love the Lord your God with all your heart, with all your soul, with all your mind, and with all your strength.' This is the first commandment." Mark 12:30*
> *"And the second, like it, is this: 'You shall love your neighbor as yourself…" Mark 12:31*
> **"That the most important commandments are:**
> **"To love Me, your God, above everything else, and to love your fellow man** *your neighbor* **the same way you would like to be loved.**
> **"In truth, the commandment, is only one: To love."**

My God, what did Jesus mean when He said:

> *"Go into all the world and preach the gospel to every Creature." Mark 16:15*
> *"And these signs will follow those who believe: In My name they will cast out demons; they will speak with new tongues;" Mark 16:17*
> *"they will take up serpents; and if they drink anything deadly, it will by no means hurt them; they will lay hands on the sick, and they will recover." Mark 16:18*
> **"That every person who believes, accepts and lives Jesus' teachings can accomplish all the above works."**

My God, who are these *unclean spirits* and *demons* Jesus talks about in the following verses, and why they do exist?

"And when He had called His twelve disciples to Him, He gave them power over unclean spirits, to cast them out, and to heal all kinds of sickness and all kinds of disease . . ." Matthew 10:1

"Heal the sick, cleanse lepers, raise the dead, cast out demons..." Matthew 10:8

". . . In My name they will cast out demons. . ." Mark 16:17

"My son, the *unclean spirits,* **as well the** *demons,* **are souls or spirits—the Creative Power—of certain people who during their last life on earth experienced tragic events and passed on in a dramatic way.**

"Instead of waiting to be reincarnated in the body of a new-born, these souls infiltrate a living human being in the hope of finding help and peace immediately.

"The soul of an unclean spirit or of a demon is not any different than any other soul existing in the universe.

"They are all the expression and manifestation of My essence.

"The only difference between them is the nature of the thoughts/seeds harboring in their Creative Power."

"The unclean spirit or demon's Creative Power is saturated with more negative, dangerous, deadly and destructive thoughts/seeds."

∼୨

My God, what did Jesus mean when He said:

"A disciple is not above his teacher, nor a servant above his master." Matthew 10:24

"It is enough for a disciple that he be like his teacher, and a servant like his master." Matthew 10:25
"That all human beings are equally created and are the same. Indirectly, Jesus is stating that He was not any better or any different than His disciples or any other man that is living in this world."

～๑

My God, what did Jesus mean when He said:

"A prophet is not without honor except in his own country, among his own relatives, and in his own house." Mark 6:4
"That a person who grows spiritually and becomes *Enlightened, - Prophet, -* **is not accepted by the people from his own town, as well as by his own family members."**

"My God, why would family members and friends do that?"
"Because of their ignorance, My son."

"My God, would You please explain?"
"My son, most people don't understand that I am Energy and that they are the expression and manifestation of My Energy, and that they are endowed with the same attributes that I am.

"Most people believe:

- **That I am an individual;**
- **That I am the only divine being that exists in the universe, capable of doing so-called miracles;**

- That I live like a king in a place called heaven;
- And that man is an inferior being under My control.

"Consequently, it is almost impossible for them to comprehend and accept that a child they saw coming into this world as a normal and common child could grow up spiritually, become *Enlightened,* and do things that most people would consider miraculous and supernatural.
"This truth is confirmed by the following verse:
"And they said, is not this Jesus, the son of Joseph, whose father and mother we know? How is it then that He says, 'I have come down from heaven?" John 6:42
"In Jesus' case, not only He was unaccepted and rejected, but He was also declared dangerous, and for that reason they crucified Him as if He were a dangerous criminal."

I was astonished!

~⟋

My God, what did Jesus mean when He said:

"Assuredly, I say to you, whatever you bind on earth will be bound in heaven, and whatever you loose on earth will be loosed in heaven." Matthew 18:18
"That whatever the will and the mind of man conceive in the form of thoughts *whatever you bind or loose on earth* will be executed by the Omnipotence of My Creative Power *The heaven that dwells within man."*

~⟋

What did Jesus mean when He said:

"… just as the Son of Man did not come to be served, but to serve…"
Matthew 20:28
That the main purpose of humankind *the Son of Man* **is not to be flattered** *served*, **but to help** *serve* **his fellow man."**

~⁀

What did Jesus mean when He said:

"Put your sword in its place, for all who take the sword will perish by the sword." Matthew 26:52
"That whatever are the nature of man's actions, in due time, he will experience exactly the same thing. He said that, to prevent more negative experiences"

~⁀

My God, why, when the Pharisees asked Jesus,…*"Where is Your Father."*
John 8:19 …Jesus answered:

"You know neither Me nor My Father. If you had known Me, you would have known My Father also." John 8:19
"Because Jesus knew that I, God, am not an individual as commonly believed;
"And because He knew that I express Myself in every being that exists in the world, including Jesus.
"This is the reason that Jesus said: *If you had known Me, you would have known My Father also." John 8:19*

~⁀

My God, what did Jesus mean when He said:

> *"...If you abide in My word, you are My disciples indeed."*
> *John 8:31*
> *"And you shall know the truth, and the truth shall make you free."*
> *John 8:32*
> **"That is it by believing and living Jesus' teachings** *abide*
> *in My word,* **that man can learn the** *truth* **about Me and**
> **him.**
> **"And that it is the knowledge of that** *truth* **that sets man free**
> **from the bondage of his ignorance and limitation** *...and the*
> *truth shall make you free....* **and that will allow him to progress**
> **spiritually and eventually join Me—***The life***—at the moment**
> **of his trespass."**

In different words can also be said:

> **"That whoever believes and lives Jesus teachings will become**
> **attuned with the Omniscience of my Creative Power within,**
> **from where they will perceive the truth about Me, about them**
> **and about all creation, freeing themselves from the limitation**
> **imposed by man's ignorance."**

~♪

My God, what did Jesus mean when He said:

> *"An eye for an eye and a tooth for a tooth." Matthew 5:38*
> **"That whatever man does to others—good of bad—in time**
> **the same will be done to him."**

~♪

My God, was Jesus a unique and special divine being, as we have been taught to believe, or was He a common person, similar to any other man who comes into this world?

"My son, after all the things I allowed you to perceive, you should know that Jesus was indeed a common person, not any different from any other person who lives on the face of the earth.
"The only difference between Jesus and other people is that Jesus, in the course of His life, was able to learn and understand the following:

- **That man is not what he seems to be to the eyes and beliefs of most people: A helpless creature at the mercy of the apparent arcane and mysterious forces of My will and nature;**
- **That man is indeed the expression and manifestation of My Divine essence and nature;**
- **That man is one with Me;**
- **That man is My Divine creature;**
- **That man is Divine;**
- **That man is able to accomplish any task or anything he put his mind to.**

"Man's greatest enemy is his ignorance in not understanding who he truly is and his lack of awareness that he controls, and is responsible at all times for his life, his destiny and his experiences, good and bad."

"My son, it is for all the above reasons that Jesus, up to the last moment of His life, in the attempt to help His fellow man, dedicated all His time teaching what He had learned and what He knew."

My God, if the truth is universal, constant and eternal, and can only be perceived exclusively and directly from the Omniscience of Your Divine Creative Power dwelling in man, why is there a difference between the terms that Jesus used to express the truth and the terms used by You to make me perceive the same truth?

"My son, as you know, people throughout the world make use of specific words, expressions, and structures peculiar to their own tongue. The sum of these features, as used in speech, gives origin to and constitutes the spoken language of a given people at a given time in history."

"When man prays, he expresses himself through the words and expressions peculiar to his own language. Hence, in order for Me to reply to his prayers, I have to respond in that particular tongue; otherwise he would not be able to understand Me. That, My son, is the reason that truth is often expressed and perceived through different words, terms, and connotations."

My God, what is the message that the Apostle John is trying to convey with the following verse:

"No one has seen God at any time. The only begotten Son, who is in the bosom of the Father, He has declared Him." John 1:18
"My son, the verse, has two messages.
"The first one, is that nobody can say they have seen Me at any time.

"The second one is that Jesus is My only Son *The only begotten Son.*

"Now, while the message expressed in the first part expresses the truth, the message expressed on the second part does not represent the truth, because as you already know, every human being who comes into the world, is My son, My *begotten Son.*"

"My God, I believe that what You are allowing me to perceive is the truth, but why did John express it the way He did?
"Because He never fully and truly understood the truth of Jesus' teachings."

"How can we prove that?"
"By John's own words, My son."

"My God, would You be more specific, please?"
"In the beginning of chapter one, verse three, the Apostle John, states:
All things were made through Him, and without Him nothing was made that was made." John 1:3
"Then in verse eighteen states that Jesus is My only son, *the only begotten Son*—per se that only Jesus is My Divine son.
"These two different statements prove that John did not quite understood the essence of Jesus' teachings.
"This is why in verse eighteen, he states, *The only begotten Son, who is in the bosom of the Father, He has declared Him,* leading people to believe that Jesus was indeed My only Divine son, *the only begotten Son."*

"My son, Jesus was well aware that He was not *the only begotten Son,* and that all humanity is My *begotten Son.* He attested to that when He addressed Me as the Father of Mankind in the Lord's Prayer—*Our father....*"

"Jesus knew that He was not a superior being, but He was a common human being, and that the only difference between Him and other people was awareness of the truth, and the fact He already had achieved Enlightenment.

"Jesus was well aware that anyone has the potential to become like Him, as stated on the following verse:

"… Most assuredly, I say to you, he who believes in Me, the works that I do he will do also; and greater works than these he will do…" John 14:12

~~~

After this perception, I thought:

"Could Jesus have been any more specific that He is not any different than any other man, and that every human being is equally created and that whoever believes in Him—meaning that whoever practices His teachings—will reach *Spiritual Enlightenment,* and whoever reaches *Spiritual Enlightenment* will do the works that He (Jesus) was doing and can do even greater works than the ones He did?"

While I was thinking that, I perceived the following:

"What you are thinking, My son, is the truth, and that truth is proved by the works done by many *Enlightened* people who belonged to different religions and who came before or after Jesus."

"My son, you must understand, remember, and recognize that every man who comes into the world is equally created, he is the materialization and manifestation of the essence of My nature, My Energy, he is one with Me, he is

My son, *My begotten son,* **and he is** *in the bosom of Me,* **the Father."**

~

After these perceptions, my inquiries continued, and I asked:

"My God, why did Jesus say to His disciples that He was empowering them when He already knew that the Omnipotence and the Omniscience of Your Creative Power was already within them as part of the makeup of their beings?"

"And when He had called His twelve disciples to Him, He gave them power over unclean spirits, to cast them out, and to heal all kinds of sickness and all kinds of disease." Matthew 10:1

"Heal the sick, cleanse lepers, raise the dead, cast out demons." Matthew 10:8

"And why did He teach that when they wanted a favor from You, to ask in His name, when He already knew that it was the Omnipotence and the Omniscience of Your Creative Power within that does the work?"

"Most assuredly, I say to you, whatever you ask the Father in My name He will give you." John 16:23

"My son, before I will let you perceive the reasons Jesus said that He empowered His disciples and told them to ask Me favors in His name, it is important that you know, and understand that His disciples were having difficulty in fully understanding the nature of His teachings."

"The disciples had a hard time understanding that the creation, including the body of every man who comes into the world, is the materialization and manifestation of the essence of My nature, My Energy...

"All things were made through Him, and without Him nothing was made that was made." John 1:3
... and that every human being is created equally."

"What they truly believed was that Jesus was indeed My only Divine Son, equal to Me, and the only one in the world to be endowed with all My Divine power, and the only one who could do what is known as miracles.
"The disciple Simon Peter proves this when He said:
"... we have come to believe and know that You are the Christ, the Son of the living God." John 6:69
"The disciples believed they couldn't do the works that Jesus did.

"Confronted with this dilemma, Jesus had the idea to tell his disciples that He empowered them, hoping to make them believe that because now they were empowered by Him, they could do also the works that He was doing.

"It was a stratagem to induce the disciples to pray, to ask and to act.

"Jesus knew that if they would begin to do so, their prayers, and the object of their desires in the form of thoughts/seeds, once sowed in My Creative Power within them, were going to be manifested in their life in the form of experiences.

"Those experiences, in time, would allow the disciples to perceive and understand the truth that He was teaching.

"The reason why Jesus told His disciples to ask Me favors in His name, was the same that induced Jesus to tell the disciples that He empowered them, a stratagem to induce the disciples to pray, to ask and to act."

"My God, could You be more explicit?"

"My son, Jesus knew that the disciples truly were convinced and believed that Jesus was indeed My only Divine son, and that I would never say no to someone who asked Me favors in His name.
"There again, I will repeat what I said before: It was a stratagem to induce the disciples to pray, to ask and to act."

My God, how should we see the disciples?

"As people who never truly understood Jesus' teachings and message!
"This truth is proved by the fact that, after Jesus' death, the disciples, instead of dedicating their time and energy to teaching how to live Jesus' doctrine, concentrated and dedicated all their effort to the exaltation and glorification of Jesus as a Divinity to be worshiped.
"The consequence of that is that two thousand years after Jesus' supreme sacrifice on the cross, people are still living in ignorance and suffering."

After the above perceptions, I asked: My God, how should we see Jesus?

- **"As an Enlightened man who understood My true nature, the true nature of man, how We are related, and how We work together in unison, as proved by His teachings and His works."**

"Therefore I say to you, do not worry about your life, what you will eat or what you will drink; nor about your body, what you will put on." Matthew 6:25
"But seek first the kingdom of God and His righteousness, and all these things shall be added to you." Matthew 6:33

- **As a common and humble man;**
- **As a brother;**
- **And as a man who was equal to everybody.**

"Jesus proved that He was a *common and humble man,* **when he washed and wiped His disciple's feet.**
"After that, He poured water into a basin and began to wash the disciples' feet, and to wipe them with the towel with which He was girded." John 13:5

"Jesus proved that we are all *brothers* **when He said:**
"And He stretched out his hand toward His disciples and said, Here are my mother and my brothers!" Matthew 12:49
"For whoever does the will of my Father in heaven is My brother, and sister, and mother." Matthew 12:50

"Jesus proved that we are all *equal* **when He said:**
"A disciple is not above his teacher, nor a servant above his master." Matthew 10:24
"It is enough for a disciple that he be like his teacher, and a servant like his master." Matthew 10:25

At this perception with astonishment I said: Wahoo!

My God, how we should see Man?"

"As the being who he truly is, a Divine being made by the essence of My Divine nature: My Divine Light, My Divine Energy. "Man should also be seen as a triune being who carries within him the trinity of My divine essence and nature: the will, the mind and the Omnipotence and Omniscience of My Creative Power."

After this perception, the only thing that I was able to say was: Wahoo!

My God, can You help me to understand, why generally speaking, people from all over the world, from all the times, have developed the tendency to worship You?

"Because they believe that I am a superior being living outside of the sphere of their existence, and they are inferior beings living under My direct control. "Because they don't understand that they are the expression and manifestation of My essence, My Energy, and that we are one and the same."

My God, can You help me understand who is a true Prophet?

"A person who has reached true Enlightenment." "My God, why does a person who reaches *Enlightenment* is called *Prophet?*" **"Because he is able to understand the truth about Me, him and the creation;**

"And because he is capable of using consciously and at will the Omnipotence and the Omniscience of My Creative Power within him to accomplish things that the average person considers supernatural and miraculous."

My God, why do people also worship the so-called Prophets and Saints?

- "Because they believe they are *superior divine beings*, capable of acting as a liaison between Me and them;
- "Because they believe that I would easily ignore and deny their request for favors, but I would not ignore and deny the request of a Prophet or a Saint;
- "And because, they think and believe it will make it easier for them to get favors from Me."

One night as I lay in bed resting, I visualized the interior of the little church *dell'Immacolata* in Via Roma, in Ribera, where I was baptized and confirmed, where I began to learn about Jesus and God, and where, until I emigrated, I went to the Holy Mass.

Then my vision continued to tour some of the most magnificent churches that I have had the privilege and the joy to visit, such as Saint Peter in Rome, Santa Maria delle Grazie in Florence, the Duomo in Milan, and San Joseph in Montreal.

While I was absorbed in remembering those beautiful edifices, I formulated the following question:

"My God, what is the proper way to see a church—as an edifice?"

Here is what I perceived:

"My son, before I let you perceive the object of your desire, you need to answer My questions.

"Can you explain with your own words what a school is?"
"A school is a place, an edifice, where people called students go to learn things."

"Well said, My son!

"Now, can you explain with your own words, what represents in your opinion an edifice called a church?"

After I reflected for a while, I noticed that I didn't have a clear idea and a specific opinion on how to describe what represented an edifice called a church, so I answered in the following way:

"My God, I believe that at this moment You already know that I don't know what truly represents for me an edifice called a church.
"What I can say is what I have been taught, and what I have been reading and hearing.
"An edifice called a church is Your home, the place where You live, My God.
"It is also the place where people go to worship You, and go to perform rites for You, with the hope that You'll be pleased.
"In return for their devotions, their prayers and the performance of their rites, they expect that You will be merciful and that You will grant their wishes, Your protection, Your love and Your grace."

"My son, what you have been taught to believe—which is what most people also believe—is incorrect.

"The edifice called a church should be looked upon the same way as an edifice called a school, with the exact same function: "A place where people should go to learn the truth about the spiritual message of their enlightened leaders: Jesus, Mohammed, Buddha, etc."

"The learning of their messages should bring awareness and understanding about the followings:

- Who I am;
- Who man is;
- How we are related and connected;
- How we work in unison;
- How to use consciously the Omnipotence and the Omniscience of My Divine Creative Power that dwells within man;
- And how to have a life full of true joy, peace and success."

"The belief that an edifice called a church is My home or the place where I live is incorrect.
"As you already know, My son, the essence of My nature is Energy, and I express Myself through all creation.
"My Home is in every little or big thing that exists in the universe, include man's body."
"All things were made through Him, and without Him nothing was made that was made." John 1:3
"Do you not know that you are the temple of God and that the Spirit of God dwells in you?" 1 Corinthians 1:16
"Or do you not know that your body is the temple of the Holy Spirit who is in you, whom you have from God, and you are not your own?" 1 Corinthians 6:19

"My son, considering the fact that I am not an individual, worshiping Me, praising Me and making offerings and rites to honor Me and to please Me as an individual is a waste of time, because it does not allow Me to respond to the pleas of the people.

"What makes Me answer man's plea, and what makes man's wishes come true, is formation of thoughts/seeds of his desires."

"Most of the time, when people worship Me, perform rites in My honor, or praise Me, they are not expressing the object of their desire;
"Therefore, they are not creating anything in the form of thoughts/seeds.

"Now if a person does not create anything with his mind in the form of thoughts/seeds, he does not transmit anything to the Omnipotence and the Omniscience of My Creative Power that dwells in him.
"Consequently, My Creative Power has nothing to manifest in his life.

"This is the reason why people who continuously worship Me or praise Me or perform rites in My honor rarely see their pleas answered, giving them the impression that I don't listen to their pleas and that I don't care for them.

"The process could be compared to a farmer who pretends to obtain a crop from the soil of his farm by solely worshiping, praising and doing rites to the soil without sowing in the soil the seeds of the plants that he wants to grow. "

After the above perception, I asked:

"My God, could You give me a practical example that is easy to follow that shows how the Omnipotence and the Omniscience of Your Creative Power that dwells in man responds to the action of his will and of his mind?"
"My son, a practical example of it is the way a vehicle—such a car or a truck—responds to the command of its driver."

"As the will and the mind of the driver chooses the road in which the vehicle is going to travel;
"In the same fashion the will and the mind of a person, consciously or unconsciously, chooses the journey of his life.

"As the vehicle responds continuously to the direction imposed by the driver;
"In the same fashion the Omnipotence and the Omniscience of My Creative Power within man responds and manifests continuously what will and mind (of man) creates in the form of thoughts/seeds.

"As the vehicle does not have the ability to choose the road on which to travel and needs the cooperation and the guidance of the driver;
"In the same fashion the Omnipotence and the Omniscience of My Creative Power within man does not have the ability to manifest in a person's life anything without the cooperation and the guidance of the will and the mind of man.

"As the driver needs to focus all the time on his driving to avoid steering the vehicle off the road;

"In the same fashion man, to avoid unpleasant experiences, needs to control at all the times what the will and the mind are creating in the form of thoughts/seeds.

"As going off the road will create a bumpy ride that could lead the vehicle to crash and to put an end to the trip;
"In the same fashion, the creation of negative thoughts/seeds by the will and the mind will create negative experiences that could lead to the end of a person's journey.

"As the vehicle follows at all time the direction of the driver;
"In the same fashion the Omnipotence and the Omniscience of My Creative Power that dwells in man follow and execute to perfection the orders imposed on them by what has been created and conceived in the form of thoughts/seeds by man's will and mind.

"As the driver, to have a safe and pleasant journey, must focus his attention at all the time to keep the vehicle on the road;
"In the same fashion a person to have a life full of joy, peace and success, must continually monitor and control the actions of his will and mind and make sure that they are continuously creating and conceiving only good and positive thoughts/seeds."

Wahoo! I was amazed and very thankful!

My God, why did Jesus say:

"... It is to your advantage that I go away; for if I do not go away, the Helper will not come to you; but if I depart, I will send Him to you." John 16:7

"Because He was aware His disciples were having a hard time understanding, accepting and living His teachings. Consequently, instead of relying upon themselves, they continuously relied on Jesus' assistance.

"This is what was preventing the disciples from becoming in tune with the Omnipotence and the Omniscience of My Creative Power *the Helper* within them."

"If Jesus were to leave *but if I depart*, the disciples could no longer rely on His help. "That would have forced them to pray deeply and earnestly.

"And, as you know, My son, by your own experiences, deep and earnest prayer is what put man in touch with the Omnipotence and the Omniscience of My Creative Power within *the Helper, the Teacher* learning all there is to learn about the apparent mystery of life.

"This knowledge is what frees man from the bondages of the limitation imposed by his ignorance."

~~~

My God, what did Jesus mean when He said:

"However, when He, the Spirit of truth, has come, He will guide you into all truth; ...and He will tell you things to come." John 16:13

"My son, to understand the message of the above verse, first you need to understand that the *Spirit of truth* that Jesus refers to is in reality the Omniscience of My Creative Power within', the only true *Teacher* of man.

"The message is:

"When a person is in tune with the Omniscience of My Creative Power within *the Spirit of truth* not only he will perceive from it the truth about everything in the universe, but also he will be able to perceive events that may take place in the future *He will tell you things to come.*"

After this perception, I asked:

"My God, if *the Spirit of truth* is synonymous for the *Omniscience of Your Creative Power* and is part of the essence that forms the human body, why does Jesus say, *when He, the Spirit of truth, has come*—giving the impression that *the Spirit of truth* does not reside within and is not part of the human body?"

"My son, in the past I let you perceive that Jesus never wrote down what he believed and professed, and that what is known about His life and works has been handed down mostly by the writings attributed to John, Matthew, Mark, Luke, and Paul.

"I also let you perceive that over the centuries, these writings have gone through many transcriptions, translations, and adaptations.

"Consequently, they do not reflect precisely, word-for-word, the terms and expressions that Jesus expressed during the course of His life. In order to grasp the true message of Jesus' teachings, you cannot rely on current biblical literature and its literal interpretation, but rather you must catch the true essence and spirit of His thoughts.

"The right interpretation for the words *when He, the Spirit of truth, has come* is that when man becomes aware that the

Spirit of truth, **the** *Omniscience of My Creative Power,* **abides in the human body, from it he can perceive events that may take place in future times."**

"My God, why are You saying *events that may take place in future times* and You do not say that *will take place?"*
"Because it is not sure if those events will take place or not."

"Why is it not sure?"
"Because a person, through the use of his will and mind, has the power to change the course of those events."

~~

After this perception, the word *clairvoyance* came to my mind, so I asked:

"My God, can you let me perceive what *clairvoyance* is?"
"*Clairvoyance* **is the capacity of a person who in the past or present life has evolved spiritually to the point that he is able to synchronize himself consciously and at will with the Omniscience of My Creative Power within, perceiving events that happened in the past or that may be happening in the near or distant future."**

"My God, is there any substantial difference between what is known as *clairvoyance* and the ability of a person, as Jesus said, *to perceive from the Omniscience of Your Creative Power within* events that may take place in the future? *He will tell you things to come."*
"No, My son. Both express the same thing and the same truth. Jesus stated and proved on different occasions that he who believes in Him and His teachings will be able to learn to enjoy this privilege."

"My God, why are many people afraid of people who claim to be clairvoyant?"
"Because of their ignorance, My son."

~~⌐

My God, why did Jesus say:

"My doctrine is not Mine, but His who sent Me." John 7:16
"Because Jesus was well aware that His teachings *His doctrine* **was inspired by the Omniscience of My Creative Power dwelling in Him** *His who sent Me.*
"The same way that you've experienced. As you now know, it is the Omniscience of My Creative Power that dwells in you that is allowing you to perceive the answers to all your questions."

~~⌐

My God, what did Jesus mean when He said:

"But you, do not be called 'Rabbi'; for one is your Teacher, the Christ, and you are all brethren." Matthew 23:8
"And do not be called teacher; for One is your Teacher, the Christ." Matthew 23:10
"That the only true teacher of man is the *Christ*—**the Omniscience of My Creative Power that dwells in him**—**the only universal source that allows to perceives the truth about all the apparent mystery of the world.**

~~⌐

My God, why did Jesus say:

"I can of Myself do nothing..." John 5:30
"Because He was aware that all His works were performed by the Omnipotence and the Omniscience of My Creative Power that dwelt in Him, and not by Him as Jesus, as the people believed and believe even today."

~♫

My God, what did Jesus mean when He said:

" ... I have come that they may have life, and that they may have it more abundantly..." John 10:10
"That He came into the world to show the truth about who I am, who is man, how we are connected, and how we work in unison, so people can enjoy life better, be happier and be more successful. *...and that they may have it more abundantly..." John 10:10*

~♫

My God, what did Jesus mean when He said:

"I have come as a light into the world, that whoever believes in Me should not abide in darkness..." John 12:46
"That He came into the world to explain the truth about My nature, man's nature, and how we are connected together, so people wouldn't have to stay *abide* **anymore in ignorance** *darkness.***"**

~♫

My God, why did Philip say to Jesus:

"…Lord, show us the Father, and it is sufficient for us." John 14:8
"Because He, as well the other disciples *us*, believed that I am an individual, living in a place of the universe called heaven, from where I control My creation in the same fashion a monarch controls his kingdom.
"Because of this belief, they thought that I could be introduced like a person is introduced to another person.

"It is another demonstration that Philip, the other disciples, and many people of today have difficulty in understanding and accepting that I, God, do not have a specific form with which I can be introduced, and that I express Myself through the essence of the body of every person that lives in the world, Jesus included."

"The above truth is confirmed by Jesus in the following verses:
"Have I been with you so long, and yet you have not known Me, Philip? He who has seen Me has seen the Father, so how can you say, "Show us the Father?" John 14:9
"Do you not believe that I am in the Father, and the Father in Me? The words that I speak to you I do not speak on My own authority; but the Father who dwells in Me does the works." John 14:10
"Believe Me that I am in the Father and the Father in Me, or else believe Me for the sake of the works themselves." John 14:11
"Most assuredly, I say to you, he who believes in Me, the works that I do he will do also; and greater works than these he will do…" John 14:12

"And these signs will follow those who believe: In My name they will cast out demons; they will speak with new tongues;" Mark 16:17

"They will take up serpents; and if they drink anything deadly, it will by no means hurt them; they will lay hands on the sick, and they will recover." Mark 16:18

~~~

My God, why did Jesus say:

"For assuredly, I say to you, whoever says to this mountain, Be removed and be cast into the sea, and does not doubt in his heart, but believes that those things he says will be done, he will have whatever he says." Mark 11:23

"therefore I say to you, whatever things you ask when you pray, believe that you receive them, and you will have them." Mark 11:24

"To make His disciples aware that for a person to see his prayers answered, he needs to believe they will be answered.

"Whatever things you ask when you pray, believe that you receive them, and you will have them". Mark 11:24

"And to warn them that the Omnipotence of My Creative Power within man does not have the ability to discern the difference between what is right from what is wrong in the eyes of man.

"That the task, the job of the Omnipotence of My Creative Power within is to execute and manifest whatever is created

by the will and the mind of man in the form of thoughts/ seeds, good or bad."

"For assuredly, I say to you, whoever says to this mountain, 'Be removed and be cast into the sea', and does not doubt in his heart, but believes that those things he says will be done, he will have whatever he says." Mark 11:23

~~~

While I was savoring my learning, there came to my mind the episode when Jesus' mother and brothers went to look for him.

"While he was still talking to the multitudes, behold, His mother and brothers stood outside, seeking to speak with Him." Matthew 12:46
"Then one said to Him, 'Look, Your mother and Your brothers are standing outside, seeking to speak with You." Matthew 12:47
"But he answered and said to the one who told him, 'Who is my mother, and who are my brothers?" Matthew 12:48
"And He stretched out his hand toward His disciples and said, 'Here are my mother and my brothers!" Matthew 12:49
"For whoever does the will of my Father in heaven is My brother, and sister, and mother." Matthew 12:50

Once more, not being able to understand Jesus' behavior, I asked:

"My God, why did Jesus ignore His mother and His brothers?"
"Because He was upset with them."

"My God, how could Jesus get upset with His mother and His brothers, when the core of His teachings were forgiveness and love?"

"Because even though He had already reached Enlightenment, He still was a common human being, and as such, He was subject to the same emotions of a human being."

"My God, I think that I understand what You allow me to perceive, but so I don't misinterpret the perception, could You be more specific?"

"My son, before I answer your question, I want you to answer My questions, and then, if needed, I will let you perceive the reasons that induced Jesus to act the way He did."

"My son, can you describe what you wish for your children?"

"That they grow healthy and honest; that they go to school; that they will choose a good profession; and that they will marry the girl of their dreams so they'll have children and their own family."

"My son, can you describe how you'd feel if one of your children left home and you didn't know if he would ever be back, and if you would be able to see him ever again?"

"I would be sad, my God, and my heart would weep."

"My son, how would you react if your son came home after many years, as healthy as could be and single?"

"My God, I don't think that I would be able to describe my joy and my happiness."

"My son, after your initial joy over his return, what would you expect from him?"

"That he find a job, get married and start his own family."

"What would be your reaction if he told you he wasn't interested in finding a job, that he wasn't interested in finding a wife, and that he wasn't interested in having his own family?"
"I would be very disappointed."

"My son, what would you think if your son told you that he is the son of God (that he is My son), that he is equal to Me, and that he and I are the same?"
"That he had lost his mind."

"Why?"
"Because I saw him grow for nine months inside his mother's womb and because I witnessed his birth."

"So you wouldn't agree with Him when he says that he is My son, that he and I are one and that he is equal to Me?"
"That is correct, My God."

"My son, this is exactly what did happen between Jesus and His family."

"When Jesus, after seventeen years, went back home, Joseph and Mary were very happy to see Him.
"However, after being back for a while, Jesus refused to work, and He began to state and preach that I, God, was His father, that He was part of Me, that He was equal to Me, and that He and I are one and the same.

"His parents, incapable of understanding Him, rejected His claims, thinking and believing that He was out of His mind.

"Mary and Joseph's reaction created friction between them and Jesus to the point that Jesus, frustrated for not being understood and accepted, decided to leave home, breaking their relationship.

"When Mary learned where He was preaching, accompanied by Her other sons, went to look for Him hoping for a reconciliation, but Jesus ignored them.

"When the man brought to Jesus' attention their presence, He said:

"… Who is my mother, and who are my brothers?" Matthew 12:48

" As to say: who cares about them!

" And He stretched out his hand toward His disciples and said, 'Here are my mother and my brothers!" Matthew 12:49

"For whoever does the will of my Father in heaven is My brother, and sister, and mother." Matthew 12:50

"As to say: the people who understand and accept Me are My brother, and sister, and mother.

"My son, Jesus' behavior was the consequence of the misunderstanding and the rejection by His family of His teachings and His beliefs."

After all the above perceptions, I felt that most of the questions that had plagued me for most of my life have been answered. Deep in my heart, I felt a relief and a joy that I never experienced before.

Finally, I could say without any shadow of doubt that I understood the essence of Jesus's doctrine, as well His message of love for mankind.

One day, while working, as I was savoring my new understanding, the following question popped into my mind:

"How was it possible that all the religious leaders of Christianity that I knew, in spite of the fact they had spent most of their lives studying the sacred scriptures, never perceived the *truth* the way I was allowed to perceive?"

After I debated this question for quite long time and being incapable of finding an answer that would satisfy my inquiry, I posed the question to God within, or per se to the Omniscience of the Creative power of God Within Me.

Here is the response to the question:

"My son, the reason why most of the religious leaders of Christianity—as well as people who have dedicated their lives to studying the Sacred Scriptures—never understood who truly I am, as well as who truly is man, is due to the following reasons:

- "They never understood the fact that I am Light (Energy);
- "That all creation is the manifestation and materialization of My Light (Energy);
- "That man is also the manifestation of My Light (Energy);
- "That he is part of Me, and that we are one and the same.

"Also My son, what prevents them from perceiving what you have perceived is the fact that they truly believe that I am an individual, a superior being, living in some place in the sky, from where I govern and control all creation in the same fashion a monarch, a king, or a political dictator governs his kingdom.

"They think and believe that they are inferior beings whose most important task in order to gain My favors is to adulate, serve and please Me with the performance of ceremonies, offerings and rites, just like peoples do with a king.

"Failure to do so means that I become angry and I will punish them severely.

"Consequently, with their mindset in those beliefs, when they are reading the Scriptures, they do so mechanically; they don't reflect and pay attention to the meaning of the words they are reading, thereby missing the true message My words convey."

After this perception, the name of my manuscript, *Journey of a Healer,* came to my mind.

I still was concerned that people would be misled, making them think that I was the one who was performing the healing, when I was fully and perfectly aware that the healing is performed by the Omnipotence of the Creative Power of God within, so I began to pray for clarification.

Here is what I perceived:

"My son, the reason why the title *Journey of a Healer* is appropriate and is not going to mislead your readers is because you are not who you think you are, the body that in this life is identified with the name Paolo Ficara.

"As you already know, you are the manifestation of the infinity of My Essence and Nature: My Light, My Energy.

"It is for this reason that in *Journey of a Healer* you should not see the *journey* of you as Paolo Ficara, but you should see the *journey* **of the Omnipotence and Omniscience of My Creative Power within you, that as you know, is the true healer of all spiritual and physical imperfections."**

"All things were made through Him, and without Him nothing was made that was made." John 1:3

"Do you not know that you are the temple of God and that the Spirit of God dwells in you?" 1 Corinthians 1:16

"Or do you not know that your body is the temple of the Holy Spirit who is in you, whom you have from God, and you are not your own?" 1 Corinthian 6:19

"Do you not know that your bodies are member of Christ?" 1 Corinthian 6:15

"But you, do not be called 'Rabbi'; for One is your Teacher, the Christ, and you are all brethren." Matthew 23:8

"And do not be called teachers; for One is your Teacher, the Christ." Matthew 23:10

~~~

After these perceptions, I began to think of the name that I was inspired to give to the Center, as well as to the format of the logo that represents it.

As the reader may remember, at the time I felt the name as well as the logo was appropriate, even though I was not able to understand the reasons.

Infused by a great desire to understand, I began to pray, knowing that my prayer would be answered.

Here is the sum of what I perceived:

"My son, *Universal Center for Self-Enlightening and Self-Healing,* **the name that I inspired you to give to the center, as well the** *logo,* **are appropriate, because they portray in a graphic way,**

the nature of My essence, the nature of the essence of man, and the path that man needs to follow."

At this perception I asked: "My God, how is that? Can You be more specific?"

"My son:

- **The globe and the silhouette (man), symbolize My Creation, through which My Light, My Energy, - the essence of My Nature - expresses itself, and takes form and shape;**
- **The Light, the Energy, surrounding the silhouette (man), is a reminder to mankind that his essence and nature is Light, Energy: My Light, My Energy, and that he is made in My image and likeness and not the other way around;**
- **The glow of light at the center of the forehead of the silhouette (man), symbolizes the *seat*, *the center*, of the *will* and of the *mind*, the Creative branch of My essence;**
- **The glow of light at the center of the chest symbolizes the *seat*, per se the *center*, wherein abides the Omniscience and the Omnipotence of My Creative Power within man, the executive branch of My essence.**
- **The silhouette (man), in the meditative posture, symbolizes: *Meditation* and *Prayer*.**

"The message is:

- **That all creation, including man's body, is Energy, My Energy;**
- **And that It is through *Meditation* and *prayer*, that man can get in tune with:**

"The *Omniscience* of My Creative Power within him, that as you already know, is the *source*, per se the *sit*, the *center*

of My knowledge; the only true *universal teacher* of man, from where he perceives and learns the truth about all the mystery of My nature. This stand for: *Self-Taught, per se Self-Enlightening."*

"And the *Omnipotence* of My Creative Power within, the *source*, the *seat*, the *center* of the power of My divine essence, through which, man can heal himself and others from all the spiritual and physical imperfections.
It stands for: *Self-Healing!*

"All the above My son, is *Universal*. It is *Universal,* because is the same for every human being who comes into the world.

"My son, *Universal Center for Self-Enlightenment and Self-Healing*, symbolizes also, the *Physical Place of the Center*—any place or building, - where people meet to learn the teachings of the Enlightened, and where they can share, their experiences and their knowledge, with the only purpose to help each other to grow spiritually.

"I remind you, that the center should not be a place to *worship Me*, instead should be a place where they can learn about Me.

"As you already know, *worshiping Me is worthless* and *a waste of time*, while the knowledge of who I am, and how to contact Me, allows man to get his prayers answered, his goals achieved and in time consciously aware of our unity, and oneness.

"I hope My son, that now you understand why, name and logo - *Universal Center for Self-Enlightening and Self-Healing*, - are appropriate."

At this point, what can I say?

Once more, I was happy, astonished, and overwhelmed, by my perceptions, and very thankful!

~

While I was contemplating on all the above perceptions, I began to think very strongly about the events that led to the passing of my brother Gioacchino.

The pain caused by his unexpected departure is still burning very strong inside me.

One of the things that I was incapable of understanding is the fact that although he felt the healing energy of God, and he improved, his improvements were only temporary.

I never stop asking myself why. Why? Why? Why didn't he get another chance to live?

Hoping to bring some light into this painful experience, I formulated the following prayer:

> *"My God, in this moment, I know that You know the pain I am suffering in my heart.*
> *"It is for this reason that I pray that You will help me understand why, although Gioacchino perceived Your healing energy and felt better, his improvements were only temporary, and why he didn't get another chance."*

After a while, I perceived:

"Because it was time for him to return home, My son."

"Why was it time?"

"My son, even with the degree of your spiritual development, it is almost impossible for you to understand the complexity of the events that cause the passing on of a human being."

"My God, I am perfectly aware that my spiritual make up at the moment doesn't allow me to perceive and understand a lot of things. However, I truly believe that if You want, like many other time in the past, You can find the way to allow me to perceive the basics of the object of my desires."

Here is the sum of my perceptions:

"My son, I remind you, that the essence of man is energy, My energy; and that My energy is the life of life, is eternal, lives forever and never dies.

"I also remind you that the understanding that man has of death—as the end of the cycle of life—is wrong. It is wrong, because man, in being the manifestation of My energy, is eternal and lives forever.

"My son, what man calls death, in true reality is only a change of form, from visible to invisible, just like the water, when the liquid becomes vapor.

"The evaporated water, under the different conditions of temperature, returns in the form of water, snow, ice or hail;
"Likewise, as I let you perceive in the past, the spirit of man returns again to fulfill another part in the stage of My Creation;
"The process continues until he become consciously aware of My true entity, of his true entity, how we work in unison as one, and until he becomes Enlightened.

"My son, in regard to the reason why Gioacchino was allowed to perceive My healing energy while the two of you were praying together was to prove to you both that your love for each other was above the differences that from time to time arose between you.

"The reason Gioacchino wasn't healed is because that would have delayed his passing on, and with it, the spiritual progress of his soul."

"For this reason, you should stop grieving, and you should pray for his spiritual development."

After these perceptions, although I am still missing my brother immensely, deep inside I felt more at peace with myself and more willing to accept the harsh reality of life, knowing that as drastic and painful as some of life's events are, they lead us to the understanding of who truly is man and God, how we can experience Divine Love, and how we can reach eternal life.

CHAPTER 52

Jesus' Most Important Message
Jesus' Most Valuable Message
and Meaning of Faith
Jesus' Greatest Achievement
Explanation of the Most Important Commandments

One evening as I was comfortably lying on the sofa absentmindedly watching TV, the following questions surfaced in my mind:

- **What was Jesus' greatest achievement?**
- **What was Jesus' most important message?**
- **Why, according to Jesus, were the most important commandments of God's divine law to love God with all our heart, soul, and mind, and to love our neighbors as ourselves?**

After mulling over these questions for a few days, I realized that it was impossible for me to answer them. Consequently, I formulated the following prayer:

"My God, everything Jesus tried to convey to His followers through word and deed seems extremely far-reaching, so it's impossible for me to classify His messages in terms of importance and thus find answers to my queries.

"Being aware that I cannot resolve this problem, I ask for your merciful help."

Here is the sum of my perceptions.

Jesus' Greatest Achievement

My son, Jesus' greatest achievement was having made known the *truth* and having given witness to that same *truth*.

"My God, what is the *truth*?" I asked.

- That the essence of My nature is made of Light, Energy;
- That the essence of My Light, My Energy was, is, and shall always be;
- That the Light, the Energy, has no cause, while at the same time is the cause of everything that exists in the universe;
- And that the Divine essence of My Creative Power is an intrinsic part of the Light, of My Energy.

"My God, how did Jesus bear *witness* to the *truth*?"

"By showing and proving that He understood the nature of My true essence, the true essence of man, and the true relationship existing between man and myself.

"By admitting and teaching that the works He performed and the essence of His teaching were not His, but Mine, since they were performed by the Omnipotence and the Omniscience of my Creative Power that dwelled in Him.

"And by doing all the things man can do when he's attuned to the Omnipotence and Omniscience of my Creative Power dwelling in him:

- Healing the sick;
- Restoring life to the dead;
- Multiplying fish and bread;
- Changing water to wine;
- Causing a fig tree to wither;
- Knowing the future *(clairvoyance)*,... and so on.

"My son, Jesus' truth is also proved by the works performed by all other humans who have undertaken the path of spirituality and have reached Enlightenment, regardless of the place or time in which they lived and the religious affiliations to which they claimed to be part of.

Jesus' Most Important Message

My son, the most important message conveyed by Jesus is:

- His affirmation that He was My Divine son—the expression of My essence—that He and I are one and the same.

"I and My Father are one." John 10:30
"...believe the works, that you may know and believe that the Father is in Me, and I in Him." John 10:38

- His affirmation, that all people coming into the world are also My Divine children, one with Me, just as Jesus was, because they are also the expression and manifestation of My essence, My Light, My Energy."

"In him was life, and the life was the light of men." John 1:4
"All things were made through Him; and without Him nothing was made that was made...." John 1:3

- **And His affirmation, that anyone who has** *Faith* **in Him and believes, accepts, and practices diligently what He taught, will realize the truth about Me, about him, and the relationship existing between us. He will become Enlightened, will be able to perform the same works as Jesus, and at the moment of his trespass, will be reunited to Me for the rest of the times.**

"But as many as received Him, to them He gave the right to become children of God . . . " John 1:12

Hoping to have a clearer understanding of what *faith* truly is, I asked:

"My God, would You clarify the true essence of what is often defined as *faith*?"
"My son, *faith* **can be defined as man's effort to accept un-conditionally, information, precepts, or phenomena that are unseen, unknown, and undemonstrated to him. The word** *faith* **is synonymous with the word** *trust*.**"

Having grasped the above perceptions, I thought I fully understood the message contained therein.

At the same time, however, in order to avoid further doubts, I felt the need for practical examples, so I asked:

"My God, could You please give me some practical examples?"

"My son, whenever someone calls you for an estimate on a job, what do you ask them?"

After a brief pause, I replied, "Name, telephone number, job address, and directions to the location of the job."

"And then what do you do?"
"I make an appointment, then drive to meet the potential client at the address I have been given."

"At this point, My son, what assurance do you have that the directions provided to you will take you to the right destination?"
"I don't have any assurance, my God."

"Then why would you follow the directions?"
"Because I trust the person and because I believe the directions are correct."

"Can you tell Me now if there is any difference between affirming that you *trust* the man's information and that you have *faith* in the man's information?"
After a moment of reflection, I replied, "No, my God. In essence, the words *trust* and *faith* in this case mean and result in exactly the same action."

"Well said," replied the perception.

"Now, My son, I want you to know that *faith* and *trust*, from a religious point of view, mean exactly the same thing— accepting and scrupulously following—with unconditional *trust*—the teachings of Jesus or the teachings of any of the great spiritually-developed men or women who have populated the earth throughout history.
"Hence, My son, just as accepting and following faithfully the directions of the client will take you to the asphalt job;
"Likewise, by accepting, believing, and scrupulously and faithfully practicing the teachings of Jesus or the teachings of any Enlightened person, man will become aware of life's true

essence and nature and the things they have in common, and they will be led to Me."

Following this perception, I asked:

"My God, what is the difference between *doubt* and *faith*?"
"*Doubt* is the *wandering* of the mind. It is a temporary occurrence and it passes.

"*Faith*, on the other hand, is synonymous of *trust*, is the acceptance and the living of what man perceives instinctively from the Omniscience of My Creative Power dwelling in him, or what he may learn from others, in the form of suggestions, or teachings, *is steadfast* and *eternal.*"

"My God, how can we prove that?"
"By carefully examining the experiences and events of your own life or anyone's life."

"My God, can You help me do so?"
"My son, do you remember when you instinctively and obstinately left your native Ribera and moved to Montreal, believing that by so doing you could reunite your family in one place?
"Time proved that the *trust* or *faith* in your instinct was the right thing to do.

"Do you remember when, upon your return from James Bay, instead of using the money you had earned to invest in a business venture—as you had originally planned—you decided to follow your inner intuition, from what you then called 'the voice of the heart,' and bought the two house apartments instead?

"Once more, that *trust* or *faith* in your instinct proved to be the right thing to do.

"Do you remember when, having read for the first time about the mechanism of thought processes, you questioned their veracity?

"Then, when your son Nino was born and the doctor found the fibroma in Pina's uterus, you reconsidered your original reaction and began to pay attention to the nature of your own thoughts, which put to the test the veracity of what you had learned?
"That unconscious *trust* or *faith* in the author of that book, little by little, led you to the healing experiences, to the fruition of your youthful dreams in Ribera, and to the understanding of the apparent mystery of life.

"Do you remember when Steve—your brother Ignazio's school buddy—talked to you about Yucca Valley, and how the voice of your heart made you perceive that you had to go live there, and how you instinctively followed this perception with *faith--trust* and determination—ultimately making that town your home?
"You now have the results of that important decision. And I could go on and on.

"Do you realize, My son, that in making all these decisions and taking them to completion, you did everything instinctively by having *faith,* or by *trusting* your intuition, hoping everything would turn out for the best?

"Do you realize that every morning when you get up and face a new day, there is no guarantee what you will experience during the course of that day?

"Do you understand that the only thing spurring man to go on is *hope* and *faith-trust* in My Divine Providence, which he instinctively perceives from the Omniscience of My Creative Power that dwells in him?

"My son, do you realize that most decisions made by humans about things that they neither see nor know are based upon unconditional *faith-trust* by listening to their own instincts or by listening to other people's advice?

"Wasn't this the *faith, truth,* Jesus tried to teach his disciples?

"Wasn't this the lesson Jesus taught Thomas when the latter doubted his resurrection?
"Thomas, because thou have seen Me, you have believed. Blessed are those who have not seen, and yet have believed." John 20:29

"My God, what must one believe?"

- That the essence of My divine Creative Power dwells in man;
- That *the Heavenly Father, the Comforter, the Holy Ghost, the Voice of the Heart, the Christ, and the Creative Power,* are synonymous terms used by man to define and describe the essence of My Divine nature;
- That man's body as well as all creation, represents the temple through which I express and manifest Myself;
- And that whoever listens and lives out Jesus' teachings or the teachings of any Enlightened one—regardless of their professed religious affiliation—in due time will perceive the truth; will be able to consciously use the Divine and Infinite Omnipotence and Omniscience of My Creative Power that dwells within him; will become Enlightened, and at the moment of their trespass, will be reunited forever to My Divine Essence.

"Jesus confirms all this on the following citations:

"Then Jesus said to those Jews who believed Him: If you abide in My word you are My disciples indeed." John, 8:31

"And you shall know the truth, and the truth shall make you free." John 8:32

"Most assuredly I say to you, He who believes in Me, the works that I do he will do also; and greater works than these he will do…" John 14:12

"And He said to them: Go into all the world and preach the gospel to every creature." Mark 16:15

"He who believes and is baptized will be saved; but he who does not believe will be condemned.

"And these signs will follow those who believe: In My name they cast out demons; they will speak with new tongues;" Mark 16:17

"They will take up serpents; and if they drink anything deadly, it will by no means hurt them; they will lay hands on the sick, and they will recover." Mark 16:18

Jesus' Most Important Commandments

My God, according to Jesus, the most important commandments of Your Divine law are:

"You shall love the Lord your God with all your heart, with all your soul, and with all your mind." Matthew 22:37

"You shall love your neighbor as yourself." Matthew 22:39

"My God, I understand the importance of loving You, but why we should love our neighbors as ourselves?"

"My son, as you already know, the essence of My nature is Light, Energy.

"You also know that My Light, My Energy is the life and the essence of man.

"The neighbor in reality is Me, God, expressing through every living man."

"When Jesus taught people to love their neighbor, he was actually teaching them to love Me, your God.

"And when Jesus taught people to love Me, your God, in reality He was teaching them to love all humankind, because I express myself through the lives of everyone in the world.

"In reality, the commandment is only one:

"To Love all the time, everyone and everything existing on the face of the planet."

"My God, why did Jesus place so much importance on the acts of *Prayer* and of *Love?*"

"Because He knew they are the only tools at man's disposal that can help him achieve understanding, enlightenment, and finally, experience My Divine Love."

After this perception, I asked:

"My God, is there any conceptual difference between *Your Divine Love* and *Jesus' Love?*"

"My son, as I allowed you to perceive in the past, *My Divine Love* represents the Harmony of My Energy.

"*Jesus' Love*, on the other hand, represents man's emotions, the essence of which expresses the warm flow of goodness, and the summation of all good things in the universe that man desires for himself and others.

"It is the *living of the above teachings* that will allow him to reach and experience *My Divine Love.*"

Although I thought, I understood the intended message of Jesus' teachings and the reasons for all His actions, my reason made me wonder.

With the hope that I could somehow free myself of my doubts, I formulated and asked the following question:

"My God, are there other people who had the same experiences as Jesus?"
"Yes, My son."

"Who are they?"
"All those who over the course of their lives achieved the highest spiritual development—Enlightenment—and who, directly or indirectly, influenced the beginning or the expansion of what you call religion or spiritual movement.

"You may want to do some research on the beliefs and teachings of the world's major religions and Prophets as well as on some philosophers who left their mark on the history of civilization.
"You will find the veracity of what I have allowed you to perceive."

CHAPTER 53

BELIEFS, TEACHINGS AND QUOTES OF
THE WORLD'S MAJOR RELIGIONS

After the perceptions I described on the previous chapter, I started to think about the time and effort involved in such a project, and became concerned. The following day, I drove Pina to San Diego, where she attended a fundraiser for disadvantaged people.

While I was waiting for her, I decided to call Roberta Edgar, who at the time was helping me edit my manuscript. I shared with her my latest perceptions and my concerns about accomplishing what I had perceived. She told me she would do some research on the Internet to help me out.

That evening when I got home and looked at my electronic mail, I found several emails from Roberta, which I read immediately.

She had found the following from Wikipedia, the free Encyclopedia:

Beliefs, Teachings and Quotes of the World's Major Religions, Past and Present.

CHRISTIANITY:

"Therefore, whatever you want men to do to you, do also to them, for this is the Law and the Prophets." Matthew 7:12

"And just as you want men to do to you, you also do to them like-wise." Luke 6:31

BUDDHISM:

"...a state that is not pleasing or delightful to me, how could I inflict that upon another?" (Samyutta Nikaya v. 353)
"Hurt not others in ways that you yourself would find hurtful." (Udana-Varga. 5:18)

HINDUISM:

"This is the sum of duty: do not do to others what would cause pain if done to you." (Mahabharata 5:15)

ISLAM:

"None of you [truly] believes until he wishes for his brother what he wishes for himself." (Number 13 of Imam "Al-Nawawi's Forty Hadiths.")

JUDAISM:

"...thou shall love thy neighbor as thyself." (Leviticus 19:18)
"What is hateful to you, do not do to your fellow man. This is the law: all the rest is commentary." (Talmud, Shabbat 31a)
"And what you hate, do not do to anyone." (Tobit 4:15 6)

BAHA'I WORLD FAITH:

"Ascribe not to any soul that which thou wouldst not have ascribed to thee, and say not that which thou doest not. Blessed is he who preferred his brother before himself." (Baha'u'llah)

"And if thine eyes be turned towards justice, choose thou for thy neighbor that which thou choosiest for thyself." (Epistle to the Son of the Wolf)

BRAHMANISM:

"This is the sum of Dharma [duty]: Do naught unto others which would cause you pain if done to you." (Mahabharata, 5:1517)

CONFUCIANISM:

"Do not do to others what you do not want them to do to you." (Analects 15:23)
"Tse-kung asked, 'Is there one word that can serve as a principle of conduct for life?' Confucius replied, 'It is the word shu—reciprocity. Do not impose on others what you yourself do not desire.'" (Doctrine of the Mean 13.3)
"Try your best to treat others as you would wish to be treated yourself, and you will find that this is the shortest way to benevolence." (Mencius VII.A.4)

ANCIENT EGYPTIAN:

"Do for one who may do for you, that you may cause him thus to do." The Tale of the Eloquent Peasant, Pages 109-110 Translated by R.B. Parkinson.
The original dates from 1970 to 1640 <u>BCE</u> and may be the earliest version ever written).

JAINISM:

"Therefore, neither does he [a sage] cause violence to others nor does he make others do so." (Acarangasutra 5.101-2)

"In happiness and suffering, in joy and grief, we should regard all creatures as we regard our own self." (Lord Mahavira, 24th Tirthankara)
"A man should wander about treating all creatures as he himself would be treated." (Sutrakritanga 1.11.33)

NATIVE AMERICAN SPIRITUALITY:

"Respect for all life is the foundation." (The Great Law of Peace)
"All things are our relatives; what we do to everything, we do to ourselves. All is really One." (Black Elk)
"Do not wrong or hate your neighbor. For it is not he who you wrong, but yourself." (Pima proverb.)

ROMAN PAGAN RELIGION:

"The law imprinted on the hearts of all men is to love the members of society as themselves."

SHINTOISM:

"Be charitable to all beings, love is the representative of God." (Ko-ji-ki Hachiman Kasuga)

SIKHISM:

"Don't create enmity with anyone as God is within everyone." (Guru Arjan Devji 259)
"No one is my enemy, none a stranger, and everyone is my friend." (Guru Arjan Dev: AG 1299)

SUFISM:

"The basis of Sufism is consideration of the hearts and feelings of others. If you haven't the will to gladden someone's heart, then at least beware lest you hurt someone's heart, for on our path, no sin exists but this." (Dr. Javad Nurbakhsh, Master of the Nimatullahi Sufi Order)

TAOISM:

"Regard your neighbor's gain as your own gain, and your neighbor's loss as your own loss." (T'ai Shang Kan Ying P'ien)
"The sage has no interest of his own, but takes the interests of the people as his own. He is kind to the kind; he is also kind to the unkind: for Virtue is kind. He is faithful to the faithful; he is also faithful to the unfaithful: for Virtue is faithful." (Tao Teh Ching, Chapter 49)

YORUBA: (NIGERIA)

"One going to take a pointed stick to pinch a baby bird should first try it on himself to feel how it hurts."

ZOROASTRIANISM:

"That nature alone is good which refrains from doing unto another whatsoever is not good for itself." (Dadistan-i-dinik 94:5)
"Whatever is disagreeable to yourself do not do unto others." (Shayast-na-Shayast 13:29)

CHAPTER 54
SUMMARIZED BIOGRAPHIES OF MOST PROMINENT PROPHETS
JESUS, BUDDHA, MOSES, MUHAMMAD

Jesus

He was born in Bethlehem, Israel, 2000 years ago. We know very little about Jesus' life for the first thirty years. One significant incident recorded about His childhood involves a trip to Jerusalem with His parents when He was twelve. Soon after arriving, He wandered off and got lost. After searching frantically, his parents found Him in the temple, explaining the *law* to the doctors and priests in attendance. From twelve until thirty, when He began teaching to the public, there is little known of Jesus' whereabouts.

As we already know, the key messages of Jesus teachings are:

- **To love God;**
- **To love everyone including our enemies;**
- **To do good deeds;**
- **To do no evil things;**
- **To pray;**
- **To not be attached to money and material things;**
- **That whoever believes, accepts, and practices His teachings will be capable of accomplishing the same miracles as He did;**
- **To recognize that the truth will set us free.**

Buddha

Contrary to what I had always believed, Buddha is not a person's name, but a title.

- **It means the one who has awakened;**
- **The one who has attained enlightenment by himself;**
- **The one that has learned to get in touch consciously with the Omnipotence and the Omniscience of the Creative Power within.**

Siddartha Gautama was the first man to become the Buddha.

He was born a prince circa 563 BCE in Lumbini in the Terai lowlands near the foothills of Himalayas, which, today, is Nepal, and located between India and Tibet. He did not become the *Buddha* (that is, *Enlightened)* until the age of thirty-five, when, hoping to find a solution to human suffering, he left his wife and child, his family, his luxurious palace, and his future role as leader of his people to study with a group of monks.

For seven long years, he practiced breath control and fasting, but without results. In the end, he convinced himself that the extreme rituals the monks practiced were not producing the answers he sought, so he left the monastery and retired to the forest to pray under a fichus tree.

One day while praying deeply, he began to recall and perceive detailed events of his previous reincarnations. From that moment on, he was able to see the good and bad deeds performed by many living entities over the course of their lifetimes.

Ultimately, he found the answers he was seeking, as well as the reason for human suffering—not only how to cure it, but to prevent it, as well.

He arrived at a state in which he felt no craving, no desire, no hatred, no hunger, no thirst, no exhaustion, no fear, no doubt, and no delusions. By then, he had progressed beyond

Spiritual Defilements and had attained Enlightenment on his own.

The cores of his teaching were that in order to attain Enlightenment, one must:

- **Purify the mind;**
- **Cultivate good;**
- **Do no evil;**
- **Practice Faithful, Deep and Mindful Prayer.**

After having attained this level of awareness Siddhartha assumed the title of Lord Buddha and went on to share his acquired knowledge with others, because he was convinced that whoever followed him, in his footsteps, as listed above, would indeed attain *Enlightenment.*

Moses

According to the book of Exodus, Moses was born to a Hebrew mother who was forced to hide him when the Pharaoh ordered all newborn Hebrew males to be slaughtered.

Set afloat on the river in order to save his life, the infant was discovered and adopted into the Egyptian royal family.

As a young man, he killed an Egyptian slave master in defense of a Hebrew who was being beaten.

In order to avoid being put to death, he fled from the region, and found a peaceful new life as a shepherd.

Years later, he was commanded by God to deliver the Hebrews from slavery.

After the Ten Plagues were unleashed upon Egypt, Moses led the Hebrews out of Egypt, parted the Red Sea in order to escape to the other side, and guided his people into the desert where they wandered for forty years.

At that point, God called Moses onto Mount Sinai where He presented him with the Ten Commandments, which thereafter became the moral code by which man was to be measured.

During the 120 years of his life, Moses wrote the five books of the Old Testament, which are called the Torah. He also delivered his people to the Promised Land.

The Ten Commandments are:

1. **Thou shalt have no other gods before me;**
2. **Thou shalt not make for thyself an idol;**
3. **Thou shalt not make wrongful use of the name of thy God;**
4. **Remember the Sabbath and keep it holy;**
5. **Honor thy Mother and Father;**
6. **Thou shalt not murder;**
7. **Thou shalt not commit adultery;**
8. **Thou shalt not steal;**
9. **Thou shalt not bear false witness;**
10. **Thou shalt not covet thy neighbor's wife (or property.)**

Muhammad
In Arabic
Mohammed, Muhammed, Mahomet

Regarded by Muslims as the last messenger and prophet of *God (Allah,* in Arabic), Muhammad was born in the year 570 AD., in the Arabian city of Mecca.

He was orphaned at a young age and was brought up by his grandfather and then by his uncle. First, he went to work as a shepherd, later as a merchant. By 26, he was married. But he never learned to read or write.

Discontented with his life in Mecca, he retreated to a cave in the surrounding mountains for meditation and reflection. It was there that at age 40 he reached Enlightenment and received his first revelation from *God, Allah.*

Three years after this event, Muhammad started preaching his revelations publicly, proclaiming that God is one, that complete surrender to Him is man's religion, and acknowledged himself as a prophet and messenger of God, in the same vein as Abraham, Moses, Jesus, and other prophets.

Muhammad acquired few followers early on, and was met largely with hostility from the tribes of Mecca.

In 622 AD, in order to escape persecution, Muhammad and his followers migrated to Yathrib, which is known in the twenty-first century as Medina.

Six years of continuous warfare between Muslim and Meccan forces culminated with the Muslim victory and conquest of Mecca.

In March 632, Muhammad led the pilgrimage known as the Hajj. A few days after returning to Medina, he fell ill and died on June 8.

Most or all of the Koran (Qur'an), was apparently written by Muhammad's followers while he was still alive. It was primarily a verbal doctrine. The written version was not completed until shortly after his death.

The core of Muhammad's beliefs and teachings are:

- **To believe, have faith, and pray to God, in Arabic: Allah;**
- **To be charitable and give to the poor;**
- **To do good works;**
- **To do no evil;**
- **To fast.**

CHAPTER 55

BELIEFS AND CREDOS OF PEOPLE CALLED PHILOSOPHERS WHO LEFT THEIR MARK ON THE HISTORY OF CIVILIZATION

EPICTETUS: "What you would avoid suffering yourself, seek not to impose on others." (Circa 100 CE)

KANT: "Act as if the maxim of thy action were to become by thy will a universal law of nature."

SOCRATES: "Do not do to others that which would anger you if others did it to you." (Greece; 5th century BCE)

SENECA: "Treat your inferiors as you would be treated by your superiors." Epistle 47:11 (Rome; 1st century CE)

In analyzing what I had just learned, I had proof that every religion from every part of the world or historical period—as different and mysterious as I had originally thought— stated and preached exactly the same thing:

> **To pray, to love, and to treat our fellow man just the way we would like to be treated.**

The various statements made by philosophers who lived centuries apart and in different parts of the world professed the same philosophies as their more ecclesiastical counterparts.

Jesus, Siddhartha Gautama (Buddha,) Moses, and *Muhammad* all followed the same basic principles in order to attain Enlightenment:

- **Detachment from material things;**
- **Practice of solitude and quiet;**
- **Practice of deep and mindful prayer.**

At this point, everything became very clear to me, and I felt a powerful sense of understanding of not only Jesus' teachings and works, but also of the teachings and works of all the Enlightened Ones.

My discoveries were both amazing and incredible to me.

The solution to all man's problems, the attainment of Enlightenment, and the experience of *Divine Love* is linked to:

- **Forgiveness;**
- **Mindful Prayer;**
- **And the expression of Love without conditions and expectations.**

Jesus and all the other Enlightened Ones were aware of this, which is why in their teachings they so strongly emphasized *Forgiveness, Prayer* and *Love.*

Once more, I was overwhelmed!

CHAPTER 56

MAN'S GREATEST MISTAKE AND DRAMA

A few days after receiving this perception, I asked myself the following:

Since the beliefs, teachings, and credos of men like *Moses, Siddhartha Gautama (Buddha), Jesus, Muhammad*—**as well the ones from all the Enlightened ones from those religions not mentioned here—are virtually the same, how can we explain the fact that in the course of time their leaders did not make fervent attempts to make alliances and teach their universality?**

It occurred to me that such an act might have led to a universal understanding of the common truths that are expressed in all religions, to the acceptance and respect for everyone's beliefs and to a commonality of purpose among all people on earth that surely would have led them to experience peace, harmony and prosperity.

Hoping to perceive the reasons behind my inquiries, I began to pray.
After a few days of praying, I perceived the following:

"My son, the reason why the major religious leaders over the centuries never formed such an alliance is that they never fully understood the message of their Enlightened predecessors.

Consequently, instead of recognizing and looking at them as professors from whom they could learn and in time follow—just as students do in school—they recognized them as Special Divine Beings.

"This recognition led to *Idolatry* and *Fanaticism*.

"*Idolatry* and *Fanaticism*, My son, are the two things that have prevented religious leaders from seeing and recognizing that the teachings of all the Enlightened Ones are universal and the same."

"My God, what is man's worst enemy?"
"Ignorance, My son."

"Why?"

- Because ignorance precludes man from achieving Enlightenment;
- Because it is the source and the cause for man's perpetual suffering;
- And because it is the divider between man and Me.

Soon after that, I perceived:

"Do you remember, My son, the response from the priest in Joshua Tree, when many years ago you shared with him your healing experiences and your desire to pray for the sick people of the parish?"
"Yes, My God."

"What did he say?"
"That the people were conservative and they didn't believe in that kind of stuff."

"Do you know why he gave you that answer?"
After a moment of reflection, I answered, "Not exactly, My God."

"My son, despite the fact that he had been a priest for over fifty years, he never understood the message of Jesus when He said to His disciples:
"Go into all the world and preach the gospel to every creature." Mark 16:15
"He who believes…will be saved; but he who does not believe will be condemned.
"And these signs will follow those who believe:
"In My name they will cast out demons; they will speak with new tongues;" Mark 16:17
"They will take up serpents; and if they drink anything deadly, it will by no means hurt them; they will lay hands on the sick, and they will recover." Mark 16:18

CHAPTER 57
Retirement - More Doubts - Understanding

Since my four-way bypass heart surgery and up to the present moment, March 25, 2011, I have been fatigued with pain in my joints, making me incapable of working with the same intensity that I had before surgery.

My cardiologist, as well other doctors I consulted, ordered all kinds of tests such as blood analysis, x-rays, cat scans, MRIs, and an echocardiogram, but every one of them was negative.

According to medical science, there is nothing wrong with me, and they can't understand why I have those malaises.

I began to pray, with the hope that I would be healed through prayer.

But regardless of how hard I tried, I was not able to get in touch with the Omnipotence and the Omniscience of the Creative Power within me, and consequently, my malaises continued to affect me.

What was very strange was that during this same period of time, when I prayed for people who requested my prayers, I was able to get in touch with the Creative Power within, and the people for whom I prayed received help.

I couldn't understand why God, the Omnipotence of the Creative Power Within, would not respond to prayers for my healing, while at the same time He responded to my prayers to heal others.

These experiences made me wonder a lot, and I was frustrated, confused and perplexed.

Occasionally, I thought that maybe what I had learned as the *truth* wasn't the total *truth,* and there are times when we have no control over the nature of our experiences and we are not able to change them regardless of how hard we may try.

What was strange about the entire thing was that while my mind was in complete turmoil, my being was at peace.

Two contrasting and opposite feelings.

How could that be?

During this period of my life, what hurt me the most were the cynical comments of some family members and friends, who would sometimes sarcastically say:

- **"Why don't you pray God to heal you?"**
- **Or, "If what you are professing is the truth, why is then that you're not able to heal yourself?"**
- **Or, "Why is it that God does not answer your prayer and heal you?"**

Pina, as well our children Pino, Nino and Paolo Jr., along with their spouses, surrounded me with all the love they could express. They suggested that because I was already sixty-five years old, it was time for me to consider retirement and to do some traveling and enjoy life in a different way.

Their unconditional love, as well as their continuous encouragement, made it easier for me to look forward, accept the reality of my new life, and finally go into retirement, which I did in January 2011.

Since then, I made my number one priority to finish the third volume of *Journey of a Healer.*

While doing so, I felt that I could not finish it until I was able to understand the following:

- **How did I get cardio-vascular disease?**
- **Why, after the surgery, did I encounter complications and continue to experience health problems?**
- **And why did God (the Creative Power within), choose not to respond to my pleas and prayers to heal me, while at the same time, He responded to my prayers when I prayed for other people.**

After thinking on those questions continuously day and night for a considerable amount of time, I was not able to perceive what I wanted to know.

I decided to ask the help of the Omniscience of the Creative Power within, and so I formulated the following prayer:

"My God, You who are the essence of the Omniscience of the Creative Power within me, in this moment, I know that You know that I can't finish the work that You inspired me to do until I am able to understand clearly the reasons for my problems.
"It is with humility and sincerity that I ask You to allow me to perceive:

- *The truth about the nature of my malaises;*
- *The truth about why You are not responding to my pleas and my prayers to heal me in a miraculous way;*
- *And why, while You are ignoring my prayers for personal healing, You respond to my prayers to help the people for whom I pray."*

After approximately ten days of intense prayer, I perceived the following:

> **"My son, by now you should already know that the nature of your experiences are caused by the working of your will, mind and Creative Power within.**
> **"The ultimate purpose of those experiences is to lead you to the fulfillment of your goals and dreams."**

After this perception, I asked:

> "My God, how can sickness, suffering and not having my prayers answered, lead me to the fulfillment of my goals and dreams?"
> **"My son, before I let you perceive the object of your desires, it is important that you know and understand the cycle of life is subordinated at all time to the working of the laws of My nature, which can be described as balance, moderation, and fulfillment.**
>
> **"Whoever consciously or unconsciously breaks the rules of My laws will alter the harmony of the organs that constitute his body, with the consequence that the body becomes inharmonious and therefore sick.**
>
> **"My son, your passion and love for food and the enjoyment that you get from it are one of the causes of your problems.**
> **"The reason why you had cardiovascular problems is because for many years, you indulged in overeating eggs, cheese and meat, with the consequence that your arteries got plugged.**
> **"The purpose of it is to teach you moderation."**
>
> **"Your physical suffering that became more intense after the surgery is due to the following:**

- **Your inability to master total control over your emotions and eating habits;**
- **The attachment you still have for material things;**
- **The unfolding of the negative thoughts/seeds that are still harbored deep inside My Creative Power dwelling within you;**
- **And the excessive wear and tear on your body due to your intense physical work.**

"The purpose of all the above is to remind you that:

- **You are not living to the fullest, the things that I allowed you to perceive in the course of your search;**
- **To inspire you to conduct a more balanced life;**
- **And to teach you that to achieve and fulfill your remaining goals and dreams, you need to try harder."**

After I evaluated the above perceptions, I noticed there was no reference to my *age* as a probable cause for my problems.

I always believed that *age* had a lot to do with the pain and suffering experienced by our bodies. In fact, it seems like they walk hand in hand, and that the older we get, the greater are pain and suffering.

Intrigued by the fact that there was no reference to this reality, I formulated the following question:

"My God, in looking at life in general, it seems that a great deal of pain and suffering are inflicted by what is called *old age*.
How is it that in what You allowed me to perceive there is no reference that my *age* could be co-responsible for my malaises?"

Here is the response to my question:

> **"My son, to the eyes of most people,** *old age* **represents the part of the life cycle that leads to the inevitable decline of the vitality of the body and to an increase of physical sufferings.**
> **"Although the progressive decline of every living thing is a part of the nature of the cycle of life that I master-planned for this dream world of Mine, the suffering is not, and should not be a part of man's life.**
>
> **"My son, by now, you should know that man's suffering is a by-product of his ignorance; it is self-inflicted and can be avoided and overcome.**
> **"The ultimate purpose of man's suffering is to spur and inspire him to seek with a greater determination the path that leads to the understanding and living of the truth.**
> **"It is understanding and living the truth, My son, that helps man to overcome and defeat the pain suffered by his body."**

Although I understood everything I perceived, in my mind was still not clear on how pain and suffering could be avoided, especially during the period of old age.

Therefore, I formulated the following prayer:

> *"My God, I know that You know, that in this moment, I still have difficulty in understanding.*
> *"It is for this reason, that with humility and with all the sincerity that I can express in my being, I ask You to have mercy on my intellectual incapacity, and help me to understand Your message so I can free myself of my doubts."*

After a few days of prayers, here is what I perceived:

"My son, although all appearances lead to the belief that the sufferings of the body of man are inevitable and insurmountable, and have no apparent purpose, I need to inform you that those beliefs are wrong.
"They are wrong, because man's sufferings can be prevented, avoided and overcome, while at the same time they play a very important role in leading people to the realization of their goals and dreams."

At this perception, I replied:

"My God, I believe that what You are allowing me to perceive it is the truth, but how can we explain that the reality of life seems to be opposed to what I just perceived from You?
"Why does life seem to be haunted by pains and sufferings?"
"My son, for you to be able to understand, first you need to remember that the essence of the body of man is made with the essence of My Divine Light, Energy.

"It is also important, My son, that you always remember that My Divine Light, Energy, is never, and I say never, subjected to pain, suffering and limitation.

"Now, before we continue, I want you to answer the following question:

"What do you experience when, while praying or meditating, you are in tune with the Omnipotence and the Omniscience of My Creative Power within you?"

After I reflected for a few minutes, I answered, *Peace, joy* and *harmony,*
My God."

> **"Did ever occur to you that while praying or meditating,
> and while being in tune with the Omnipotence and the
> Omniscience of My Creative Power within you, you experi-
> enced no pain or suffering?"**
> Immediately, I answered: "No, My God."

> **"Do you know why, My son?"**
> After I reflected for a while, I answered, "No, My God."

> **"My son, when you are in perfect tune with My Creative Power
> within you, you never experience pain or suffering because
> during that time, you allow the infinity of My pure energy to
> flow through your entire being, becoming one with it."**

> **"When this occurs, you lose awareness of your physical be-
> ing, and with it you all the pain and suffering, and you can
> only feel the essence of My Divine being, which is peace, joy
> and harmony.**
> **"This is the reason why, while in prayer or in deep medita-
> tion, you never feel any sense of pain and suffering."**

> **"Now, due to the fact that you have not yet reached the state
> of consciousness called Enlightenment, those moments last
> only for as long you stay perfectly tuned to My Creative
> Power within you, and disappear the moment that connec-
> tion is broken."**

> **"My son…**

- "When you become at all times consciously aware that the essence of your true nature is energy and that you are an integral part of My essence and not a separate entity;

- "When you learn to see in every man, as well as in every little or big thing existing in the universe, the essence of My nature as well as the essence of your nature;

- "When you learn to love every person and every living creature existing in the universe equally, unselfishly and with the same intensity, without expecting anything in return;

- "Only then, you will be able to stay consciously in tune all the time with My Creative Power within you;

- "You will be able to feel My Divine love in the form of Divine joy, Divine peace and Divine harmony;

- "You will never again experience limitation, pain and suffering;

- "You will be able to use consciously and at any time the Omnipotence and the Omniscience of My Creative Power within you;

- "And you will feel to be an integral part of all My Creation."

"I remind you, My son, that man's greatest enemy is ignorance of his true heritage, ignorance of the truth, and his inability to live the *truth*.

"The *truth* I did allow you to perceive in the course of your search is the same *truth* lived, professed and shared by all the people who in the course of their lives have achieved Enlightenment."

"My son, always remember, that it is not the *knowledge of the truth* that frees man from the bondage of his limitations and the sufferings of life, but the *living of the truth.*"

"It is the *living of the truth* that allows man to grow from a *human being to a divine being;*
"And from *ignorance to Enlightenment.*"

"An eloquent demonstration of this truth has been giving to the world by Jesus, Mohammad, Moses, Siddhartha Gautama (Buddha), Saint Francis of Assisi, Padre Pio of Pietralcina, Brother Andrew of Montreal, just to name a few that are known to you, My son."

After the above perception, I asked:

"My God, why did Your Creative Power within me not respond to my prayers and my pleas, and You chose to not heal me in what is known as a miraculous way?"

Here is the response:

"The reason why My Creative Power within you did not respond to the pleas of your prayers to heal you, My son, was because of the *implementation of My law of fulfillment,* which has the purpose to lead you towards the realization of the goals, dreams and desires of your life."

"My God, how is that possible? Could you please be more explicit?"
"My son, for you to be able understand and see the veracity of what I just allowed you to perceive, we need to go back

in time and analyze together the goals that you wanted to achieve in the course of your life."

"If you recall, as a child what you wanted the most was:

- To understand the apparent mystery of My nature and the apparent mystery of how I operate;
- To understand the nature of man and his strange and mysterious behavior;
- And to understand the reason man seems to be subordinate to pain and suffering.

"As a young man, what you wanted most was:

- To reunite your family in a place where you could work and prosper together;
- To have your own business;
- To make enough money that you could afford the things that your parents could not afford during your childhood.

"As an adult what you wanted the most was:

- To evolve spiritually to the point that you could become consciously enlightened so that at the moment of your passing you will be reunited to the essence of My nature and consciousness for the rest of times;
- And to share your experiences with your fellow man, with the intent that they could learn from your struggles and mistakes and be led to a smoother, better and more fulfilled life.

"My son, if you notice, you did achieve what you wanted as a child and what you wanted as a young man.

"Now what is remaining for you to achieve is what you want as an adult:

- To evolve spiritually to the point that you can become consciously enlightened so at the moment of your passing you can be reunited to the essence of My nature and consciousness for the rest of times;
- And to share your experiences with your fellow man, with the intent that they can learn from your struggles and mistakes and be led to a smoother, better and more fulfilled life.

"My son, I remind you that these last two goals are not only the most important goals of a person's life, but are also the hardest to achieve.
"They are the hardest because they require without any distraction all the effort, attention, dedication, and willpower that a person can muster.

"My son, if after the surgery you were healed completely, you were going to continue to dedicate most of your time working for your paving company, leaving little time for prayer, healing and meditation, with the consequence that the achievement of your most important goals were in jeopardy.

"*My law of fulfillment*, the working of the Omnipotence and Omniscience of My Creative Power within you was aware of that, and it was for this specific reason that you were not allowed to be healed, forcing you into retirement.

"My son, it is important that you see your retirement not as inevitable decline in the cycle of your life, but as that interval of time that offers you the greatest opportunity to focus your effort, devotion and attention on prayer and meditation, the only things capable of helping you develop and increase your spiritual awareness, which are indispensable for realizing the last two and most important goals of your life."

After all the above perceptions, I felt *ashamed, astonished and moved.*

I felt *ashamed* because after what I was allowed to perceive over the course of years, I still harbored within myself feelings of doubts.

I was *astonished* because once more I had a demonstration of how incredibly perfect is the nature of God's law and the way it works.

I was *moved,* because one more time I had the demonstration that even when I was incapable of understanding and still doubting, the Omniscience and the Omnipotence of God's Creative Power within continued to create for me the right conditions so I could be directed to the path that will eventually take me to the realization of my ultimate goals.

I was also *moved,* because I was assured that in our *journey* we are never alone, helpless, or abandoned to ourselves.

Instead, we are continuously sustained and directed by the essence of the Omnipotence and the Omniscience of God within us, making me understand more clearly than ever that when *we trust and have faith in Him and allow His Spirit to guide us, in due time, we will be safely led to*:

- **The realization of all our goals and dreams;**
- **The purification of our Soul and Spirit;**
- **And ultimately, we will be led to join Him, so we can be with Him and part of Him for eternity to enjoy forever the blessing of His Divine Love.**

Paolo Ficara
Joshua Tree, CA.
2017

Paolo & Pina Ficara
Joshua Tree, CA. 2017

CHAPTER 58
COMMITMENT - THANKS - PRAYER - HOPE

After all the above perceptions, deep in my being, I sensed a feeling of peace that I had never experienced before; a peace so deep that it's impossible to describe with words.

Finally, all my life questions had been fully answered, and I understood the truth about the apparent mysteries of God, Man and Creation.

Now I can say without hesitation and without doubt that the key that unlocks the door to the path that leads us to the fulfillment of our goals and dreams, and ultimately to Enlightenment, is within us, always at hand, ready to be used at any time.

This path can be described as:

- **Sincere prayer and meditation;**
- **And constant expression and manifestation of our devotion and love to God within us, to our fellow man and to all Creation.**

At this point, before I end this book, I want to summarize what I believe I learned during the course of my search.

"I begin by saying that the entity we address to as God is not an individual with a specific and defined form as commonly believed by most people;

"In reality, God is the essence of the Light, the Energy, that makes up every atom in the universe, the building-stones that give life and form to every living and non-living thing in all of creation.
It is for the above reason that we should see God in every big or little thing existing in the universe, and we should nourish unconditional respect, devotion and love for all creation;

"God does not live in some place in the universe called heaven or paradise, but lives in the heart and in the body of every man and living thing in the universe;

"God does not govern His creation with force and fear the way a monarch governs his kingdom;
God governs His creation with the infinite power of His love (Harmony), the intrinsic part of His nature;

"We should not see God as an individual who wants to be worshiped as an idol;
But rather as the Almighty living force that gives life to our life as well as to the life of every living creature in the universe;

"We should not see our self as an unhappy, inferior, weak and powerless being;

"Instead, we should see our self as a happy, humble and powerful divine being, because, our essence and nature is made with God's Divine Light, Energy, and as such, we are Divine, capable of accomplishing any task we want;

"We should understand once and for all, that we have been created in God's image, and not the other way around;

"We should not fear God, because in being the expression and manifestation of God's essence, we are part of God, and consequently, to fear God is to fear our self;
"Instead, we should fear the nature of our negative emotions and actions in the form of thoughts as well as deeds, our most dangerous deadliest enemies;

"For the same above reasons, we should not harbor toward God an attitude of servility;
"What we should do instead, is embrace, harbor and live the teachings of unselfishness, forgiveness, equality and love, conveyed to us by all the Enlightened people who have been living in this world during the course of time."

Now I can truly say and affirm that a very important cycle of my life has come to an end and that a new one is about to begin, that I believe is going to be greater, more exiting and more rewarding than this past one, and for this reason I am going to say the following prayer of thanks:

"My God, in this moment, with all the sincerity and humility that my heart can express, I thank You for having constantly helped and inspired me in my quest to find the truth.
"I thank You also for being the constant guiding light that has allowed me to understand with absolute certainty:

- *That You are in me;*
- *That You are a part of me;*
- *That You are the substance of my substance;*
- *That You are the Energy of my energy;*

- *That You are the Life of my life;*
- *That You are the essence of my body and of my spirit.*

My God, I now implore and pray to You to strengthen:

- *My weak traits;*
- *And my determination and will, so I may keep seeking You with greater and greater earnestness and determination.*

I ask You:

- *To continue to protect me from the illusions of the world;*
- *To give me the strength and courage and wisdom to live out the truth that You allowed me to perceive;*
- *To make of me the most humble of Your creatures;*
- *To transform me into a benevolent instrument of Your essence;*
- *And most important, I pray You to arouse and increase within me the Love I bear for You, as well the Love I bear for all mankind, and to allow me to perceive, feel and manifest the infinity of Your Divine Love.*

To conclude, I hope, my God, this work that I am about to complete, which in reality is Your work, is going to reach out and touch every human being in the world, firing into their hearts a brilliant flame of Love for:

- You;
- Mankind;
- And all Your Creation.

LOVE, LOVE, AND MORE LOVE

IS THE TRUE RULER OF THE UNIVERSE,

THE ANSWER, TO ALL HUMAN SUFFERINGS,

THE ONLY PATH THAT LEADS TO...

PEACE, TRUE PROSPERITY, REALLY
HAPPINESS, AND GOD!

With Many Blessings dedicated to Mankind.
Paolo Ficara
Joshua Tree, Ca.
May 14, 2014

www.ingramcontent.com/pod-product-compliance
Lightning Source LLC
Chambersburg PA
CBHW060449090426
42735CB00011B/1952